THE OVEN BIRDS

American Women on Womanhood, 1820–1920

Gail Thain Parker was born in Chicago on February 8, 1943. She was educated at Harvard where she received her Ph.D. in 1969. Currently an Assistant Professor of History and Literature, she was the first Harvard faculty member to teach a course specifically about women. The author of articles on Jonathan Edwards, Mary Baker Eddy and William Dean Howells, she is in the process of finishing a book on mind cure in America and is beginning another on Charlotte Perkins Gilman. She lives in Cambridge with her husband and five-year-old daughter.

THE OVEN BIRDS

American Women on Womanhood, 1820–1920

EDITED BY GAIL PARKER

ANCHOR BOOKS

Doubleday & Company, Inc.
Garden City, New York
1972

Anchor Books edition: 1972
Library of Congress Catalog Card Number 72–171338
Copyright © 1972 by Gail Thain Parker
All Rights Reserved
Printed in the United States of America

CONTENTS

THE OVEN BIRD[*]

There is a singer everyone has heard,
Loud, a mid-summer and a mid-wood bird,
Who makes the solid tree trunks sound again.
He says that leaves are old and that for flowers
Mid-summer is to spring as one to ten.
He says the early petal-fall is past,
When pear and cherry bloom went down in showers
On sunny days a moment overcast;
And comes that other fall we name the fall.
He says the highway dust is over all.
The bird would cease and be as other birds
But that he knows in singing not to sing.
The question that he frames in all but words
Is what to make of a diminished thing.

[*] "The Oven Bird" is taken from *The Selected Poems of Robert Frost* (New York, 1965), p. 76.

THE OVEN BIRDS

American Women on Womanhood, 1820–1920

INTRODUCTION

Within the last ten years, historians of American feminism have come to agree that something vital went out of the organized woman's movement in the 1890s when Elizabeth Cady Stanton and Susan B. Anthony abandoned the field to the new "realists" in the suffrage ranks. Mrs. Stanton and her co-workers had scorned compromise—they were more than willing to sacrifice popularity to Truth—while the second-generation feminist leaders, or so the story goes, prided themselves chiefly on their organizational skills. Carrie Chapman Catt and Anna Shaw were good at keeping records and scheduling speaking tours, but they never were able to articulate a distinctly feminist ideology.

Elizabeth Stanton felt confident that open debate between the advocates of woman's rights and their opponents was the best possible way to educate the public. If thousands of American women were suffering under outmoded divorce laws, then avowed feminists had to be willing to broach the shocking subject, and to take the consequences. In contrast, women like Mrs. Catt sought to avoid more controversial issues and to concentrate instead on getting the vote. The National American Woman Suffrage Association, a conglomerate which grew out of the merger of the two wings of the woman's rights movement in 1890, sponsored a convention each year, and it was at the convention in 1896 that Mrs. Catt and her cohorts won a decisive victory. At that time they moved, and managed to pass, a resolution disavowing any connection between the National Association and Elizabeth Stanton's latest publication, a heretical Woman's Bible. Susan Anthony had tried to warn Mrs. Stanton that she could only damage woman's cause by trying to give the story of

Adam and Eve a feminist moral, but when it came to a vote on the convention floor, Miss Anthony stepped down from the chair to speak out against those who would censure a sister rather than risk offending orthodox Protestants—or anyone else.

It is somewhat baffling, then, to find Susan B. Anthony choosing Carrie Catt to succeed her as president of the National Association. Perhaps she felt that an infusion of *Realpolitik* was necessary to keep the woman's movement alive. After years of lobbying, the chances of getting a federal suffrage amendment seemed slimmer in the nineties than ever before, and many of the younger suffragists turned their attention to state referenda. Mrs. Catt had organized the Idaho campaign with notable success in a decade when only one other referendum (in Colorado) was won. In the long run, however, it is less important to understand what Susan Anthony saw in Carrie Catt, than to estimate whether the sensitivity of second-generation suffragists to what was popular, acceptable, and nice did real damage to the integrity of the woman's movement. My own feeling is that it did.

Woman suffrage as Mrs. Catt described it was just one of a number of strategies devised by middle-class citizens eager to keep their hands on the levers of political power. Instead of demanding the vote for women as a basic human right, the new suffrage leaders requested it in order to preserve a white, native-born, voting majority. Under Mrs. Catt's leadership there was little in the official suffrage movement that appealed specifically to women. They *were* going to be enfranchised, but their enfranchisement had been redefined. No longer the first step in a long process of emancipation, the vote had become the be-all and end-all of the woman's movement. And although women would go to the polls, it was their male relatives, the politic suffragists were careful to point out, who stood to gain the most from the Nineteenth Amendment. The good citizen, in other words the family man, could effectively double his voting power by enfranchising his wife.

Obviously it would be wrong to mistake Carrie Chapman

Catt for the villain in the piece. Known as the "Big Boss" to her co-workers, Mrs. Catt was realistic about what she had to contribute to the woman's movement. Campaigning on white supremacy in the South and native supremacy in the North, dissociating the National Association from its more radical elements, and, above all, performing these machinations without self-dramatization, she seems an appropriate heroine for William Dean Howells—perhaps Silas Lapham's older daughter Penelope come of age. Unlike the earliest American feminists, Mrs. Catt left no memoirs; she apparently felt no need to pull her life into focus, or to project it larger than life-size. She was a massively capable woman, but never a heroine, even in her own eyes.

Mrs. Catt believed that she and her contemporaries lived on a different scale from the "great-souled" workers in the first years of the woman's movement. Recent historians have pointed to this devolution in the movement's leadership to explain why 1920 and the vote marked the end of a campaign rather than the beginning of a revolution. Yet, characteristically, they have overlooked the fact that historians trained to think in terms of paradox were not the first to perceive declension in the female line. In fact, in the years after the Civil War large numbers of American women came to believe that they were lesser beings than their grandmothers, and mothers, and great-aunts.

The selections in this anthology were chosen, in part, to document this pervasive post-war sense that they just didn't make women like they used to. Catharine Beecher's statistics on female health, Sarah Orne Jewett's attempts to memorialize a disappearing breed of omnicompetent New England women, Charlotte Perkins Gilman's fascination with genealogies, all reflect their feelings of inadequacy. Yet these women did more than reveal their inferiority complexes, they suggested (if sometimes inadvertently) just what it was that had gone out of their lives, leaving them emotionally—and physically—impoverished.

Given the fact that most of the women who left memoirs or wrote fiction in the nineteenth century were ladies—women who had been exempted or had exempted themselves from physical drudgery—I was prepared to find that their jeremiads sprang out of a sense of alienation from the real work of the world. They were marginal figures, the vicarious consumers of Veblen's description, their only function to be decorative and sensitive. It soon became clear, however, that there were serious flaws inherent in a socio-economic explanation. In the first place, many of the women who appear in this anthology were self-supporting (and sometimes family supporting) and were proud of it. And in the second, their laments cannot be readily translated into the jargon of industrial revolution and status upheaval—they had their own ideas about how their experiences differed from those of earlier generations. Catharine Beecher went out of her way to discredit the theory that disability followed economic dysfunction; working-class women, she had discovered, were as sickly as their more affluent sisters.

But instead of trying at this point to extract the moral of these woman's stories from their own words, let me first summarize that moral as simply as possible. With varying degrees of clarity, Catharine Beecher, Harriet Beecher Stowe, Sarah Orne Jewett, Jane Addams, and Charlotte Gilman recognized that they were suffering for want of heroines. Their matrilineal piety was an attempt to fill the vacuum, to provide themselves with role models. Yet to define their need does not automatically explain their choice of satisfactions. Why were their grandmothers more meaningful to these women than the Amazons, than Ruth, than Joan of Arc, or Jane Eyre?

Many American women in the years after the Civil War thought of the ante-bellum period as a time of great causes and great commitments when even the most ordinary people had been larger than life-size. And they sensed, often without being able to be very articulate about it, that there was a real connection between ante-bellum heroism and the Romantic and Sentimental conventions which had dominated pre-war literature. It is hard to be compellingly articulate about these connections even now. Obviously people are not what they read, any more than they are what they eat. But women like Harriet Beecher Stowe and Sarah Orne Jewett could imagine what Mrs. Stanton knew to be true—she, and other women of her generation, had been sustained in a variety of radical causes by a sense of themselves, a sense of their own potentialities and options, that they had taken from the poems and novels that they read. And Stowe and Jewett, while pioneering in their own writings in a species of literary realism, still found the image of the Romantic—or Sentimental—heroine compelling. In short, the women whose thoughts have been collected in this anthology suggest to our generation that the history of American feminism and literary history must be studied simultaneously if any sense is to be made of the rise and fall of the woman's movement in America.

The years immediately following the Civil War, like those after World War I, were marked by a widespread devaluation of heroism. In the 1920s Ernest Hemingway described the nausea which the words "sacred," "glorious," and "sacrifice" inspired in him. Similarly, in the 1870s and 1880s, William Dean Howells and Henry James found themselves unable to respond to the Romantic stereotypes of pre-Civil War literature. Grand causes, great figures, and holy zeal seemed to belong to an earlier, more innocent age. Henry James saw the Civil War as a rite of initiation which had "introduced into the national consciousness a certain sense of proportion and relation, of the world being a more complicated place than it had hitherto seemed, the future more treacherous, success more difficult. . . . The good American," he prophesied, "in days to come, will be a more critical person than his complacent and confident grandfather."[1]

When James wrote his biography of Hawthorne and made these prophetic remarks, he felt certain that modern Americans would be neither cynical nor skeptical, but prepared

[1] Henry James, *Hawthorne* (New York, 1880), pp. 139-40.

for life as it really was. They would be something more than their forefathers—more observant, more flexible, more broadly competent. It is intriguing, then, to see how much less sanguine James was about the modern age and sensibility only seven years later, in 1886, when he turned from literary history to discuss contemporary feminism in *The Bostonians*. To be sure, James qualified his condemnation of the post-war era in *The Bostonians* by putting his most derogatory remarks first into the mouth of a reactionary Southerner, and then into the mind of his feminist, Olive Chancellor. Basil Ransom lamented that the "whole generation is womanized; the masculine tone is passing out of the world";[2] while Miss Chancellor, who agreed that the age was "relaxed and demoralized," "looked to the influx of the great feminine element to make it feel and speak more sharply."[3]

Yet while these forays into sexist analysis neatly canceled each other out, James did not try to redress the balance when Olive Chancellor turned her back on contemporary life to sketch a brief history of the woman's movement in America. Her tone was elegiac, and James did a great deal behind the scenes to give that tone maximum resonance. The movement, as Miss Chancellor envisioned it, was embodied in Miss Birdseye, a veteran reformer who had begun her career by "carrying the Bible to the slave" and, in consequence,

> had spent a month in a Georgian jail. She had preached temperance in Irish circles where the doctrine was received with missiles; she had interfered between wives and husbands mad with drink; she had taken filthy children, picked up in the street, to her own poor rooms, and had removed their pestilent rags and washed their sore bodies with slippery little hands. . . . It struck Miss Chancellor . . . that this frumpy little missionary was the last link in a tradition, and that when she should be called away the heroic age of New England life—the age of plain living and high thinking, of pure ideals and

[2] Henry James, *The Bostonians* (London, 1886), III, p. 52.
[3] *Ibid.*, I, p. 194.

earnest effort, of moral passion and noble experiment—
would effectually be closed.[4]

Of course James was poking fun at this credulous zealot,
"a confused, entangled, inconsequent, discursive old woman,
whose charity began at home and ended nowhere," but the
condescension in Olive Chancellor's account reflected more
on her own neurotic refinement than on the somewhat slov-
enly selflessness of Miss Birdseye.

In the opening pages of *The Bostonians* James carefully
pointed out that Miss Chancellor, instead of being better
capable of coping with life than her progenitors, was in fact
less competent and more conflicted. Only the memory of her
mother (who "always chose the positive course") had inspired her to make contact with her southern cousin, Basil
Ransom. Left to herself, "Olive had a fear of everything. . . ."[5] However, James did not depend on this aside
to establish the theme of declension in the female line. He
set the third and final book of *The Bostonians* on Cape Cod,
primarily, or so it would seem, to play on the parallels between the degenerate condition of New England ports and
the degenerating strength of the great ante-bellum causes,
particularly the woman's movement.

Miss Birdseye had gone to the Cape for a rest (ending in
death), accompanied by Olive Chancellor, Olive's inspired
protégée Verena, and a female physician, Dr. Prance. These
women, the saving remnant of American feminism, had rented
a cottage in

> Marmion [which] called itself a town, but . . . was a
> good deal shrunken since the decline in the shipbuilding
> interest; it turned out a good many vessels every year, in
> the palmy days, before the war. There were shipyards
> still, where you could pick up the old shavings, the old
> nails and rivets, but they were grass grown now, and the
> water lapped them without anything to interfere.[6]

[4] *Ibid.*, II, pp. 36–37.
[5] *Ibid.*, I, p. 19.
[6] *Ibid.*, III, p. 81.

Basil Ransom, who had come to Marmion to court Verena, was given a guided tour of the town by Dr. Prance. "Dr. Prance," admittedly claustrophobic in a summer cottage with three feminists, "didn't say the place was picturesque or quaint, or weird;" but Ransom "could see that was what she meant when she said it was mouldering away. Even under the mantle of night he himself gathered the impression that it had had a larger life, seen better days."[7]

As if this setting were not enough to produce an atmosphere of shrunken hopes, James used the season itself to highlight Olive Chancellor's sense that the "heroic age of New England life" was a thing of the past.

> There were certain afternoons in August, long, beautiful and terrible, when one felt that the summer was rounding its curve, and the rustle of the full-leaved trees in the slanting golden light, in the breeze that ought to be delicious, seemed the voice of the coming autumn, of the warnings and dangers of life.[8]

It is barely possible that James was parodying Sarah Orne Jewett here, or if not Jewett specifically, the burgeoning school of New England local colorists. Decaying coastal towns and late summer days were a favorite stage setting for these writers, generally women, whose most compelling creative impulse was a kind of preservationism. They were determined to record American life in its most eccentric and savory forms, before it became a perfectly homogenized product. James' description of Ransom's New York City neighborhood, ending as it does in a series of olfactory puns, is even more likely to have been an intentional parody of the genre than his elegiac descriptions of Cape Cod.

> The two sides of the [grocery] shop were protected by an immense penthouse shed, which projected over a greasy pavement . . . , an open cellar-way yawned be-

[7] *Ibid.*, III, p. 81.
[8] *Ibid.*, III, p. 127.

neath the feet of those who might pause to gaze too fondly on the savoury wares displayed in the window; a strong odor of smoked fish, combined with a fragrance of molasses, hung about the spot; the pavement, toward the gutters, was fringed with dirty panniers, heaped with potatoes, carrots, and onions; and a smart, bright wagon, with the horse detached from the shafts, drawn up on the edge of the abominable road (it contained holes and ruts a foot deep, and immemorial accumulations of stagnant mud), imparted an idle, rural, pastoral air to a scene otherwise perhaps expressive of a rank civilization.

James' humorous intent becomes even clearer in his lame apology for having made so much of a neighborhood grocery store; "I mention it not on account of any particular influence it may have had on the life or thought of Basil Ransom, but for old acquaintance sake and that of local color; besides which, a figure is nothing without a setting. . . ."[9]

Henry James never insisted that his characters were the products of their environment, but he did have a sense of aesthetic congruity which made it seem appropriate to him that his retrograde Southerner should live in a backwater of New York City and that Miss Birdseye should die on the New England coast surrounded by other relics of a lost heroic age. And what is finally more intriguing here than the possibility that James was parodying a certain group of female authors, is the feeling he had that the elegiac note was the only true one for a post-Civil War study of American feminism. James had half guessed what female Jeremiahs like Catharine Beecher and, later, Charlotte Perkins Gilman knew in their bones. The national devaluation of moral heroism had been devastating to the woman's movement in general, and had left Miss Beecher and Mrs. Gilman, as well as Olive Chancellor, without any way to cherish or even acknowledge their own strongest feelings.

[9] *Ibid.*, II, pp. 43–44.

The later suffragists' inability to formulate a distinctively feminist ideology reduced the National Association to a kind of ladies' auxiliary of the Progressive movement. Carrie Chapman Catt and her cohorts believed that the enfranchisement of women, a disproportionately well-educated and native-born voting bloc, would introduce that element of responsibility into the electorate that others sought to institutionalize through primary elections and the powers of referendum and recall. Yet in truth, even the most radical first-generation American feminists never had a real analysis of the position of women. Instead, they had relied on an antinomian complex of ideas, largely drawn from Romantic and Sentimental literature, to fill the ideological vacuum.

This complex of ideas suggested to them that they had to trust their own intuitions about what was right and what was wrong. Strong feelings were holier than man-made laws or social conventions, and if these women felt in their hearts that they were being treated unfairly it was their sacred duty to protest. It was no coincidence that a disproportionate number of early feminists were Quakers. Not only were Quaker meetings the first enclaves in American society in which women were encouraged to speak out in public, but the faith behind that encouragement, faith that each individual, regardless of sex, had to act according to his inner lights, was just another way of phrasing the more broadly disseminated message of Romantic-Sentimental literature. Men and women could not rely on codes and conventions to keep them in the paths of righteousness. To deny women property rights, or custody of their children, or the vote, seemed to the early feminists tantamount to denying that they had immortal souls.

Unquestionably, then, Elizabeth Stanton and her contemporaries got invaluable support from the popular belief that Truth could only be known on the basis of internal experience, but they failed to provide for a time when American feminism would need to have an analysis of its own. Mrs. Stanton's humorous self-perception kept her from indulging in anachronistic role playing, and she knew when it was time to drop the Romantic heroine routine and to look to Theodore Roosevelt's imperialistic posturing for inspiration. Still, for all her mental agility, she was unable to make the woman's movement as a whole less vulnerable to changes in cultural style. In Madame de Staël and her heroine Corinne, in Charlotte Brontë and George Sand and George Eliot, Elizabeth Stanton found the data for her thesis that real greatness was an option for women as well as for men. And she could not help but fear that Literary Realists with their antiheroines would undermine the ability of American girls growing up after the Civil War to imagine woman's full potential. In 1883 she wrote in her diary that while William Dean Howells' "women . . . may be true to nature, . . . as it is nature under false conditions, I should rather have some pen portray the ideal woman, and paint a type worthy of our imitation."[10]

Howells conceived of Realism as a mental purgative for the American reading public which as far as he could tell was four-fifths female and thoroughly depraved in its taste. Yet while it is not difficult to see an anti-feminist animus in Howells' (and James's) writings, it is hard to imagine that either of them ever really appreciated how devastating their literary reforms might be to the future of feminism. Frances Willard, long-time president of the Woman's Christian Temperance Union, was even more outspoken than Elizabeth Stanton on the subject of Realism. "The writer of the W. D. Howells and Henry James school" was to her mind the enemy of the ideal woman of the twentieth century, as well as of the contemporary activist. "Not more 'conventional' was the style of art known as 'Byzantine,' which repeated with barren iteration its placid and colorless 'type,' than are the pages of this dreary pair whose books," she could only hope, "will put a period to the literary sentence

[10] Theodore Stanton and Harriot Stanton Blatch, eds., *Elizabeth Cady Stanton, As Revealed in Her Letters, Diary and Reminiscences* (New York, 1922), II, p. 213.

of the age."[11] Where would American girls find heroines, how would they be fired to struggle for woman's cause, if they were raised on Howells' and James's uninspiring pap?

Howells was ready to dismiss feminine resistance to the Realists' anti-heroines as just one more example of women's inability to face the facts about their own sex, or anything else. But he missed the point that Mrs. Stanton and Miss Willard were willing to concede—in the absence of living models, women were dependent upon fictional characters to enlarge their conception of the potentialities of their kind. Literature was a great factor in the socialization of women, and without novels (and poems) which portrayed women on an heroic scale, whole generations of nascent feminists might be stunted in their development. James was far more acute on this point than Howells (or later Jacobites), although he was clearly repelled by the need American women felt to canonize members of their sex and make the veteran campaigners, the Miss Birdseyes, their inspiration as the Romantic-Sentimental ideology lost credibility.

It meant something to Carrie Chapman Catt to be able to evoke the memories of those suffragists who were in the field before the Civil War. She could hope to make her battle plans inspirational through frequent reference to the dead and dying heroines of the cause. But her own thoughts were not shaped by the ideals of those heroines—she never really believed in the inner light or the potential sublimity of women's souls, and seemed instead to live her life by Howells' dictum that while "the present" is "not so spacious . . . as either the past or the future, . . . it's all we have." "Every day *is* the day of small things. . . ."[12]

Nonetheless, it is unfair continually to measure Mrs. Catt against Elizabeth Stanton and to find her wanting, for Carrie Catt would probably never have entered the larger-than-life-

[11] Frances E. Willard, *How to Win: A Book for Girls* (1888), quoted by Aileen Kraditor, ed., *Up from the Pedestal* (Chicago, 1968), pp. 316–17.

[12] William Dean Howells, *A Modern Instance* (Boston, 1881), p. 469.

size dimension even if she *had* believed every word of de Staël's *Corinne*. She actually was much closer in temperament to the Sentimentalists than to the more audacious Romantics. The Sentimentalists were soft-spoken reinterpreters of orthodox religious beliefs, generally only covertly interested in social rearrangements. Yet although Sentimental and Romantic authors can be distinguished easily enough in retrospect, there was a significant overlap in their viewpoints—and in their audiences. Mrs. Stanton, for example, was convinced that Madame de Staël was "a magnificent creature," yet she was delighted by the tearful effusions of Felicia Hemans whose *Records of a Woman* were "a worthy contribution to high-minded womanhood from the pen of a brilliant poetess. . . . How pleased I am," she confided to John Greenleaf Whittier, "when I see one of my sex doing anything well. . . ."[13]

Mrs. Stanton did not discriminate between Hemans and de Staël, in part, as she admitted, because she cherished any female who could write or speak intelligently. But it is important not to gloss over Elizabeth Stanton's major insight—that underlying the morally unexceptionable writings of the Sentimentalists was a fundamentally feminist reinterpretation of Calvinism. Madame de Staël had suggested that it was possible for a woman to be Byronic—at least if she were willing to die young. In a more devious and yet not dissimilar way, Sentimental authors undercut the monopoly on the word of God that orthodox Christians had awarded to an all-male ministerial corps.

Sentimentalism restructured the Calvinist model of salvation, making the capacity to feel, and above all to weep, in itself evidence of redemption. As women like Felicia Hemans and Lydia Huntley Sigourney saw it, the transformation from hardheartedness to grace might more easily be accomplished by reading a poem than by listening to a sermon. For the purposes of most American feminists, then, Romanticism and Sentimentalism were interchangeable, pro-

[13] Stanton, II, p. 15.

viding them with a potentially revolutionary ideology by suggesting that women, perhaps even more than their husbands and sons, could have direct and powerful access to the great Truths of the universe. Women were potentially magnificent souls; they could write, preach, and at the very least deserved to vote.

Of course, this ideology, if exaggerated, could become a new way to justify keeping women in their place. Faith in the supreme validity of pure feeling was a powerful weapon against laws and conventions. Yet, pushed too far, it fed into a definition of women as, at best, too good for this world, and at worst, hysterical. In fact, much of the crippling gentility that characterized the woman's movement by the end of the nineteenth century was simply an outgrowth of a Sentimentalism gone sexist. It was one thing to say that women could have direct access to heaven through their sacred feelings, and quite another to insist that women were generically purer and more spiritual than men. The former line of argument could be used to gain leverage against a male-dominated social order; the latter was a trap which women helped to prepare for themselves. Most second- and third-generation suffragists did not call for the vote on the grounds of an equal right to develop their full capacities as human beings; instead, they insisted on their pre-eminent purity as reason in itself to award them the ballot. They campaigned on the basis of what they embodied—not in terms of their right to explore.

However, this degeneration of Sentimentalism from a potentially feminist assault on religious orthodoxy to a slur word for all that made women unfit for full citizenship, cannot be understood in isolation from the widespread devaluation of the heroic style in literature, and in life. And while the idea that women could somehow gain power by exploiting their own emotional resources had within it the counterproductive notion that women were ever at the mercy of their impulses, the corruption of the Romantic-Sentimental ideology into a reaffirmation of the status quo was not somehow fated from the beginning. Certainly many feminists failed to keep the faith, but in a very real sense their cultural environment had failed them.

My purpose in these introductory pages is not to argue the inevitability or un-inevitability of the decline of the American taste for moral heroism after the Civil War, but simply to assert this decline as a fact, for the point of the anthology is not to visit an elaborate historical over-explanation on the heads of a group of women, but to listen carefully to what several women had to say about the way they saw themselves, the way they remembered their mothers and grandmothers, and the hopes they had for future generations. And it is my belief that all of the women represented here, with varying degrees of self-awareness to be sure, recognized the importance of the Romantic-Sentimental complex of ideas, either as a vital component of their self-definition, or as a cultural given that had enabled earlier generations of women simultaneously to value their own feelings and to insist upon their rights.

Unquestionably, women after the Civil War idealized the ante-bellum period as a high point in the development of their sex. Some of their descriptions of their mothers and grandmothers seem as far-fetched as any of the nineteenth-century lore about Daniel Boone and Davy Crockett. But there was a consistent element in their tall tales that was missing in the male-oriented mythos; a wistfulness not only about their female progenitors' strength and competence, but about their ability to show feeling. Above all, what the Romantic-Sentimental ideology had done for women was to provide them with a way to argue for legal reforms on the basis of passionate convictions. Women like Catharine Beecher and Harriet Beecher Stowe envied their mothers and grandmothers their mental as well as their physical health, insofar as they guessed that earlier generations of women had been able to demand change while still keeping in touch with their own inner needs.

Henry James made much of the constant mortification of taste that Olive Chancellor was forced to undergo as part of her dedication to a better future. She had to emerge from her

Back Bay mansion and endure the grime and glare of Miss Birdseye's public parlors. Yet this mortification is a trivial thing in comparison to the radical surgery James performed on Olive Chancellor's personality in the act of creating her. Carefully separating the two components of a healthy and functioning psyche—the urge to manipulate and the need to be dependent—James made Miss Chancellor the embodiment of the will to power while endowing her protégée, Verena Tarrant, with an almost holy passivity. Olive was pure Svengali; Verena pure Trilby. But there had been a time, or so women like Catharine Beecher and Charlotte Perkins Gilman would have us believe, when women in fact had "had it all together."

We are accustomed to thinking in terms of dichotomies—between career and home, for example, between a relentless future-orientation and the ability to live each day for itself. Yet women who could believe in the Romantic-Sentimental ideology were convinced that their emotional capacity in itself fit them to be full citizens of this world and the next. They did not have to choose between being Olive Chancellor; or Verena Tarrant; they could demand their political rights without trying to conceal from the world or from themselves, that they had feelings—of love and grief and indignation—because those feelings were in themselves proof that women were the equals of anyone.

II

As Thomas Carlyle's wife later remembered, Lydia Sigourney had caused a sensation when she arrived unexpectedly at their house one afternoon. The Carlyles and their guests "had all set in to be talkative and confidential—when this figure of an over-the-water-Poetess" burst in,

> beplastered with rouge and pomatum—bare necked at an age which had left *certainty* far behind—with long ringlets that never grew where they hung—smelling marvellously of camphor or hartshorne and oil—all glis-

tening in black satin as if she were an apothecary's puff
for black *sticking-plaster*—and staring her eyes out to
give them animation.[14]

The contrast between Mrs. Sigourney's own image of herself
as a "flowret," struggling for existence in a cruel world, and
this eyewitness account, is in its own way as striking as the
contrast between the hyper-feminine role of Sentimental
poetess and the way in which women like Lydia Sigourney
worked out their urge to male impersonation within the forms
of their art. The "American Hemans" and her sister Sentimentalists could have lucrative careers without being accused
of behaving in an unladylike fashion. Whatever success they
had was understood to be confirmation of their tender sensibilities and not the mark of unbecoming ambition.

'Twas But a Babe illustrates the kind of transsexual role
playing that the Sentimentalists indulged in. When the poem
begins, Mrs. Sigourney is a kindly passerby who comes upon
a new grave and asks, "Who goeth to his rest in yon damp
couch?/ The tearless crowds pass on—''twas but a babe.'" Ap-
palled by their callousness, she cries—what of a mother's love,
a mother's woe; what of the father whose agonized prayer is
heard only by God? This then is her cue, and quietly, between stanzas, the motherly stranger is transformed into the
Great Sympathizer, and Mrs. Sigourney speaks, if not precisely with the voice of God, with all the assurance of an experienced clergyman. "Trust to Him," she calls, "whose
changeless care . . . Passeth a mother's love." The child is
with cherubim and seraphim; "Can ye not hope? When a few
hasting years their course have run,/ To go to him, though he
no more on earth/ Returns to you."[15] Mrs. Sigourney was not
satisfied merely to hint that poem might be as efficacious as a

[14] Quoted by Gordon Haight, Mrs. Sigourney: *The Sweet of
Hartford* (New Haven, 1930), pp. 57–58.
[15] Lydia Huntley Sigourney, *Poems* (Philadelphia, 1836),
pp. 142–43. See also, Gail Thain Parker, "Mary Baker Eddy
and Sentimental Womanhood," *New England Quarterly*, XLIII
(March, 1970), 3–18.

sermon; she wanted to know the satisfactions of ministerial status at firsthand.

In her short story "The Father," she did not bother to change behind the scenes, but spoke out from the first with a man's voice. Nevertheless, the first page of the story reads more like the confessions of a career woman than anything else.

> . . . As my path was among the competitions and asperities of men, a character combining strong elements might have been in danger of becoming indurated, had it not been softened by the domestic charities. . . . I was anxious that my home should be the centre of intellectual and polished society, where the buddings of thought should expand unchilled and those social feelings which are the life blood of existence flow forth, unfettered, by heartless ceremony. —And so it was.[16]

Only gradually does the reader realize that the piece is not to be a candid appraisal of one woman's priorities, but the story of a father whose best self is elicited by the perfect dependency of his daughter.

A man's love for his son, according to Mrs. Sigourney, is mixed with ambition and inevitably tinged with impatience, while father and daughter may have a species of romance based on "the sex in hearts." The girl's gentle and mysterious womanhood "sublimate[s] his aspirations," while the support and protection she claims make him aware of his oneness with the universal principle of love. She is not only his greatest earthly joy, but, potentially, his salvation. "I was determined to take my seat in the sacred pavilion of intellect, and superintend what entered there," the father remembers, although in fact he goes beyond education to thought-control. "It was *for my sake*, that she strove to render herself the most graceful among women,—*for my sake*, that she rejoiced in the

---

[16] Lydia Huntley Sigourney, "The Father," in *The Young Ladies' Offering* (Boston, 1840), pp. 5–6.

effect of her attainments."[17] Yet according to the canons of Sentimentalism the father cannot be saved vicariously. His relationship with his daughter is at best a preparation; she weans his affections from the follies of this world and introduces him to the possibilities of perfect self-effacement. Before he can become worthy of God's grace she must die, and he must learn to weep.

After her death the father continues to get up in the morning and go to work, but every evening he seeks his daughter's grave.

> While the stars looked coldly on me, I spoke to her fondly and earnestly, as one who could not be denied. I said, "Angel! who art mine no longer, listen to me. Thou, who art raised above all tears, cause *one tear* to moisten my burning brow. Give it to me, as a token that thou hearest me, that thou hast not forgotten me."[18]

What the father does not know is that well-hidden friends have been watching every night with him, afraid his grief may shade into necrophilia. And finally it is their tender concern that saves him. Once he realizes that he has not been alone in his vigils, he becomes as helpless as an infant; the "torrents of tears flowed." By acknowledging his dependence on human love, he implicitly accepts the Redeemer, and when the story ends has reason to hope for a family reunion in heaven.

This is the Sentimental formula in full. In fact, Mrs. Sigourney was such a consummate practitioner of her art that it apparently satisfied all her deepest needs, for her interest social reform was minimal. She did favor the education of young ladies, oppose tight-lacing and strong drink, and support the Colonization Society, whose members hoped to solve America's race problem by sending the slaves back where they came from. In her poem *The African Mother at her Daughter's Grave*, the mother's grief is a sure sign that she has a soul

[17] *Ibid.*, pp. 7–9.
[18] *Ibid.*, pp. 14–15.

and can be emancipated from earthly cares.[19] The abolition of slavery was beside the point. Suffering was the key to the kingdom of heaven, and alleviating pain was consequently far down on Mrs. Sigourney's list of priorities. What *was* important was that the sufferer be educated to understand how his agony was related to Christ's agony on the cross. It was therefore the white man's burden to Christianize Africa, and Lydia Sigourney hoped to accomplish this mass conversion by sending educated ex-slaves back to Liberia to spread the Word.

Mrs. Sigourney's Sentimentalism was, if covertly feminist, hardly a call to unorthodox action. Through an adroit manipulation of Sentimental formulas she could simultaneously fulfill her ambitions and experience the solaces of a passive dependence on the Lord. Yet other women, not so fortunate as to have reconciled career and domesticity, fame and reputation, could not share Mrs. Sigourney's complacency. Their inner voices were not silenced by tears and promises of heaven; told to value their own feelings they felt compelled to speak out against laws and codes that violated their holy intuitions.

Lydia Maria Child, for example, never found perfect repose within her art. She was fascinated by Swedenborg's belief in the existence of precise correspondences between nature and the spirit, and more specifically, by the possibility that the correspondence between Fourier's plan of society and Swedenborg's description of life among the angels meant that Fourier had been sent to earth "to answer the prayer, 'Thy kingdom come on earth as it is in heaven.' "[20] Yet while she was intrigued by the prospect of social reorganization, she was even more charmed by the effect a lively sense of correspondence had on her perceptions here and now. "There *was* a time," she wrote in the first of her *Letters from New York*, when the blind beggar sitting before the mansion of the slave trader, when street cries and horse carts

[19] Sigourney, *Poems*, pp. 116–18.
[20] Lydia Maria Child, *Letters from New York*, I (New York, 1852), pp. 273–74.

would have passed me by like the flitting figures of the magic lantern, or the changing scenery of a theatre, sufficient for the amusement of the hour. But now I have lost the power of looking merely on the surface. Everything seems to me to come from the Infinite, to be filled with the Infinite, to be tending toward the Infinite.[21]

In short, Swedenborg's philosophy gave Mrs. Child a way to justify her own overwhelming interest in the contemporary scene. She could concentrate on local color only when she knew that her observations could be translated into spiritual terms on a moment's notice. For example, after praising the public gardens in New York, she goes on to point out "that in this worst emporium of poverty and crime, there are, *morally* speaking, some flowery nooks, and 'sunny spots of greenery.'" She has in mind the leaders of the Washington Temperance Society who scorn political maneuvering in order to follow "the Genius of Temperance" and the ways of sweet persuasion. Mrs. Child is deeply moved by the sight of a Washingtonian procession with banners and fire companies, military organizations, and troops of boys. "It was a beautiful pageant," she reflects in her *Letters,*

and but one thing was wanting to make it complete; there should have been carts drawn by garlanded oxen, filled with women and little children, bearing a banner on which was inscribed, WE ARE HAPPY NOW! I missed the women and the children; for without something to represent the genial influence of domestic life, the circle of joy and hope is ever incomplete.[22]

To Mrs. Child's way of thinking, no individual was so vicious that he could not be saved by maternal influence, or the influence of a maternal surrogate such as the Genius of Temperance—or the Virgin Mary. Like Mrs. Sigourney, she believed that brokenheartedness, not doctrinal purity, saved.

[21] *Ibid.,* I, p. 14.
[22] *Ibid.,* I, pp. 19–21.

It is not surprising then that she admired the Catholic Church for its refusal to engage in theological debate, and its ability to inspire the unquestioning faith of the Irish servant girl. To be sure, the Church was full of Popish absurdities, but Mrs. Child loved the faithful Irish all the more for their credulity. Their sympathy for the plight of slaves everywhere seemed to her the natural overflow of warm hearts. "Not in vain is Ireland pouring itself all-over the earth," she wrote in 1842. "Divine Providence has a mission to fulfil; though a mission unrecognized by political economists. There is ever a moral balance preserved in the universe, like the vibrations of the pendulum. The Irish, with their glowing hearts and reverent credulity, are needed in this cold age of intellect and scepticism." "Africa," she continued, "furnishes another class, in whom the heart ever takes guidance of the head;" and women, "on whose intellect ever rests the warm light of the affections, are obviously coming into a wider and wider field of action."[23]

Here, Mrs. Child's scorn for intellect must be read as the climax of a sustained defense of the downtrodden. Actually her allegiance to impulse was more ambiguous. The elaborate ways in which she worked out the doctrine of correspondence suggest how important it was to her to have a sense of intellectual mastery. Yet sometimes even Swedenborg's formulations were not enough, action not analysis was called for, and Mrs. Child was left face to face with her sympathetic energies. On one of her frequent walks through the city streets, she encountered two young boys fighting over some pennies. Nearby sat an emaciated woman who might have been their mother. "Poor forlorn wanderer!" muses Mrs. Child.

> Pence I will give thee, though political economy reprove the deed. They can but appease the hunger of the body; they cannot soothe the hunger of thy heart; that I obey the kindly impulse may make the world none the bet-

[23] *Ibid.*, I, p. 244.

ter—perchance some iota the worse; yet I must needs follow it—I cannot otherwise.[24]

Mrs. Child's scruples, her fear that charity might undermine character, were overcome by her desperate need to do something, to respond. The origin of her inhibitions, however, is perhaps more realistically located in her upbringing as a proper lady than in her vicarious allegiance to an ethic of self-help. One of the saddest sights to her (as to Jane Addams more than a half-century later) was a "young girl, born of wealthy and worldly parents; full of heart and soul, her kindly impulses continually checked by etiquette, her noble energies repressed by genteel limitations. She must not love until her parents have found a suitable match; she must not laugh" or run or work lest she be thought vulgar. "A very few, the noblest and strongest, can throw off shams and lead a comparatively true life without defensiveness." For the few who "accomplish this difficult task," Lydia Child felt "even more respect than . . . for those who struggle upward under the heavy burden of early poverty."[25]

For all her sympathy with the generous Irish, and Africans, and those women of whom the best that could be said was that they were affectionate, Mrs. Child was no egalitarian. Underlying her broadmindedness was a firm conviction that she, and women like her, were in the vanguard of spiritual evolution. She could tolerate Tom, Dick, and Harry in the faith that exposure to literature, music, flowers, and virtuous women would transform them into "Mr. Thomas, Richard, and Henry. In all these things," she lectured her audience, "the refined should think of what they can *impart*, not of what they can *receive*."[26]

Lydia Child's praise for the single standard was of a piece with this elitism; as far as she was concerned men were in sad need of all the virtues commonly prescribed for women.

[24] *Ibid.*, I, p. 97.
[25] *Ibid.*, II, pp. 280–81.
[26] *Ibid.*, I, p. 18.

That the feminine ideal approaches much more to the
gospel standard, than the prevalent idea of manhood, is
shown by the universal tendency to represent the Saviour and his most beloved disciple with mild, meek expression, and feminine beauty. None speak of the bravery, the might, or the intellect of Jesus; but the devil is
always imagined as being of acute intellect, political
cunning, and the fiercest courage.[27]

Yet not all of Mrs. Child's thwarted impulses were merciful
and supportive. She usually identified with a hermaphrodite
Jesus who suffered the little children to come unto him, but
sometimes she longed to lash out at that old slave trader, the
devil, and furtive acts of charity could not satisfy her.

Mrs. Child's *Letters* were a species of free association; she
wandered from observation to interpretation and back again.
Yet when her meanderings are charted they have a logic of
their own. Her account of the temperance parade is first supplemented by a short treatise on the domestic affections. Then
she has a vision of John the Baptist preparing a pathway
through the wilderness. And, finally, she comes back to the
parade to work out its correspondences. "Within the outward
form I saw, as usual, spiritual significance. The men's bodies
were being weaned from drink, so their souls were approaching those fountains of living water. . . . The music, too, was
revealed to me in fullness of meaning." It was military in
character, and as much as she loathed war, her "heart leaps
at the trumpet call and marches with the drum." With complete faith in her inner promptings, she concludes that martial music must be

the voice of resistance to evil, of combat with the false;
therefore the brave soul springs forward at the warlike
tone, for in it is heard a call to its appointed mission.
Whoso does not see that genuine life is a battle and a
march, has poorly read his origin and his destiny. . . .
It is right noble to fight with wickedness and wrong;

[27] *Ibid.*, I, p. 246.

the mistake is in supposing that spiritual evil can be overcome by physical means.[28]

In *The Bostonians*, James predicted that the militant feminists would never be able to live with victory—they were too fond of the fight.

> The world was full of evil, but she [Olive Chancellor] was glad to have been born before it had been swept away, while it was still there to face, to give one a task and a reward. When the great reforms should be consummated, when the day of justice should have dawned, would not life perhaps be rather poor and pale?[29]

Certainly the sense of anticlimax that followed the passage of the Nineteenth Amendment makes this observation seem prophetic, but as long as women like Lydia Maria Child—and Angelina Grimké Weld—clung to the vocabulary of religious struggle they were never without a cause to focus their energies. Sin was everywhere.

The martial note was not Mrs. Child's most consistent one, but it is easy to see in Angelina Weld the sacred rage that overflowed Sentimental formulas and fed into abolitionism and the woman's movement. Mrs. Weld was a Quaker convert. Unlike those of her contemporaries who followed their inner lights into feminism, she followed her feminist impulses straight to the inner light. But she was never able to confine herself to speaking out in meeting and, with her sister, was the first woman to take to the lecture platform. Mrs. Weld's "Appeal to the Christian Women of the South" is a perfect example of the kind of Sentimentalism that led to heretical action, as opposed to Mrs. Sigourney's more solipsistic art.

At the beginning of the "Appeal" her tone is sisterly and imploring; she has "*not* written in the heat of passion or prejudice, but in that solemn calmness which is the result of conviction and duty." She will speak hard truths gently.

[28] *Ibid.*, I, p. 21.
[29] James, *The Bostonians*, I, p. 243.

I have felt for you at this time, when unwelcome light
is pouring in upon the world on the subject of slavery;
light which even Christians would exclude if they could,
from our country, or at any rate from the southern portion of it, saying, as its rays strike the rock bound coasts
of New England and scatter their warmth and radiance
over her hills and valleys, and from thence travel onward over the Palisades of the Hudson, and down the
soft flowing waters of the Delaware, and gild the waves
of the Potomac, "hitherto shall they come and no
further. . . ."[30]

But this sweet compassion is not to last, and with almost in-
decent haste, Mrs. Weld transforms herself from the motherly
friend of conscience into the One who comes to judge. Only
ten pages into her "Appeal" she announces that "the *guilt of
the North* is increasing in a tremendous ratio as light is pouring in upon her on the subject and the sin of slavery."[31] Here
the warm rays of truth come as a judgment; "the sun of righteousness." And less than twenty-five pages into her "Appeal"
even this sun is wholly obscured by the

dark cloud of vengeance which hangs over our boasting
republic. Saw you not the lightning of Heaven's wrath,
in the flames which leaped from the Indians' torch to
the roof of yonder dwelling, and lighted with horrid
glare the darkness of midnight? Heard you not the thunders of Divine anger . . . ?[32]

Unlike Mrs. Child who sometimes stumbled over her own
anger in the course of her ramblings, Angelina Grimké Weld's
prose built inexorably to self-righteous rage. She marshalled
her facts and arranged them into lists—the six different ways
by which Jews became servants, the four laws specially designed to protect Jewish females in servitude—framing these

[30] Angelina Grimké Weld, "An Appeal to the Christian Women
of the South" (New York, 1836), p. 2.
[31] *Ibid.*, p. 10.
[32] *Ibid.*, p. 24.

lists with a rhetorical question, does this sound like American slavery? Women had always numbered among the army of martyrs, according to Angelina Grimké Weld, and it was now up to southern women to read, pray, speak, and act as Miriam and Deborah and the female members of anti-slavery societies had done before them. Slavery was sin, there could be no compromise with sin, every Christian not only had to preach abolition but to practice immediate emancipation. Laws forbidding such action violated conscience and could be broken with impunity. Who could doubt, Mrs. Weld asked in 1836, that all that stood between America and a righteous God was the "mighty engine of *moral power,*" in other words, the Bible and peace and temperance and abolition societies. "Who does not believe," she questioned her audience, "that if these societies were broken up, their constitutions burnt, and the vast machinery with which they are laboring to regenerate mankind was stopped, that the black clouds of vengeance would soon burst over our world . . . ?"[33]

Once Mrs. Weld got the stage her sacred rage could be sustained and channelled only by a reconstruction of the old evangelical drama—a vengeful Jehovah speaking through His impassioned ministry. She was never authentically Quaker in her rhetoric. And what she meant by the power of moral suasion was very different from what Lydia Maria Child meant by it—or Lydia Sigourney, or Catharine Beecher. Mrs. Child put her faith in the influence of the domestic affections; no man could resist the gentle pressure of a godly woman. Most of the Sentimentalists who usurped ministerial prerogatives coveted the right to comfort the sick at heart. Unlike Angelina Weld they did not want to be revivalists, female Charles Grandison Finneys, winning souls by asserting the merciless power of the Lord. They were the allies of the gentle Jesus with the golden curls. Catharine Beecher, however, had yet another alternative in mind; she would accept the notion of "sex in hearts" and of a special sphere for women, but then go on to insist on professionalizing the fe-

[33] *Ibid.,* p. 27.

male role so that women could have the status of doctors
and lawyers and preachers while maintaining a sexual
monopoly on the power of virtue.

Catharine Beecher was perhaps the greatest female anti-
Romantic in America. Unlike Angelina Weld and the Sentimentalists she did not believe for a minute that strong belief
flowed directly into passionate speech and action. She had a
far more mechanical conception of the way the human mind
worked than their images of gushing and flowing—tears,
words, good deeds implied. Catharine Beecher's watchword
was common sense; her great gift, as she saw it, was faculty.
She believed that ends and means were separable and she was
more than willing to move by indirection. Her attack on the
suffragists was characteristic. Miss Beecher deplored the fact
that a "large portion of those who demand woman suffrage
are persons who have not been trained to reason, and are
chiefly guided by their generous sensibilities." As far as she
could tell, they wrote and talked

> as if *reasoning* were *any kind* of writing or talking which
> tends to convince people that some doctrine or measure
> is true and right. And so they deal abundantly in excit-
> ing narratives and rhetorical declamations, and employ
> words in all manner of deceptive senses.[34]

Catharine Beecher believed St. Paul when he insisted on
the subordination of women, yet she also believed that the
meek would inherit the earth. And she had a scheme for hastening the day of inheritance. An opponent of evangelical
religion which depended upon an abrupt spiritual crisis to
bring the soul to God, she had a more gradual, a thoroughly
domesticated model for salvation. The real business of the
world went on in the home—the family state—and that business was bringing children to Jesus. Government outside the
home was a trivial concern; the future of the nation depended

[34] Catharine Beecher, "An Address to the Christian Women of
America," *Woman Suffrage and Woman's Profession* (Hartford,
1871), p. 200.

not on women's getting the vote, but on their staying home
and leading the young aright. There was a perfect division of
labor; man was

> the head, protector, and provider—woman the chief edu-
> cator of immortal minds—man [was] to labor and suffer
> to train and elevate woman for her high calling, woman
> to set an example of meekness, gentleness, obedience,
> and self-denying love, as she guides her children and
> servants heavenward.[35]

Catharine Beecher believed that even slavery was best abolished by a wise patience and the tactical use of moral suasion.
It is not surprising that Angelina Grimké Weld took her to
task as a sneak. In a volume of *Letters to Catharine Beecher
in Reply to an Essay on Slavery and Abolitionism,* Mrs. Weld
summarized her own understanding of human psychology, an
understanding remarkably like that of Jonathan Edwards.
"Real Abolitionists," she wrote there

> know full well, that the slave never has been, and never
> can be a whit the better for mere abstractions, floating
> in *the head* of any man; and they also know, that *prin-
> ciples,* fixed in the heart, are things of another sort. The
> former have never done any good in the world, because
> they possess no vitality, and therefore cannot bring forth
> the fruits of holy, untiring effort; but the latter live in
> the lives of their possessors, and breathe in their words.
> And I am free to express my belief that *all* who really
> and heartily approve our *principles,* will also approve our
> *measures;* and that, too, just as certainly as a good tree
> will bring forth good fruit.[36]

The aggressive tone which Catharine Beecher found repellent
in anti-slavery tracts, appealed to Mrs. Weld as a sure sign of
"uncompromising integrity and fearless rebuke of sin. . . ."

[35] *Ibid.,* p. 181.
[36] Angelina Grimké Weld, *Letters to Catharine Beecher in Reply to an Essay on Slavery and Abolitionism* (Boston, 1838), p. 6.

Beecher's model for coaxing the wayward into the paths of
virtue as a mother would coax a child seemed to her critic
little better than cheating the sinner out of his sin.[37]

Even more repulsive from Angelina Weld's point of view
was Catharine Beecher's analysis of the sources of woman's
power. " 'Woman is to win everything by peace and love;' "
Mrs. Weld mimicked,

> 'by making *herself* so much respected, &c, that to yield
> to *her* opinions, and to gratify *her* wishes, will be the
> freewill offering of the heart.' This principle may do as
> the rule of action to the fashionable belle, whose idol is
> herself; whose every attitude and smile are designed
> to win the admiration of others to *herself*. . . . But to
> the humble Christian, who feels that it is truth which
> she seeks to recommend to others, truth which she wants
> them to esteem and love, and not herself, this subtle
> principle must be rejected in holy indignation.[38]

Having worked herself up this far, Angelina Grimké could
not stop, and her final indictment of Catharine Beecher is not
only typical of her rhetoric, but in its own way a perfect sum-
mary of the differences between the two women.

> Hast thou ever asked thyself, what the slave would think
> of thy book, if he could read it? Dost thou know that
> from the beginning to the end, not a word of compas-
> sion for *him* has fallen from thy pen? Recall, I pray, the
> memory of the hours which thou spent in writing it!
> Was the paper once moistened by the tear of pity? Did
> thy heart once swell with deep sympathy for thy sister
> in *bonds*? Did it once ascend to God in broken accents
> for the deliverance of the active . . . ?
> I greatly fear that thy book might have been written
> just as well, hast thou not had the heart of a woman. It
> bespeaks a superior intellect but paralyzed and spell-
> bound by the sorcery of a worldly minded expediency.

[37] *Ibid.*, pp. 35, 42–43.
[38] *Ibid.*, pp. 104–5.

. . . Farewell! Perhaps on a dying bed thou mayest vainly wish that *Miss Beecher on the Slave Question* might perish with the mouldering hand which penned its cold and heartless pages.[39]

It is probably impossible to read Catharine Beecher without sharing some of Mrs. Weld's feelings. Her whole scheme to professionalize woman's traditional role and make self-sacrifice a science was rooted in a desire to replicate male career patterns. Having acknowledged a difference between the sexes, she hoped to capitalize upon it by developing an independent power base for all women. It is hard to know just what Catharine Beecher could have meant by "self-effacement" when, for example, in her "Address to Christian Women of America" she switched abruptly from preaching about the family state, to promoting the sales of her books. And her emulous animus is even more naked at the end of that speech when she digresses to talk about hygiene.

She introduces the topic with a long quote from a "regularly educated American physician" whose first thoughts are to the point—the standard, male, medical education does not teach the laws of nature and health. But Miss Beecher does not stop quoting here. She allows the doctor to speak on and on in her lecture, drawing an infernal picture of the medical student's life. And when at last she interrupts his monologue it is with a strangely inconsequent remark. Instead of concluding with her physician-spokesman that professional education is a waste of time (and often of health), she calls to

the women of our country to ask for benefactions, both private and legislative, to secure equal advantage for their professional duty as health-keepers, such as have so long and liberally been bestowed on men to train them for their professions?[40]

[39] *Ibid.*, pp. 128–29.
[40] Beecher, *Address,* pp. 195–96.

There is always a double bind in Catharine Beecher's reasoning. She simultaneously tried to make the role of the Victorian woman, that of mother, teacher, cook, and nurse, seem a divine given *and* to insist that the role could only be mastered in heavily endowed schools of domestic science. Catharine Beecher represents the moment of transition between the cosmology of Sigourney and Child and that of Carrie Chapman Catt, between a Romantic-Sentimental valuation of women as souls, and a strategic realism. Elizabeth Stanton was a transitional figure too, but her primary allegiance to self-expression gave her considerable mental agility, while Catharine Beecher got caught straddling the fence. Her ideas of the family state and the role of women were a kind of distilled Sentimentalism, but her commitment to reason and status politics were something else again.

Certainly her political strategy—power through purity—was the basic ploy of the degenerating woman's movement. Yet there was a kind of logic to the later suffragists' position that Catharine Beecher's antisuffragism lacked. If purity was power Carrie Catt wanted to know some of the pleasures of power now; she would not wait forever for her reward. In the nineteenth century the vote was perhaps not more immediately accessible than the perfect sexual apartheid Catharine Beecher longed for, but at least it provided an excuse for action, for a campaign that could channel some of the energies generated by the Sentimental conception of female superiority. In contrast, in order to effect a more perfect separation of the spheres women would have to become less aggressive than ever before, without any real guarantee that home management could be a sufficient outlet for moral genius. Mrs. Sigourney could weep and know the pleasures of a career. Lydia Maria Child had Sentimentalism, plus Swedenborg, plus a modified Manicheanism to help her release her pent-up feelings. Angelina Grimké Weld clung to evangelical models to phrase her hostility against slaveholders and Miss Beecher, Elizabeth Cady Stanton recommended vituperation to all women as the key to well-being, but Catharine Beecher never got the message. It is not surprising then to discover that

Miss Beecher, with all her self-repressive strategies, was rarely well herself, and was preoccupied with disease among the members of her sex.

The report she wrote on the appalling state of female health in America might be dismissed as a particularly ludicrous illustration of her determination to deal scientifically with woman's traditional role. Certainly there seems to be little gained by compiling figures based on such categories as "feeble," "quite feeble," "not well," "sickly," "very delicate."[41] But her observations do add another dimension to the laments of women after the Civil War that they were somehow less competent and in touch with their own needs than their grandmothers had been. Unquestionably, Sentimental role playing, when sundered from a valuation of moral heroism, was physically debilitating to many women. The compensations of invalidism were a constant temptation to ladies incapable of writing poems and yet as interested as Mrs. Sigourney ever was in exercising social control.

Helpless, suffering, pure, the woman who was never quite well wielded terrific power in the home where she was almost invariably being nursed. To give her credit, Catharine Beecher was repelled by the status of the "never well," and hoped to substitute her vision of a trained corps of home hygienists for the legions of the bedridden. Still it seems wonderfully appropriate that her own most cherished health reform was to provide fresh air in homes and schools. She was never so scientific, or so eloquent, as when she was describing ways to insure perfect ventilation. And who can wonder that she often felt claustrophobic?

Unlike her sister, Harriet Beecher Stowe wanted to vote. Many suffragists hoped Mrs. Stowe, the most famous woman in America, would become a feminist leader. But she disappointed them, and they never really understood the limits of her commitment. For Catharine Beecher voting was anathema because it signified a candid display of sexual

41 Catharine Beecher, "Statistics of Female Health," *Woman Suffrage and Woman's Profession*, pp. 121–33.

rivalry. Projecting her own power jealousies and adding them
to the animosities actually expressed by men, it is no wonder
that she feared the results of an open contest. Separate but
equal spheres were a psychological necessity for someone as
caught up in status politics as Catharine Beecher was.

Mrs. Stowe perceived the devolution of American womanhood just as her sister did, and "Heartily wished for the
strength and ability to manage my household matters as my
grandmother of notable memory managed hers." But she
feared "that those remarkable women of the olden times are
like the ancient painted glass,—the art of making them is lost;
my mother was less than her mother, and I am less than my
mother."[42] She sensed, as did Mrs. Sigourney, Mrs. Child,
and Mrs. Weld, the necessity for integrating ends and means,
feeling and action, and she found her own solution, if a temporary one, in writing *Uncle Tom's Cabin*.

Like her sister, with whom she produced the compendious
American Woman's Home, Harriet Beecher Stowe was interested in ventilation, nutrition, and co-operative laundries. In
previous generations, she assured her readers,

> a trained housekeeper knew just how many sticks of
> hickory of a certain size were required to heat her oven,
> and how many of each different kind of wood. She knew
> by a sort of intuition just what kind of food would yield
> the most palatable nutriment with the least outlay of
> accessories in cooking. She knew to a minute the time
> when each article must go into and be withdrawn from
> her oven; and if she could only lie in her chamber and
> direct, she could guide an intelligent child through the
> processes with mathematical certainty.[43]

Yet Mrs. Stowe did not become mired in the contradictory
notion that female intuition needed to be professionalized.
She believed in domestic education and deplored the fact the

[42] Harriet Beecher Stowe, *Household Papers and Stories, The
Writings of Harriet Beecher Stowe*, VIII (Cambridge, Mass.,
1896), p. 98.

[43] *Ibid.*, p. 98.

girls were no longer being taught to sew in school, but her imagination was never really gripped by endowed institutions devoted to a scientific cult of domesticity. She instead tried to heal the sundered lives of women by infusing their everyday actions with a higher meaning. Rather than advocating a direct expression of selfhood like Mrs. Stanton, Mrs. Stowe hoped to spiritualize trivia through an act of faith. Homemaking could become a full expression of the noblest woman's gifts if only she understood the larger meaning of her duties.

In a group of essays entitled *Household Papers*, Mrs. Stowe assumed the personality of a male journalist who used his wife and daughter to provide him with material for a regular column on the home. Women, according to this observer, had shown themselves capable of great endurance and self-sacrifice during the Civil War and now had the even larger responsibility of reconstructing the nation. They were the real architects of society; they alone could insure that America would not follow the corrupt ways of the Old World. The journalist's horror of social sophistication is reminiscent of Lydia Child's vision of New York as the New Babylon. But where Mrs. Child was interested in making a life of direct sympathy for the poor a real option for wealthy women, he, or rather Mrs. Stowe, had a more narcissistic solution. Instead of opening up the wellsprings of Christian charity, Harriet Stowe after the Civil War was more interested in the revivification of ladylike behavior, a project not unlike putting the Christ back into Christmas. "A noble-hearted woman puts a noble meaning into even the commonplace details of life," according to her journalistic spokesman. "Viewed in this light, even the small, frittering cares of woman's life—the attention to buttons, trimmings, thread, and sewing-silk—may be an expression of their patriotism and their religion."[44]

Interestingly enough, his daughter's friends are not convinced that they can save the nation by plain living.

"I'm sure," said Humming Bird, "we all would like to be noble and heroic. During the war, I did so long to

[44] *Ibid.*, p. 382.

be a man! I felt so poor and insignificant because I was nothing but a girl!"

"Ah, well," said Pheasant, "but then one wants to do something worth doing, if one is going to do anything. One would like to be grand and heroic, if one could; but if not, why try at all? One wants to be *very* something, *very* great, *very* heroic; or if not that then at least very stylish and very fashionable. It is this everlasting mediocrity that bores me."

Of course the journalist-Stowe cannot let this retrograde thinking go unchecked, and after reminders that Grant and Sherman needed privates—and women—to win the war, he sketches a new battle plan. "A whole generation" had had "the luxury of thinking heroic thoughts and being conversant with heroic deeds;" now women must unite to keep out the contagion of fashionable luxury and frivolity. They could join ranks once more to establish a *cordon sanitaire* against French manners.[45]

On one level these injunctions seem a transparent and probably harmless way to try to recreate the fervor and idealism of the war years. But they have a psychological as well as a political or pseudo-political reality which seems less innocent. The young girls longing for life on a heroic scale, craving immediate dramatic satisfactions rather than the rewards of death or national destiny, are belittled to begin with by their names. They are not Corinnes or Zenobias, but twittering little creatures—Humming Bird and Pheasant. And they are being asked to find fulfillment in a cause that makes no real contact with their need for a sense of personal worth.

More frightening than the denigration of these young girl's dreams, however, is the saga of sainthood told in another essay by the journalist-Stowe entitled "The Cathedral." In this parable Aunt Esther is the perfect embodiment of that self-abnegation which is at the heart of Mrs. Stowe's emphasis on being "truly noble and heroic in the insipid details of every-

[45] *Ibid.*, pp. 383–84.

day life. . . ."[46] Aunt Esther had been born with a vehement, impulsive nature. "Devoted as she always seemed to the mere practical and material, she had naturally a deep romance and enthusiasm of temperament which exceeded all that can be written in novels. . . . She never saw her hero, and so never married." Family cares, the tending of the young, were particularly irksome to her and yet she had devoted her life to caring for sick children and the well children of sick mothers. Above all, she had had a passionate desire for travel, and a short time before she dies murmurs to a friend, "All my life my desire to visit the beautiful places of this earth has been so intense, that I cannot but hope that after my death I shall be permitted to go and look at them."[47] Only in heaven could she play the Romantic heroine or even trace the steps of such a woman.

It comes as no great surprise then (as in the case of Catharine Beecher) that she for whom "life was a constant repression" suffered from "much ill health" and "a tendency to depression of spirits, which at times increased to a morbid and distressing gloom."[48] Of course Aunt Esther learned to suppress every outward manifestation of these trials; saintly self-abnegation did not allow even the mixed pleasures of a periodic invalidism. Harriet Beecher Stowe knew what these pleasures were and cultivated a fashionable delicacy herself. But significantly, she seems never to have been capable of the perfect repression practiced by Aunt Esther. As a young woman she read *Corinne* and was entranced by the subtle worldliness of Madame de Staël's heroine of whom she wrote: "Her fancy was changeful; talent, especially in a woman, creates a zest for variety that the deepest passion cannot entirely supply. A monotonous life, even in the bosom of content, dismays a mind so constituted. . . ."[49] Unquestionably Harriet Beecher identified with this passionate creature and

[46] *Ibid.*, p. 414.
[47] *Ibid.*, p. 420.
[48] *Ibid.*, p. 422.
[49] Quoted by Constance Rourke, *The Trumpets of Jubilee* (New York, 1927), p. 93.

lamented the fact that her own throbbing sensibilities had never had room to develop in the overcrowded homes she lived in all her life. Unlike the saintly Aunt Esther, she rebelled against her lot; her genius did not find perfect sublimation in domesticity.

Constance Rourke in *The Trumpets of Jubilee* has hypothesized that Mrs. Stowe "had been caught in the toils of a formula as harsh and unyielding as any physical institution of bondage," and that it was this experience which gave *Uncle Tom's Cabin* its uncanny power. She had been dominated first by her father's Calvinism and then by the dogmatism of Calvin Stowe. In marriage she felt the additional pressures of too many children and not enough money. The "endless restraints imposed by the Fugitive Slave Law" were the

> final image of restriction. . . . Ardent and tired and overwrought, in that sensitive state where the imagination grows fluid, where inner and outer motives coalesce, she had taken bondage as her theme and had become obsessed with its conditions, morbidly obsessed by the concomitant punishment, the terrible infliction of pain. . . .[50]

With the enormous success of *Uncle Tom's Cabin*, Mrs. Stowe entered on a new phase of her life. She was no longer confined by domestic circumstances; she had the opportunity to visit Corinne's Italy and to patronize the great. Yet she seemed, in Constance Rourke's words, "to be repeating an endless pattern. After her romantic flights, once again, as in the earlier years of her marriage, she was caught within the net of weary personal responsibilities. . . ."[51] She had to write to meet her debts and could no longer afford a Romantic view of Europe. It is at this point that we have come upon her in *The Household Papers*, inveighing against knickknacks and chicken salad, and writing, both in these essays and the *Amer-*

[50] *Ibid.*, p. 108.
[51] *Ibid.*, p. 131.

ican Woman's Home, of furnaces and ventilation and how to frame chromos with crossed strips of native wood.

The Civil War was not only a time of national heroism for Mrs. Stowe, but the period of her own greatest triumphs. Reconstruction was anticlimactic on every front. A nativist crusade against European sophistication seemed to her one way in which the old zeal might be recaptured; it was a way of reconnecting domestic virtue and confrontation politics. But Harriet Stowe's own fundamental pessimism about ever making the connections again can be seen in Aunt Esther, and more particularly in Aunt Esther in heaven. When she wrote *Uncle Tom,* Mrs. Stowe had portrayed life after death in terms of blissful repose; Tom deserved a rest. But what Aunt Esther deserved was a Romantic journey to satisfy her unsatisfied impulses. It would have been too horrible to imagine her slipping into a dreamless sleep.

Sarah Orne Jewett, unlike Mrs. Stowe (and Henry James) did not get personal and political history confused. She lamented the passing of a larger and more independent race of men and women, particularly women, but she was not caught up in any scheme to restore the old fervor—or to find satisfaction in the grave. Hers are the satisfactions of preservation; the squirrels know by instinct to gather nuts for the hard winter; Mrs. Goodsoe in "The Courting of Sister Wisby" has a "dreadful graspin' fit" for mulleins, it seems as if she knows she's "goin' to need 'em extry." And Sarah Orne Jewett, in the person of a sophisticated younger woman home only for a vacation invites her reader "to share the winter provision."

> This was one of those perfect New England days in late summer, where the spirit of autumn takes a first stealthy flight, like a spy, through the ripening countryside, and, with feigned sympathy for those who droop with August heat, puts her cool cloak of bracing air about leaf and flower and human shoulders. Every living thing grows suddenly cheerful and strong; it is only when a little maple that has second-sight and foreknowledge of coming desolation to her race—only then

does a distrust of autumn's friendliness dim your joyful
satisfaction.[52]

But Sarah Orne Jewett is no James Agee. She is not the spy,
the sophisticated intruder; she cannot despoil any more than
she can save. Everything has a reality outside her consciousness; her stories are constructed but seemingly not projected.
And this gives "The Courting of Sister Wisby" its unique
documentary value, preserving intact the late nineteenth-
century sense that something had gone out of the lives of
women.

Mrs. Goodsoe, who is full of arcane lore about herbal healing, admits that she cannot hold a candle to her mother, a
woman who not only cured with herbs, but, when the need
arose, by tears. Many years before, a widow in the neighborhood had lost all her children in a single week and yet remained dry-eyed. Mrs. Goodsoe's mother (or perhaps it was a
neighbor woman, for they were apparently interchangeable
in their wisdom) felt certain that the widow would lose her
reason if she did not find emotional release, so she arranged
to have the local Irishman, a warm-hearted "creature" from
the pages of Lydia Maria Child, come and play on his fiddle.
He could break hearts with a tune, and no sooner had he
begun to play than the little woman crawled into Mrs. Goodsoe's mother's lap and cried herself into a "blessed sleep." At
this point in the story the younger woman's eyes fill with tears,
but she feels so uncomfortable about her losing her self-
possession that she immediately makes a cynical remark.[53]
The moral of the story seems clear; pure sentiment is too powerful for modern women to handle. In the process of getting
ahead in the world, of becoming smart and up-to-date, they
have lost the ability to really feel. Eccentricity, or at least a
healthy selfhood, Sarah Orne Jewett seems to be saying, was
the source of those deep human sympathies which all New

[52] Sarah Orne Jewett, "The Courting of Sister Wisby," *Great
Modern American Stories*, William Dean Howells, ed. (New York,
1920), pp. 193, 190.
[53] *Ibid.*, pp. 198–99.

Englanders, but particularly women, had felt before the Civil War.

The second half of Mrs. Goodsoe's tale shows the harder side of the New England matriarchy; the great women of the past could be shrews as well as Sentimentalists. Yet when the story ends we are back with Mrs. Goodsoe and back inside nature. The note of melodrama at the beginning in the little maple's horror is never sounded again, and when we last see her, Mrs. Goodsoe is planning to plant the peach pits the younger woman has brought and to live to see them grow and bear fruit. Miss Jewett does not have suggestions for national rebirth; she laughs with Mrs. Goodsoe and her visitor when they catch themselves feeling penitent about progress. Her sole object seems to have been to record the history of an earlier generation of women whom she believed to have been more knowing, and feeling, than herself.

Mrs. Goodsoe's sly feminism is evident not only in her failure to remember a single masterful man, but in her jibes at modern professionals. Doctors to her are "book fools" who know less about healing than the average middle-aged woman did fifty years ago, and ministers are bores and pedants. "Now I'm a believer," she assures her young visitor, "and I try to live a Christian life, but I'd as soon hear a surveyor's book read out, figgers an' all, as try to get any simple truth out o' most sermons."[54] As far as Mrs. Goodsoe is concerned, these educated men are out of touch with reality—in other words, with nature. They lack an intuitive knowledge of the relationship between body and soul. However, Mrs. Goodsoe is not interested in founding a rival female professional class, for she knows that her lore cannot be transmitted through endowed institutions.

Elizabeth Cady Stanton was capable of a sardonic humor about the battle of the sexes very similar to Mrs. Goodsoe's; she did not need to believe in a separate sphere for women to insulate herself from her own aggressive instincts. In her *Reminiscences* Mrs. Stanton celebrated her childhood tan-

[54] *Ibid.*, p. 196.

trums as justifiable acts of rebellion against the tyranny of those in authority: "I have often listened since," she wrote, "with real satisfaction to what some of our friends had to say of the high-handed manner in which sister Margaret and I defied all the transient orders and strict rules laid down for our guidance."[55]

Her earliest memories were of her father whom she confused in her mind with the Calvinist God he worshiped. When his only son died, Judge Cady played "The Father" by Sigourney, with a significant twist. The boy had meant more to him than all his daughters put together. "I taxed my every power," Mrs. Stanton recalled, "hoping some day to hear my father say, 'Well, a girl is as good as a boy, after all.' But he never said it." Even after she had won a prize in Greek, competing against older boys in the neighborhood academy, he kissed her "on the forehead and exclaimed, with a sigh, 'Ah, you should have been a boy!'"[56] Once when she threatened to cut those codes which discriminated against women out of his law books, he offered her an alternative: "'When you are grown up, and able to prepare a speech,' said he, 'you must go down to Albany and talk to the legislators . . . if you can persuade them to pass new laws, the old ones will be a dead letter.'"[57]

Yet this was apparently only meant as a palliative, for when Elizabeth Stanton actually began to speak out for women's rights her father bitterly opposed her. "To think," she wrote Susan B. Anthony, "that all in me of which my father would have felt a proper pride had I been a man, is deeply mortifying to him because I am a woman. That thought has stung me to a fierce decision. . . . I will both write and speak."[58] Constance Rourke suggested that in championing the slave (and Lady Byron) Harriet Beecher Stowe was working out the repression she had experienced

[55] Stanton, I, p. 10.
[56] *Ibid.*, I, pp. 23–25.
[57] *Ibid.*, I, p. 34.
[58] *Ibid.*, II, pp. 59–60.

first as a daughter and then as a wife. Yet Mrs. Stowe was never able to justify rebellion in and for itself. Mrs. Stanton had been pushed farther: her father and husband did more than ignore her feelings, they directly opposed her chosen career. Her life was not to be a recurrent cycling—repression, liberation, repression—but one long, determined push against authority as such.

The letters she addressed to Susan Anthony while she was still housebound are full of explosive imagery. She was no Catharine Beecher, calling for a little air in the name of common sense. "I am at the boiling point!" she wrote. "If I do not find some day the use of my tongue . . . I shall die of an intellectual repression, a woman's rights convulsion."[59] Another letter begins with a half-lament that her "machinery" is capable of running a long time.

> Of course I may burst my boiler screaming to boys to come out of the cherry trees and to stop throwing stones, or explode from accumulated steam of a moral kind that I dare not let off, or be hung for breaking the pate of some stupid Hibernian for burning my meat or pudding on some company occasion.[60]

Mrs. Stanton was quick to see the connection between excessive self-restraint and physical weakness. In a letter to Lucretia Mott in 1852, she rejoiced in the birth of a daughter (she had already had four sons), and in her own and the child's robustness. Margaret Livingston Stanton weighed twelve pounds and Mrs. Stanton had taken to her bed only minutes before her birth, sitting up immediately afterward to change her clothes.

> Am I not almost a savage? For what refined, delicate, genteel, civilized woman would get well in so indecently short a time? Dear me, how much cruel bondage of mind and suffering of body poor woman will escape when she

[59] *Ibid.*, II, p. 41.
[60] *Ibid.*, II, p. 52.

takes the liberty of being her own physician of both
body and soul![61]

Ministers, like doctors, were fair game for her plays of wit
and displays of expertise. Elizabeth Stanton had never gotten over seeing northern churchmen hesitate to speak out
against slavery while at the same time attacking emancipated
women. When Elizabeth and Henry Stanton purchased a new
house in Boston she felt that she knew how a young minister
must feel taking charge of his first congregation. But she was
not going to play minister any more than she was going to
play doctor—or house. Significantly, the medicine she practiced on her neighbors and family was homeopathic—an anti-
authoritarian therapeutics based on infinitesimal doses. Ho-
meopaths rejected the heroic treatments which made the
patient a passive victim of his physician, and recognized the
capacity of the body to restore normal functioning with little
intervention. Mrs. Stanton's most chilling illustration of false
medical expertise was taken from the experience of the
Welds who nearly starved their first child on the advice of
an "authority" who maintained that the infant stomach could
only hold an ounce or so of milk at a time.

This near disaster may have destroyed Angelina Weld's
faith in radical dietary reform, but she never went so far as
to deny that there were divinely authorized courses of action. As far as Mrs. Stanton was concerned, however, the supposed Word of God was simply a timeworn cover for the
crudest sort of authoritarian behavior. God, she was quite
sure, had never spoken directly to man (or woman), and no
one could speak directly for Him. Her own father had refused
to acknowledge the worthiness of her female soul, and after
a fearful harrowing at the hands of the revivalist Charles
Grandison Finney, she became a freethinker once and for
all. *The Woman's Bible*, which so scandalized the conservative suffragists, was just one more manifestation of Mrs. Stanton's determination to hold nothing sacred, indeed to single

[61] *Ibid.*, II, pp. 44–45.

out the most sacred institutions for attack. "At the inauguration of our movement," she recalled in 1899,

> we numbered in our Declaration of Rights eighteen
> grievances covering the whole range of human experi-
> ence. On none of these did we talk with bated breath.
> . . . In response to our radicalism, the bulwarks of the
> enemy fell as never since. . . . But at present our asso-
> ciation has so narrowed its platform for reasons of policy
> and propriety that our conventions have ceased to point
> the way.[62]

Mrs. Stanton's radicalism had never been egalitarian. Her
Romantic valuation of each individual's potential made her
tolerant of human differences, but she herself never genuinely identified with the undeveloped. "That a majority of
the women in the United States accept the disabilities which
grow out of their disenfranchisement," seemed to her "simply an evidence of their ignorance and cowardice, while the
minority who demand a higher political status clearly prove
their superior intelligence and wisdom."[63] By the end of the
nineteenth century she was advocating an educational quali-
fication for suffrage as well as American imperialism. "What
would this continent have been if we'd left it to the Indians,"
she asked, but it was a rhetorical question.[64]

Toward the end of her life Elizabeth Cady Stanton had
begun to see the value of moderation. In retrospect she could
imagine that Lincoln, had he lived, might have handled Reconstruction more adroitly than her own chosen allies the
Radical Republicans. But she never changed her mind about
the primary importance of self-development, and was unable
to make personal compromises in the name of political expediency. It may seem regrettable that Mrs. Stanton's Romanticism shaded off into a mild form of master-racism to-

[62] *Ibid.*, p. 346.
[63] Elizabeth Cady Stanton, *Eighty Years and More* (New York,
1898), p. 318.
[64] Stanton, II, p. 341.

ward the end of her life, yet it is hard to see how she could have enjoyed the healthy self-esteem which separated her feminism from the covert self-hate of the genteel and the hyper-professional alike, if she had not had a vision of the Romantic heroine who made every woman's life seem open-ended when she explored her own inner spaces.

Jane Addams, in contrast to Mrs. Stanton, identified most strongly with people who had never developed their full potential. She supported suffrage not as a means of self-expression, but as a way of enabling women to protect those values which they embodied—succor of the weak and tenderness for the helpless. Like everyone else who argued for the vote on the basis of special female virtues, she was deeply disappointed when women proved to be as callous and militaristic as men. But in truth, her personal heroes were not women of great purity or passion, but Lincoln, Mazzini, and her father. And what she admired most about these men was their love for the common people. Jane Addams never had a conversion experience of the kind that dramatically separates saints from sinners; instead, as she tells it, one day she simply gave up the conceit of being good in her own right and turned to Christian fellowship as the outward symbol of an "almost passionate devotion to the ideals of democracy. . . ."[65]

Jane Addams' thoughts on Lincoln were confused with the tenderest memories of her own father. At Hull-House she tried to prove to first-generation Americans eager to lose their "foreignness" that Lincoln's greatness lay in "his marvelous power to retain and utilize past experience."[66] At the same time, she tried to convince the "Old Settlers" in the neighborhood that the immigrants were not so very different from the native-born by emphasizing their common experience—one of loss. Those who had come from Europe and those who had migrated from "back East" had left behind them a whole

[65] Jane Addams, *Twenty Years at Hull-House* (New York, 1911), p. 79.
[66] *Ibid.*, p. 37.

range of precious associations, a sense of rootedness, that could never be reconstructed in Chicago. One neighbor who reproached her for having so many "foreign views" on the walls, was placated by the idea that those familiar scenes meant as much to the new Americans as a Yankee notion had once meant to him, "thereby formulating the dim kinship between the pioneer and the immigrant."[67]

In fact, Jane Addams might reasonably be accused of cherishing her fellow men most for what they were missing. She quite frankly preferred to deal with naturalized citizens who still had some memory of the homeland, or with the shabby genteel who had slipped into poverty while clinging to an earlier taste for culture. She was first attracted to the building that was to become Hull-House by the purity of its Corinthian columns, and she determined to furnish it with photographs and other "impedimenta" collected in Europe, supplemented by a few pieces of family mahogany, in the belief that "the Settlement may logically bring to its aid all those adjuncts which the cultivated man regards as good and suggestive of the best life of the past."[68]

Jane Addams and her co-workers have been accused of trying to reconstitute an anachronistic village ambiance in Chicago. Yet her tendency to love her neighbors best for what they had lost was the source of a genuine respect for human differences. In the first place, while *she* felt more comfortable with mahogany furniture and her confused memories of her father and Lincoln, she cherished what reminded other people of their old homes. And in the second, well, it may only be necessary to think back to Lydia Maria Child's love of the Irish and Afro-Americans for their credulity and warm-heartedness to see how truly tolerant Jane Addams' nostalgic tastes were. Believing that the modern world needed simple and superstitious people to balance the domination of cold reason and materialism, Mrs. Child did not allow for any defections from the Sentimental ranks. A lace-curtain

[67] *Ibid.*, p. 108.
[68] *Ibid.*, p. 94.

Irish family or a black businessman would have been no more appealing to her than a grotesquely learned woman. In contrast, Jane Addams' value system allowed room for growth and change, while predicating growth on length and depth of memory. Lincoln could become President because he could remember life on the farm; she could become a career social worker because of what she could not forget about her own childhood.

Jane Addams' valuation of past experience took on a distinctly personal dimension when she wrote about declension among American women. Although a second-generation feminist, Jane Addams was a member of the first generation of college women, and she was concerned about this new group's miseducation. They had "departed too suddenly from the active, emotional life led by their grandmothers and great-grandmothers" she feared, and "somewhere in the process of 'being educated' they had lost that simple and almost automatic response to the human appeal, that old healthful reaction resulting in activity from the mere presence of suffering or of helplessness. . . ."[69]

It is in statements like these about the "snare of preparation" that Jane Addams really is the heir of Lydia Maria Child. Unlike Mrs. Child there was room in her value system for evolution; she could sympathize with the new Americans who wanted to get ahead. But this does not get around the fact that she herself always preferred those who lived in memory (whether her father who lived in her memory, or the immigrant whose drunken ravings still had a pastoral content). The helpless and weak touched her heart as the up-and-coming never could. Hidden in her valuation of mutuality was a profound self-mistrust, the mistrust of the little girl who walked into church each Sunday with her uncle so that no one would guess that such a fine-looking man as Mr. Addams had a daughter with a crooked back.

Judge Cady's open discrimination against women had driven his daughter to a passionate self-reliance. Jane Ad-

[69] *Ibid.*, p. 71.

dams' father, who "wrapt . . . [her] in his large/ Man's doublet, careless did it fit or no," left his child unable to let her feelings out, except in the direction of those distinctly smaller and weaker than herself.[70] She admired her grandmothers for their instinctive ability to respond to need, but characteristically failed to identify the other side of their competence, their ability to acknowledge their own needs. Sarah Orne Jewett was trying to preserve through art what Jane Addams hoped to keep alive through institutions—the most singular and yet broadly appealing aspects of earlier ways of life—but Mrs. Goodsoe's herbs would have lost their medicinal value had she shared Jane Addams' feeling, there is no health in me.

In *Twenty Years at Hull-House,* Jane Addams recounted her collapse after a semester in medical school as "but the development of the spinal difficulty which had shadowed me from childhood."[71] Three years earlier in *Democracy and Social Ethics,* she had had a more complicated analysis of the plight of the female college graduate whose health gives way under the strain of trying to live according to her convictions. Waiting for some worthy demand to be made on her powers, the young woman collapses and "her physician invariably advises a rest. But to be put to bed and fed on milk is not what she requires."[72] This is precisely what did happen to Jane Addams when she entered S. Weir Mitchell's hospital after her own breakdown. Dr. Mitchell specialized in a drastic rest cure in which massage was substituted for exercise, visitors and letters were banned, and the patient was fed an all-milk diet to which bland and starchy foods were gradually added. His specialty was the cure of neurasthenic women, women whose complaints were believed to be largely neurotic, by reducing them to a condition of infantile dependence on their physician.

Mitchell was outspoken in his anti-feminism and was con-

[70] *Ibid.,* p. 22.
[71] *Ibid.,* p. 65.
[72] Jane Addams, *Democracy and Social Ethics* (New York, 1907), p. 87.

vinced, among other things, that higher education was debilitating to the female. At the same time, he was determined
to reduce the pleasures of invalidism by removing the suffering woman from her home, making it impossible for her to
play upon the sympathies of her relatives. It has been suggested that the great popularity of his regimen was correlated
with its drastic quality—what could be more shocking in
America at the end of the nineteenth century than to be told
to take to your bed and do nothing? But if this explains why
exhausted businessmen were drawn to Mitchell's hospital, it
does not tell us why his methods attracted their wives and
daughters. In prescribing the ultimate in feminist put-down,
Dr. Mitchell no doubt appealed to the oppressed relatives of
the never-well, yet his directives must also have had a real
(if temporary) attraction for the neurasthenic woman herself. She could find relief from the gnawing sense that her
life was being wasted in his assurances that what she mistook
for unused potential was nothing more than diseased imagination.

Charlotte Perkins Gilman wrote a story about her experiences under S. Weir Mitchell's care, a story which William
Dean Howells, despite misgivings, chose to include in his
Great Modern American Stories (along with "The Courting
of Sister Wisby"). Howells felt he had to apologize for his
selection saying, in his introductory remarks, that he had
"shivered" over "The Yellow Wall-Paper" and still basically
agreed "with the editor of *The Atlantic* . . . that it was too
terribly good to be printed."[73] Mrs. Gilman set her story in
a nursery to underscore the determination of Mitchell and
his disciples to reduce their female patients to the docility
and dependency of childhood. Ironically, however, the former
residents of Mrs. Gilman's barred playroom were more vicious
and hostile than anything Mitchell ever bargained for; they
had gouged off the wallpaper and gnawed at the bedstead.
And it is this childish rage that Mrs. Gilman's heroine relives

[73] William Dean Howells, ed., *Great Modern American Stories*,
vii.

under the watchful eyes of her husband, brother, and serenely domestic sister-in-law. She tears the paper and bites the bed and has her moment of triumph when her horrified husband faints dead away after being forced to recognize what happens to a woman who is denied the right to be an adult.[74]

Mrs. Gilman's life story as she later told it in her autobiography suggests some of the sources of her hostility to dependence in any form. Her father deserted his family; her mother, who as a girl had been threatened by consumption and besieged by lovers, grew up to be a passionately domestic woman with a spaniel-like devotion to her absent husband. Mrs. Perkins' domestic disappointments drove her to try to protect her daughter from a similar fate by stifling every impulse to show her affection. She apparently felt, or so her daughter believed, that if Charlotte never grew accustomed to love she would never crave it. Mrs. Gilman managed to internalize her mother's stoicism, and to place even more stringent demands on herself, with the result that she achieved a kind of emotional anesthesia.

Her descriptions of her relentless self-culture sound like a more flagellatory and self-hating Benjamin Franklin. In an attempt to overcome a reputation for thoughtlessness, Charlotte Perkins methodically visited a young invalid whose infirmities repelled her. She felt certain that by sacrificing her own tastes and time to the comfort of the crippled girl she would grow to love her. "And sure enough," she wrote in her autobiography, "after a while I became quite fond of the girl." But the real climax of the tale was yet to come. "In

[74] Charlotte Perkins Gilman, "The Yellow Wall-Paper," *Great Modern American Stories*, pp. 320–37. As Mrs. Gilman reconstructed her motives in *The Living of Charlotte Perkins Gilman*, "The real purpose of the story was to reach Dr. S. Weir Mitchell and convince him of the error of his ways. I sent him a copy as soon as it came out, but got no response. However, many years later, I met some one who knew close friends of Dr. Mitchell's who said he had told him that he had changed his treatment of nervous prostration since reading 'The Yellow Wallpaper.' If that is a fact, I have not lived in vain." (New York, 1935), p. 399.

about two years I heard through a kind cousin that some old lady had said that she did like Charlotte Perkins—she was so thoughtful of other people. 'Hurrah!' said I, 'another game won!' "[75]

How little a "game" this really was to Mrs. Gilman can be seen when she herself became an invalid after giving birth to a daughter. Her "handmade character" disintegrated when she was faced with the responsibility for a wholly dependent creature. Her "riotous virtues," like her ritual body building, represented the attempts of a severely mistrustful person to make it absolutely on her own. With a father who could never be counted on and a mother who demanded a total sacrifice of independence and individuality, Charlotte Perkins' earliest training had been in mortifying her feelings, in ignoring her deepest needs. It is not hard to understand why she was unable to cope wtih the demands of a husband and infant. "Motherhood means giving. . . ." she wrote in her autobiography, and then: "Here was a charming home; a loving and devoted husband; an exquisite baby, healthy, intelligent and good; a highly competent mother [Mrs. Perkins] to run things; a wholly satisfactory servant—and I lay all day on the lounge and cried."[76]

Before she visited S. Weir Mitchell, Charlotte Gilman had sent him a complete history of her case—which he interpreted as "self conceit. He had a prejudice against the Beechers. 'I've had two women of your blood here already,' he told me scornfully." Then he put her to bed and had her fed, bathed, and rubbed. His parting advice was to live as domestic a life as possible, to keep her baby with her at all times, to "have but two hours intellectual life a day, never [to] touch pen, brush or pencil" as long as she lived.[77] There is something ludicrously misogynistic about this last injunction —a total ban not only on penis envy but on its most sublimated forms. Yet what is more appalling is the fact that Dr. Mitch-

[75] *Ibid.*, pp. 58–59.
[76] *Ibid.*, p. 89.
[77] *Ibid.*, pp. 95–96.

ell gave the same advice to Jane Addams, although European travel was to take the place of a baby in her case. Of course there were similarities between the two women; both had terrific energies they were unable to find outlets for. Both were full of self-mistrust and had great difficulty expressing affection. But left to heal themselves they did so in diametrically opposed ways.

A settlement house was a nightmare to Charlotte Gilman, an institutionalization of her worst fears about invasion of privacy. A handmade character always seemed vulnerable, and she was revolted by the prying presence of servants long before she turned her attention to the "mind-meddling" of psychiatrists. Jane Addams' preservationist tendencies were anathema to her. Mrs. Gilman did not love people best for their memories; on the contrary, she was a dedicated idol smasher, who attacked orthodox religion and that holy of holies the home.

Charlotte Perkins Gilman has been called the only genuinely radical thinker in the woman's movement since Elizabeth Cady Stanton. Certainly they shared a profound anti-authoritarianism. But Mrs. Gilman lacked the self-love that characterized Elizabeth Stanton's self-reliance. Mrs. Stanton was intrigued by experiments like Brook Farm because she believed that women would never be able to explore their full potential within the confines of the nuclear family. But Charlotte Gilman, for all her "humanitarian" socialism, had a horror of co-operative housekeeping. Mrs. Perkins had been infatuated with Swedenborg, and for a time she and her two children had lived in a communal household of the like-minded. Charlotte Gilman emerged from the experience with an abiding mistrust of the occult—and a repugnance for communal living. The doctrine of correspondence in which Lydia Maria Child had found a sanction for social sympathy had no appeal for her. Nor did she seem to consider that her thwarted mother might have needed to commune with spirits, or with other adults. Charlotte Gilman preferred to go it alone, aided by specialists in food preparation, child care, and housecleaning, whose professional touch would keep each home an immaculate sanctum where the besieged individual could pull herself together.

If Jane Addams represented Sentimentalism, in a nostalgic and therefore less virulent form, come into the twentieth century, Charlotte Gilman was the heir of the anti-Romantic Catharine Beecher in temperament as well as fact. She named her daughter Katherine Beecher Stetson, and began her autobiography with a tribute to the whole Beecher family, and significantly to the New England they lived in; "a seed-bed of progressive movements, scientific, mechanical, educational, humanitarian as well as religious."[78] Mrs. Gilman was her Aunt Catharine—without this cultural background. She had the same scientism, the same compulsive interest in physical culture and fresh air, the same inability to trust her emotions, the same paranoia rooted in a repressed knowledge of her own aggressive feelings. And, not coincidentally, Mrs. Gilman and her great aunt were the foremost Jeremiahs of American feminism.

Charlotte Gilman had been one of the few young women to speak out against censure of *The Woman's Bible* at the suffrage convention in 1896, and Mrs. Stanton always meant a great deal to her—she was woman on the old and therefore larger scale. "Of the many people I met during these years lecturing on women and economics I was particularly impressed by Elizabeth Cady Stanton. To have been with her and 'Aunt Susan,' as we called the great Susan B. Anthony, seemed to establish a connection with a splendid period of real heroism."[79] Elizabeth Stanton was not a more rigorous or scientific socialist than Charlotte Gilman, but her thoughts had a genuine coherence, the result of her lifelong commitment to a Romantic ideology. Mrs. Gilman's thoughts, like those of her great aunt, were finally not quite reasonable because of her desperate valuation of self-control, her projection of her own hostile impulses on the outside world, her privatism. Yet it seems beside the point to suggest, as Wil-

[78] *Ibid.,* p. 3.
[79] *Ibid.,* p. 216.

liam O'Neill has done in his recent book on the woman's movement in America, that what Mrs. Gilman and her contemporaries really needed was the Socialist Party.[80] Although this is not the most patronizing suggestion O'Neill could have made about what the feminists needed, it completely ignores these women's own sense of what was missing in their lives.

In the next-to-last chapter of her autobiography Charlotte Perkins Gilman described her escape from polyglot New York to the New England of her visions. Yet not precisely of her visions, for she realized that the enclaves of her "own people" were doomed to extinction, and were already dominated by a species of ancestor worship. Norwich, Connecticut, was "labeled with the names of long dead residents, not merely on gravestones, but on neat white signs hung on old houses, nailed on trees, set on the ground here and there." The Gilman's "ancient mansion" was decorated with two such signs, "on either side of the front door, one a list of ancestors, the other announcing 'Lydia Huntley Sigourney born here.'"[81] Perhaps nothing is so eloquent of what had gone out of American feminism by the end of the nineteenth century as this reduction of the Sentimental poetess from an inspirer of feeling—and ultimately of action—to an embodiment of native-born-ness.

Mrs. Gilman's own lack of contact with the Romantic-Sentimental ideology may have had as much to do with her own psychology as with broad cultural revaluations. Her father had been a librarian who often sent books when his family needed financial and emotional support, and one lasting symptom of Charlotte Gilman's breakdown was an inability to do sustained reading. This, however, does not change the fact that Madame de Staël and George Eliot and Charlotte

[80] "In retrospect, perhaps the best course for feminists would have been to join the Socialist party, which alone promised to change the American social order enough so that women could exercise in practice those rights they were increasingly accorded in principle." William O'Neill, *Everyone Was Brave* (Chicago, 1969), ix.

[81] Gilman, *Living*, pp. 324–26.

Brontë and Felicia Hemans never let Elizabeth Cady Stanton down. Nothing, not even her father's bitter opposition could undermine her Romantic faith in self-expression. There is, of course, something pathetic about Elizabeth Stanton's dependence on fictional models, and about Stowe and Jewett and Addams' wistful memories of grandmothers and great aunts. Yet their feminist mythology kept alive a reverence for women as selves, as competent, feeling, worthy beings, that legal reforms, and even the prospect of revolution could not sustain. Women who knew what they felt and could value those feelings were the only ones capable of radical belief— or action. And when women like Mrs. Stanton sensed that William Dean Howells was really the enemy, despite his well-meaning support of female suffrage, they were right. He had ridiculed their chosen heroines and then hinted that Mr. Gilman's story was too true to have been told; a genteel Realism was the last thing American feminists needed.

Lydia Huntley Sigourney was born in 1791, the only daughter of a general handyman. She later recorded an intense affection for her father: "The sweetest tears swelled under my eyelids when I thought of him. Methinks the love of a daughter for a father is distinct and different from all other love." However, her mother, who encouraged her to write a novel "in the epistolary style" at the age of eight, and Madam Lathrop, her father's employer and an avid reader of Young's *Night Thoughts*, seem to have exercised a decisive influence on Mrs. Sigourney's later choice of a career and a genre.

Dedicated at an early age to upward mobility, Lydia Huntley taught school for several years, first in Norwich, Connecticut, her birthplace, and later in Hartford. Her insistence that young girls needed rigorous mental training earned her a place just behind Emma Willard and Catharine Beecher in the front ranks of the movement to reform female education. Several of the essays in Lydia Huntley's first published work, *Moral Pieces* (1815), originally had been written for use in the classroom. Her career as a pedagogue, however, was cut short in 1819 when she married Charles Sigourney, a prosperous merchant and banker, and went to live with him and his three young children in the mansion of her early ambitious visions.

Mr. Sigourney was opposed to gainful employment for married women, and it was not until 1833, when his own financial ventures had proved unsatisfactory, that he permitted his wife to abandon her pseudonyms in the interest of sales. During the early years of their marriage Mrs. Sigourney had been publishing anonymously, often without her husband's knowledge, and dividing the proceeds between her parents and a wide variety of charitable enterprises—to aid the Greeks, the Indians, the blind, prisoners, paupers, and heathens.

Soon after Lydia Sigourney began to welcome notoriety, Edgar Allan Poe suggested that her reputation as the "American Hemans" was in fact not wholly complimentary, but implied that she plagiarized from the British poetess. Yet while Mrs. Sigourney was unquestionably imitative, she probably never actually stole material from anyone but herself. She was able to write verses on order—for the parents of a child drowned in a barrel of swine's food, for an infant at its mother's funeral—but her inspiration was spotty and she used the same themes (and even the same poems and prose passages) over and over again in order to fill the forty-odd volumes which she produced before her death in 1865.

Raised a Calvinist, Mrs. Sigourney became an Episcopalian upon marriage (another sign of her social mobility), yet she never lost her taste for a dramatic conversion experience, and despite countless assurances to bereaved parents that their loved ones were safely with cherubim and seraphim, she herself was heartsick at the thought that her son Andrew, who had been stricken with consumption while still a young man, had died unrepentant. Mrs. Sigourney had to take what comfort she could in collecting and publishing her son's private writing, complete with a detailed description of his last illness which she thoughtfully provided. Yet significantly, when her husband died, the poetess who had eulogized total strangers had not one melting word to say.

"'Twas But a Babe," Lydia Huntley Sigourney[*]

I asked them why the verdant turf was riven
From its young rooting: and with silent lip
They pointed to a new-made chasm among
The marble-pillared mansions of the dead.
Who goeth to his rest in yon damp couch?
The tearless crowd past on—"'twas but a babe."
A babe!—And poise ye, in the rigid scales
Of calculation, the fond bosom's wealth?
Rating its priceless idols as ye weigh
Such merchandise as moth and rust corrupt,
Or the rude robber steals? Ye mete out grief,
Perchance, when youth, maturity or age,
Sink in the thronging tomb; but when the breath
Grows icy on the lip of innocence
Repress your measured sympathies, and say,
"'Twas but a babe."
      What know ye of her love
Who patient watcheth, till the stars grow dim,
Over her drooping infant, with an eye
Bright as unchanging Hope of his repose?
What know ye of her woe who sought no joy
More exquisite, than on his placid brow
To trace the glow of health, and drink at dawn
The thrilling lustre of his waking smile?
Go, ask that musing father, why yon grave,
So narrow, and so noteless, might not close
Without a tear?
      And though his lip be mute,

* From the second edition of Mrs. Sigourney's *Poems* (Philadelphia, 1836).

Feeling the poverty of speech to give
Fit answer to thee, still his pallid brow,
And the deep agonizing prayer that loads
Midnight's dark wing to Him, the God of strength,
May satisfy thy question.
             Ye, who mourn
Whene'er yon vacant cradle, or the robes
That decked the lost one's form, call back a tide
Of alienated joy, can ye not trust
Your treasure to His arms, whose changeless care
Passeth a mother's love! Can ye not hope,
When a few hasting years their course have run
To go to him, though he no more on earth
Returns to you?
             And when glad Faith doth catch
Some echo of celestial harmonies,
Archangels' praises, with the high response
Of cherubim, and seraphim, oh think—
Think that your babe is there.

The Father, Lydia Huntley Sigourney[*]

"Yes,—I am he,—who look'd and saw decay
Steal o'er the lov'd of earth,—the ador'd too much.—
It is a fearful thing, to love what Death may touch."

Mrs. Hemans

I was in the full tide of a laborious and absorbing profession,
—of one which imposes on intellect an unsparing discipline,
but ultimately opens the avenues to wealth and fame. I pursued it, as one determined on distinction,—as one convinced
that *mind* may assume a degree of omnipotence over matter
and circumstance, and popular opinion. Ambition's promptings were strong within me, nor was its career unprosperous.
—I had no reason to complain that its promises were deceptive, or its harvest tardy.

Yet as my path was among the competitions and asperi-
ties of men, a character combining strong elements might
have been in danger of becoming indurated, had it not been
softened and refined by the domestic charities. Conjugal love,
early fixing on an object most amiable and beautiful, was as
a fountain of living water, springing up to allay thirst, and
to renovate weariness. I was anxious that my home should
be the centre of intellectual and polished society, where the
buddings of thought should expand unchilled, and those social feelings which are the lifeblood of existence, flow forth,
unfettered by heartless ceremony.—And it was so.

But my present purpose is to delineate a single, and sim-

* "The Father" appeared in *The Young Ladies' Offering*, an
anthology featuring the writings of "Mrs. L. H. Sigourney and
Others" (Boston, 1849).

ple principle of our nature,—the most deep-rooted and holy, —*the love of a father for a daughter.* My province has led me to analyze mankind; and in doing this, I have sometimes thrown their affections into the crucible. And the one of which I speak, has come forth most pure, most free from drossy admixture. Even the earth that combines with it, is not like other earth. It is what the foot of a seraph might rest upon, and contract no pollution. With the love of our sons, ambition mixes its spirit, till it becomes a fiery essence. We anticipate great things for them,—we covet honors,—we goad them on in the race of glory;—if they are victors, we too proudly exult,—if vanquished, we are prostrate and in bitterness. Perhaps we detect in them the same latent perverseness, with which we have waged warfare in our own breasts, or some imbecility of purpose with which we have no affinity; and then, from the very nature of our love, an impatience is generated, which they have no power to soothe, or we to control. A father loves his son, as he loves himself,—and in all selfishness, there is a bias to disorder and pain. But his love for his daughter is different and more disinterested; possibly he believes that it is called forth by a being of a higher and better order. It is based on the integral and immutable principles of his nature. It recognizes the sex in hearts, and from the very gentleness and mystery of womanhood, takes that coloring and zest which romance gathers from remote antiquity. It draws nutriment from circumstances which he may not fully comprehend, from the power which she possesses to awaken his sympathies, to soften his irritability, to sublimate his aspirations;—while the support and protection which she claims in return, elevate him with a consciousness of assimilation to the ministry of those benevolent and powerful spirits, who ever "bear us up in their hands, lest we dash our foot against a stone."

I should delight longer to dwell on this development of affection, for who can have known it more perfectly in its length and breadth, in its depth and height? I had a daughter, beautiful in infancy, to whom every year added some new charm to awaken admiration, or to rivet love. To me, it was of no slight import, that she resembled her mother, and that in grace and accomplishment, she early surpassed her cotemporaries. [sic] I was desirous that her mind should be worthy of the splendid temple allotted for its habitation. I decided to render it familiar with the whole circle of the arts and sciences. I was not satisfied with the commendation of her teachers. I determined to take my seat in the sacred pavilion of intellect, and superintend what entered there. But how should one buried beneath the ponderous tomes and Sysiphean toils of jurisprudence, gain freedom, or undivided thought, for such minute supervision? A father's love can conquer, if it cannot create. I deprived myself of sleep: I sat till the day dawned, gathering materials for the lectures that I gave her. I explored the annuals of architecture and sculpture, the recesses of literature and poetry, the labyrinthine and colossal treasure-houses of history,—I entered the ancient catacombs of the illustrious dead, traversed the regions of the dim and shadowy past, with no coward step,—ransacked earth and heaven, to add one gem to her casket. At stated periods, I required her to condense, to illustrate, to combine, what I had brought her. I listened, with wonder, to her intuitive eloquence: I gazed with intense delight upon the intellect that I thus embellished,—upon the Corinthian capital that I had erected and adorned. Not a single acanthus-leaf started forth, but I cherished and fostered it with the dews of a father's blessing.

Yet while the outpoured riches of a masculine understanding were thus incorporating themselves with her softer structure, I should not have been content, unless she had also borne the palm of female grace and loveliness. Was it therefore nothing to me, that she evinced in her bloom of youth, a dignity surpassing her sex, that in symmetry she restored the image of the Medicean Venus, that amid the circles of rank and fashion, she was the model—the cynosure? Still was she saved from that vanity which would have been the destroyer of all these charms, by the hallowed prevalence of her filial piety. It was *for my sake*, that she strove to render herself the most graceful among women,—*for my sake*, that she rejoiced in the effect of her attainments. Her gentle and just nature felt that the "husbandman who had labored, should be first partaker of the fruits." Returning from those scenes of splendor, where she was the object of every eye, the theme of every tongue, when the youthful bosom might be forgiven for inflation from the clouds of incense that had breathed upon it, to the inquiry of her mother, if she had been happy, the tender and sweet reply was, "Yes,—because I saw that my dear father was so."

Sometimes, I was conscious of gathering roughness from the continual conflict with passion and prejudice, and that the fine edge of the feelings could not ever be utterly proof against the corrosions of such an atmosphere. Then I sought my home, and called my bird of song, and listened to the warbling of her high, heaven-toned voice. The melody of that music fell upon my soul, like oil upon the troubled billows, —and all was tranquil. I wondered where my perturbations had fled, but still more, that I had ever indulged them. Sometimes, the turmoil and fluctuation of the world, threw a shade of dejection over me: then it was her pride to smooth my brow, and to restore its smile. Once, a sorrow of no common order had fallen upon me; it rankled in my breast, like a dagger's point; I came to my house, but I shunned all its inmates. I threw myself down, in solitude, that I might wrestle alone with my fate, and subdue it; a light footstep approached, but I heeded it not. A form of beauty was on the sofa, by my side, but I regarded it not. Then my hand was softly clasped, breathed upon,—pressed to ruby lips. It was enough. I took my daughter in my arms, and my sorrow vanished. Had she essayed the hackneyed expressions of sympathy, or even the usual epithets of endearment, I might have desired her to leave my presence. Had she uttered only a single word, it would have been too much, so wounded was my spirit within me. But the deed, the very poetry of tenderness, breathing, not speaking, melted "the winter of my discontent." Ever was she endued with that most exquisite of woman's perfections, a knowledge both *when* to be silent, and *where* to speak,—and *so* to speak, that the frosts might dissolve from around the heart she loved, and its discords be tuned to harmony.

Thus was she my comforter, and in every hour of our intercourse, was my devotion to her happiness richly repaid. Was it strange that I should gaze on the work of my own hands with ineffable delight? At twilight I quickened my homeward step, with the thought of that countenance, which was both my evening and morning star; as the bird nerves her wearied wing, when she hears from the still-distant forest, the chirpings of her own nest.

I sat in the house of God, in the silence of sabbath meditation, and tears of thrilling exultation moistened my eyes. I gazed upon my glorious creature, in the stainless blossom of unfolding youth, and my whole soul overflowed with a father's pride. I said, *What more can man desire?* I challenged the whole earth to add another drop to my cup of felicity. Did I forget to give glory to the Almighty, that his decree even then went forth, to smite down my idol?

I came from engrossing toil, and found her restless, with strange fire upon her cheek. Fever had lain rankling in her veins, and they had concealed it from me. I raved. I filled my house with physicians. I charged them wildly to restore her to health and to me. It was in vain. I saw that God claimed her. His will was written upon her brow. The paleness and damps of the tomb settled upon her.

I knelt by the bed of death, and gave her back to her Creator. Amid the tears and groans of mourners, I lifted up a firm voice. A fearful courage entered into me. I seemed to rush even upon the buckler of the Eternal. I likened myself unto him who, on Mount Moria, "stretched forth his hand, and took the knife to slay his son." The whole energy of my nature armed itself for the awful conflict. I gloried in my strength to suffer. With terrible sublimity, I stood forth, as the High Priest of my smitten and astonished household. I gave the lamb in sacrifice, with an unshrinking hand, though it was my own heart's blood, that steeped, and streamed over the altar.

It was over. She had gone. She stayed not for my embraces.

She was permitted to give me no parting token. The mind that I had adored, shrouded itself and fled. I knew that the seal upon those eyes must not be broken, till the trump of the Archangel.

Three days and nights, I sat by the dead. Beauty lingered there, in deep, and solemn, and sacred repose. I laid my head upon her pillow. I pressed my lips to hers, and their ice entered into my soul. I spoke to her of the angels, her companions. I talked long to the beautiful spirit, and methought, it answered me. Then I listened breathlessly, but "there was no voice, nor any that regarded." And still, I wept not.

The fatal day came, in which even that clay was to be no longer mine. The funeral knell, with its heavy, yet suppressed summons, came over me like the dividing of soul and body. There was a flood of weeping, when that form, once so replete with every youthful charm, so instinct with the joyous movement of the mysterious principle of life, was borne in marble stillness from its paternal halls. The eye of the mother that bore her, of the friend that had but casually beheld her, even of the poor menial that waited upon her, knew the luxury of tears. All were wet with that balm of sorrow, to overflowing—*all save mine.*

The open grave had a revolting aspect. I could not bear that the form which I had worshipped, should be left to its cold and hideous guardianship. At the hollow sound of the first falling clod, I would fain have leaped into the pit, and demanded her. But I ruled myself. I committed her to the frozen earth, without a tear. There was a tremendous majesty in such grief. I was a wonder to myself.

I returned to my desolated abode. The silence that reigned there was appalling. My spirit sank beneath it, as a stone goes down into the depths of ocean, bearing the everlasting burden of its fathomless tide. I sought the room where I had last seen her, arrayed in the vestments of the tomb. There lay the books which we had read together. Their pages bore the marks of her pencil. I covered my eyes from them, and turned away. I bowed down to inhale the fragrance of her flowers, and felt that they had no right to bloom so fair, when she, their culturer and their queen, was blighted. I pressed my fingers upon the keys of her piano, and started back at the mournful sound they made. I wandered to her own apartment. I threw myself on the couch where from infancy she had slumbered. I trusted to have wept there. But my grief was too mighty, to be thus unchained. It disdained the relief of tears. I seemed to rush as upon a drawn sword, and still it refused to pierce me.

Yet all this was when no eye saw me. In the presence of others, I was like Mount Atlas, bearing unmoved the stormy heavens upon his shoulders.

I went forth, amid the jarring competitions and perpetual strifes of men. I adjusted their opposing interests, while I despised them and their concerns. I unravelled their perplexities. I penetrated their subterfuges. I exposed their duplicity. I cut the Gordian knots of their self-conceit. I made the "crooked straight, and the rough places plain,"—with an energy that amazed them and myself. It was like that of a spirit, which has nothing to do with the flesh. I suffered the tumult of my soul to breathe itself out in bursts of stormy declamation. I exerted the strength of a giant, when it was not required. I scorned to balance power with necessity. The calculations of prudence, and the devices of cunning, seemed equally pitiful, and despicable. I put forth the same effort to crush an emmet, as to uproot the oak of a thousand centuries. It was sufficient for me always to triumph. While men marvelled at the zeal with which I served them, I was loathing them in my heart. I was sick of their chicanery, and their sabbathless rush after empty honors and perishable dross. The whole world seemed to me, "less than nothing, and vanity." Still, I was sensible of neither toil, nor fatigue, nor physical exhaustion. I was like one, who in his troubled dream of midnight, treads on air, and finds it strangely sustaining him.

But every night, I went to my daughter's grave. I laid me down there, in unutterable bitterness. While the stars looked coldly on me, I spoke to her fondly and earnestly, as one who could not be denied. I said,—"Angel! who art mine no longer, listen to me. Thou, who art raised above all tears, cause *one tear* to moisten my burning brow. Give it to me, as a token that thou hearest me, that thou hast not forgotten me." And the blasts of Winter, through the leafless boughs, mocking replied,—"*Give it to me,—Give it to me.*" But I wept not. Ten days and nights passed over me,—and still I wept not.

My brain was heated to agony. The visual nerves were scorched and withered. My heart was parched and arid, as the Libyan desert. Then I knew that the throne of Grief was in *the heart:* that though her sceptre may reach the remotest nerve, and touch the minutest cell where the brain slumbers, and perplex every ethereal ambassador from spirit to sense, —yet the pavilion where her darkest dregs are wrung out, the laboratory where her consuming fires are compounded, is *the heart,—the heart.*

I have implied that my intellect faltered. Yet every morning I went to the scene of my labors. I put my shoulder to the wheel, caring not though it crushed me. I looked at men fixedly and haughtily with my red eye-balls. But I spoke no word to betray the flame feeding at my vitals. The heart-strings shrivelled and broke before it, yet the martyrdom was in silence.

Again, Night drew her sable curtain, and I sought my daughter's grave. Methought, its turf-covering was discomposed, and some half-rooted shrubs that shuddered and drooped when placed in that drear assemblage of the dead, had been trampled and broken. A horrible suspicion took possession of my mind. I rushed to the house of the sexton.— "Has any one troubled my daughter's grave?" Alarmed at my vehemence, he remained speechless and irresolute.

"Tell me," I exclaimed, in a voice of terror, "who has disturbed my daughter's grave." He evaded my adjuration, and murmured something about an injunction to secrecy. With the grasp of a maniac, I bore him to an inner apartment, and bade him satisfy my question. Trembling at my violence, he confessed that the grave had been watched for ten nights.

"Who has watched my daughter's grave?" Reluctantly he gave me the names of those friends,—names forever graven upon my soul.

And so, for those ten long, wintry nights, so dreary and interminable, which I had cast away amid the tossings of profitless, delirious, despairing sorrow, they had been watching, that the repose of that unsullied clay might remain unbroken.

A new tide of emotion was awakened. I threw myself down, as powerless as the weaned infant. Torrents of tears flowed. The tenderness of man wrought what the severity of Heaven had failed to produce. It was not the earthquake, nor the thunder, nor the tempest, that subdued me. It was the still, small voice. I wept until the fountains of tears failed. The relief of that hour of weeping, can never be shadowed forth in language. The prison-house of passionate agony was unlocked. I said to God that he was merciful, and I loved him because my angel lived in his presence. Since then, it would seem, that my heart has been made better. Its aspirations are upward, whither she has ascended, and as I tread the devious path of my pilgrimage, both the sunbeam and the thorn point me as a suppliant to the Redeemer of Man, that I may be at last fitted to dwell with her for ever.

The African Mother At Her Daughter's Grave, Lydia Huntley Sigourney*

Some of the Pagan Africans visit the burial places of their departed relatives, bearing food and drink;—and mothers have been known, for a long course of years, to bring, in an agony of grief, their annual oblation to the tombs of their children.

Daughter!—I bring thee food,
  The rice-cake pure and white,
The cocoa, with its milky blood,
  Dates and pomegranates bright;
The orange in its gold,
  Fresh from thy favourite tree,
Nuts in their ripe and husky fold,
  Dearest! I spread for thee.

Year after year I tread
  Thus to thy low retreat,
But now the snow-hairs mark my head
  And age enchains my feet:
Oh! many a change of woe
  Hath dimmed thy spot of birth,
Since first my gushing tears did flow
  O'er this thy bed of earth.

There came a midnight cry,
  Flames from our hamlet rose,
A race of pale-browed men were nigh,
  They were our country's foes.
Thy wounded sire was borne

* From the second edition of Mrs. Sigourney's *Poems* (Philadelphia, 1836).

By tyrant force away,
Thy brothers from our cabin torn
　While in my blood I lay.

I watched for their return
　Upon the rocky shore,
Till night's red planets ceased to burn,
　And the long rains were o'er—
Till seeds their hands had sown
　A ripened fruitage bore:
The billows echoed to my moan,
　Yet they returned no more.

But thou are slumbering deep,
　And to my wildest cry,
When, pierced with agony, I weep,
　Dost render no reply.
Daughter! my youthful pride,
　The idol of my eye,
Why didst thou leave thy mother's side
　Beneath these sands to lie?

Long o'er the hopeless grave
　Where her lost darling slept,
Invoking gods that could not save,
　That Pagan mourner wept:
Oh! for some voice of power
　To soothe her bursting sighs;
"There is a resurrection hour!
　Thy daughter's dust shall rise!"

Christians!—Ye hear the cry
　From heathen Afric's strand,
Haste! Lift salvation's banner high
　O'er that benighted land.
With faith that claims the skies
　Her misery control,
And plant the hope that never dies,
　Deep in her tear-wet soul.

Born in 1802 in Medford, Massachusetts, **Lydia Maria Child** attended public school and had one year at a female seminary, but she believed, despite disagreements with him over Milton who asserted "the superiority of his own sex in rather too lordly a manner" for her taste at fifteen, that her brother, Convers Francis, a Unitarian clergyman, had really been responsible for her education and her choice of a literary career. Lydia Francis had published two popular novels and started a school by the time she was twenty-three, and at twenty-four founded a successful bi-monthly children's magazine, *Juvenile Miscellany.*

In 1828 she married a Boston lawyer, David Child, and they were soon converted to abolitionism. Her *Appeal in Favor of That Class of Americans Called Africans* (1833) earned her the friendship of the most notable abolitionists and undermined her popularity with the general public. The furor over her *Appeal* quickly drove the *Juvenile Miscellany* into bankruptcy, although in the 1840s she resumed her journalistic career as the editor of a New York weekly, the *National Anti-Slavery Standard.* When John Brown lay wounded in a Virginia prison, Mrs. Child wrote to the governor of that state for permission to come and nurse him. Her request, the governor's reply, and the less diplomatic retort of the wife of the author of the Fugitive Slave Law, were published in pamphlet form in 1860 as *Correspondence Between Lydia Maria Child and Gov. Wise and Mrs. Mason of Virginia* and sold over 300,000 copies.

Lydia Child continued to write children's stories after her conversion to abolitionism, and to construct historical novels, including *Philothea* (1836) which was set in the time of Pericles, and *A Romance of the Republic* (1867), her personal reading of the Civil War. Mrs. Child's *Letters from New York* were first published in 1843 and 1845; ten years later she produced three volumes on the *Progress of Religious Ideas through Successive Ages* (1855). In the 1830s she wrote several biographies of notable women, including Madame de Staël, and a *History of the Condition of Women in Various Ages and Nations* (1835). She also put considerable energy into collecting anecdotal material about the true condition of American slaves, as well as into circulating anti-slavery petitions and making warm clothing for fugitive slaves, abolitionists migrating to Kansas (to keep that territory from becoming a slave state), and, later, for Union soldiers and freedmen.

Lydia Maria Child frequently wrote to friends and to her brother of her longing to find a church in which she could rest, but her inability to ignore the discrepancy between each sect's narrow-minded zeal for particular forms of worship, and what she believed was true religious sentiment, kept her from all but a brief affiliation with the Swedenborgians. In a letter to Theodore Weld in 1880 after the death of his wife Angelina Grimké, Mrs. Child recalled the early anti-slavery days, now sacred in her memory: "All suppression of selfishness makes the moment great; and mortals were never more sublimely forgetful of self than were the abolitionists in those early days, before the moral force which emanated from them had become available as a political power. Ah, my friend," she sighed to Weld, "that is the only true church organization, when heads and hearts unite in working for the welfare of the human race!"

Lydia Child was convinced that one of the great reforms yet to be accomplished after the Civil War was the enfranchisement of women. She believed her sex could raise the moral level of national and international politics by instinctively favoring temperance legislation and international arbitration. Yet Mrs. Child did not believe that only the "best people" could be reformers, in fact, her analysis in the 1850s of what was impeding the progress of abolitionism, would, had it been written fifty years later, be fairly described as Marxian. The common man, she felt, was basically sound, he was simply being played on by merchants, bankers, and successful editors whose interests were those of the slaveowners.

However her faith in the working classes was not the product of economic analysis, but of visceral identification with the underdog. It was unquestionably difficult for Lydia Maria Child to turn her back on a successful literary career at the age of thirty and to cast her lot with the abolitionists. But, when her early comments about Milton's sexism are put together with her sense of degradation when her husband had to sign her will, and her feeling of suffocation when she heard that Charles Sumner had been beaten in the Senate and she, a woman, could do nothing about it, it seems clear that her identification with the unchosen of the earth was less a decision than a compulsion. Lydia Maria Child died in 1880.

Letters from New York, Lydia Maria Child*

LETTER I

August 19, 1841

You ask what is now my opinion of this great Babylon; and playfully remind me of former philippics, and a long string of vituperative alliterations, such as magnificence and mud, finery and filth, diamonds and dirt, bullion and brass-tape, &c. &c. Nor do you forget my first impression of the city, when we arrived at early dawn, amid fog and drizzling rain, the expiring lamps adding their smoke to the impure air, and close beside us a boat called the "Fairy Queen," laden with dead hogs.

Well, Babylon remains the same as then. The din of crowded life, and the eager chase for gain, still run through its streets, like the perpetual murmur of a hive. Wealth dozes on French couches, thrice piled, and canopied with damask, while Poverty camps on the dirty pavement, or sleeps off its wretchedness in the watch-house. There, amid the splendour of Broadway, sits the blind negro beggar, with horny hand and tattered garments, while opposite to him stands the stately mansion of the slave trader, still plying his bloody trade, and laughing to scorn the cobweb laws, through which the strong can break so easily.

In Wall-street, and elsewhere, Mammon, as usual, coolly calculates his chance of extracting a penny from war, pestilence, and famine; and Commerce, with her loaded drays, and jaded skeletons of horses, is busy as ever fulfilling the 'World's

---

* The letters excerpted here are from the two-volume 1852 edition of the *Letters* which was published in New York.

contract with the Devil.' The noisy discord of the street-cries
gives the ear no rest; and the weak voice of weary childhood
often makes the heart ache for the poor little wanderer, pro-
longing his task far into the hours of night. Sometimes, the
harsh sounds are pleasantly varied by some feminine voice,
proclaiming in musical cadence, 'Hot corn! hot corn!' with the
poetic addition of 'Lily white corn! Buy my lily white corn!'
When this sweet, wandering voice salutes my ear, my heart
replies—

'Tis a glancing gleam o' the gift of song—
And the soul that speaks hath suffered wrong.

There *was* a time when all these things would have passed
by me like the flitting figures of the magic lantern, or the
changing scenery of a theatre, sufficient for the amusement
of an hour. But now, I have lost the power of looking merely
on the surface. Every thing seems to me to come from the
Infinite, to be filled with the Infinite, to be tending toward
the Infinite. Do I see crowds of men hastening to extinguish
a fire? I see not merely uncouth garbs, and fantastic flickering
lights of lurid hue, like a tramping troop of gnomes,—but
straightway my mind is filled with thoughts about mutual
helpfulness, human sympathy, the common bond of brotherhood, and the mysteriously deep foundations on which society
rests; or rather, on which it now reels and totters. . . .

LETTER II

August 21, 1841

I like the various small gardens in New York, with their
shaded alcoves of lattice-work, where one can eat an ice-
cream, shaded from the sun. You have none such in Boston;
and they would probably be objected to, as open to the vulgar
and the vicious. I do not walk through the world with such
fear of soiling my garments. Let science, literature, music,

flowers, all things that tend to cultivate the intellect, or humanize the heart, be open to 'Tom, Dick, and Harry;' and thus, in process of time, they will become Mr. Thomas, Richard, and Henry. In all these things, the refined should think of what they can *impart*, not of what they can *receive*.

As for the vicious, they excite in me more of compassion than dislike. The Great Searcher of Hearts alone knows whether I should not have been as they are, with the same neglected childhood, the same vicious examples, the same overpowering temptation of misery and want. If they will but pay to virtue the outward homage of decorum, God forbid that I should wish to exclude them from the healthful breeze, and the shaded promenade. Wretched enough are they in their utter degradation; nor is society so guiltless of their ruin, as to justify any of its members in unpitying scorn.

And this reminds me that in this vast emporium of poverty and crime, there are, *morally* speaking, some flowery nooks, and 'sunny spots of greenery.' I used to say, I knew not where were the ten righteous men to save the city; but I have found them now. Since then, the Washington Temperance Society has been organized, and active in good works. Apart from the physical purity, the triumph of soul over sense, implied in abstinence from stimulating liquors, these societies have peculiarly interested me, because they are based on the Law of Love. The Pure is inlaid in the Holy, like a pearl set in fine gold. Here is no 'fifteen-gallon-law,' no attendance upon the lobbies of legislatures, none of the bustle or manoeuvres of political party; measures as useless in the moral world, as machines to force water above its level are in the physical world. Serenely above all these, stands this new Genius of Temperance; her trust in Heaven, her hold on the human heart. To the fallen and the perishing she throws a silken cord, and gently draws him within the golden circle of human brotherhood. She has learned that persuasion is mightier than coercion, that the voice of encouragement finds an echo in the heart deeper, far deeper, than the thunder of reproof. . . .

The other day, I stood by the wayside while a Washingtonian procession, two miles long, passed by. All classes and trades were represented, with appropriate music and banners. Troops of boys carried little wells and pumps; and on many of the banners were flowing fountains and running brooks. One represented a wife kneeling in gratitude for a husband restored to her and himself; on another, a group of children were joyfully embracing the knees of a reformed father. Fire companies were there with badges and engines; and military companies, with gaudy colours and tinsel trappings. Toward the close, came two barouches, containing the men who first started a Temperance Society on the Washingtonian plan. These six individuals were a carpenter, a coach-maker, a tailor, a blacksmith, a wheelwright, and a silver-plater. They held their meetings in a carpenter's shop, in Baltimore, before any other person took an active part in the reform. My heart paid them reverence, as they passed. It was a beautiful pageant, and but one thing was wanting to make it complete; there should have been carts drawn by garlanded oxen, filled with women and little children, bearing a banner, on which was inscribed, WE ARE HAPPY NOW! I missed the women and the children; for without something to represent the genial influence of domestic life, the circle of joy and hope is ever incomplete.

But the absent ones were present to my mind; and the pressure of many thoughts brought tears to my eyes. I seemed to see John the Baptist preparing a pathway through the wilderness for the coming of the Holiest; for like unto his is this mission of temperance. Clean senses are fitting vessels for pure affections and lofty thoughts.

Within the outward form I saw, as usual, spiritual significance. As the bodies of men were becoming weaned from stimulating drinks, so were their souls beginning to approach those pure fountains of living water, which refresh and strengthen, but never intoxicate. The music, too, was revealed to me in fulness of meaning. Much of it was of a military character, and cheered onward to combat and to victory. Everything about war I loathe and detest, except its music.

My heart leaps at the trumpet-call, and marches with the drum. Because I cannot ever hate it, I know that it is the utterance of something good, perverted to a ministry of sin. It is the voice of resistance to evil, of combat with the false; therefore the brave soul springs forward at the warlike tone, for in it is heard a call to its appointed mission. Whoso does not see that genuine life is a battle and a march, has poorly read his origin and his destiny. Let the trumpet sound, and the drums roll! Glory to resistance! for through its agency men become angels. The instinct awakened by martial music is noble and true; and therefore its voice will not pass away: but it will cease to represent war with carnal weapons, and remain a type of that spiritual combat, whereby the soul is purified. It is right noble to fight with wickedness and wrong; the mistake is in supposing that spiritual evil can be overcome by physical means. . . .

LETTER XIV

February 17, 1842

I was always eager for the spring-time, but never so much as now!

Patience yet a little longer! and I shall find delicate bells of the trailing arbutus, fragrant as an infant's breath, hidden deep, under their coverlid of autumn leaves, like modest worth in this pretending world. My spirit is weary for rural rambles. It is sad walking in the city. The streets shut out the sky, even as commerce comes between the soul and heaven. The busy throng, passing and repassing, fetter freedom, while they offer no sympathy. The loneliness of the soul is deeper, and far more restless, than in the solitude of the mighty forest. Wherever are woods and fields I find a home; each tinted leaf and shining pebble is to me a friend; and wherever I spy a wild flower, I am ready to leap up, clap my hands, and exclaim, 'Cocatoo! he know me very well!' as did the poor New Zealander, when he recognized a bird of his native clime, in the menageries of London.

But amid these magnificent masses of sparkling marble, hewn *in prison*, I am alone. For eight weary months, I have met in the crowded streets but two faces I had ever seen before. Of some, I would I could say that I should never see them again; but they haunt me in my sleep, and come between me and the morning. Beseeching looks, begging the comfort and the hope I have no power to give. Hungry eyes, that look as if they had pleaded long for sympathy, and at last gone mute in still despair. Through what woful, what frightful masks, does the human soul look forth, leering, peeping, and defying, in this thoroughfare of nations. Yet in each and all lie the capacities of an archangel; as the majestic oak lies enfolded in the acorn that we tread carelessly under foot, and which decays, perchance, for want of soil to root in.

The other day, I went forth for exercise merely, without other hope of enjoyment than a farewell to the setting sun, on the now deserted Battery, and a fresh kiss from the breezes of the sea, ere they passed through the polluted city, bearing healing on their wings. I had not gone far, when I met a little ragged urchin, about four years old, with a heap of newspapers, 'more big as he could carry,' under his little arm, and another clenched in his small, red fist. The sweet voice of childhood was prematurely cracked into shrillness, by screaming street cries, at the top of his lungs; and he looked blue, cold, and disconsolate. May the angels guard him! How I wanted to warm him in my heart. I stood looking after him, as he went shivering along. Imagination followed him to the miserable cellar where he probably slept on dirty straw; I saw him flogged, after his day of cheerless toil, because he had failed to bring home pence enough for his parents grog; I saw wicked ones come muttering and beckoning between his young soul and heaven; they tempted him to steal to avoid the dreaded beating. I saw him, years after, bewildered and frightened, in the police-office, surrounded by hard faces. Their law-jargon conveyed no meaning to his ear, awakened no slumbering moral sense, taught him no clear distinction between right and wrong; but from their cold, harsh tones, and heartless merriment, he drew the inference that they were enemies; and, as such, he hated them. At that moment, one tone like a mother's voice might have wholly changed his earthly destiny; one kind word of friendly counsel might have saved him—as if an angel, standing in the genial sunlight, had thrown to him one end of a garland, and gently diminishing the distance between them, had drawn him safely out of the deep and tangled labyrinth, where false echoes and winding paths conspired to make him lose his way.

But watchmen and constables were around him, and they have small fellowship with angels. The strong impulses that might have become overwhelming love for his race, are perverted to the bitterest hatred. He tries the universal resort of weakness against force; if they are too strong for *him*, he will be too cunning for *them*. *Their* cunning is roused to detect *his* cunning: and thus the gallows-game is played, with interludes of damnable merriment from police reports, whereat the heedless multitude laugh; while angels weep over the slow murder of a human soul.

When, O when, will men learn that society makes and cherishes the very crimes it so fiercely punishes, and *in* punishing reproduces?

'The key of knowledge first ye take away,
And then, because ye've robbed him, ye enslave;
Ye shut out from him the sweet light of day,
And then, because he's in the dark, ye pave
The road, that leads him to his wished-for grave,
With stones of stumbling: then, if he but tread
Darkling and slow, ye call him 'fool' and 'knave;'—
Doom him to toil, and yet deny him bread:
Chains round his limbs ye throw, and curses on his head.'

God grant the little shivering carrier-boy a brighter destiny than I have foreseen for him.

A little further on, I encountered two young boys fighting furiously for some coppers, that had been given them and had fallen on the pavement. They had matted black hair, large, lustrous eyes, and an olive complexion. They were evidently foreign children, from the sunny clime of Italy or Spain, and nature had made them subjects for an artist's dream. Near by on the cold stone steps, sat a ragged, emaciated woman, whom I conjectured, from the resemblance of her large dark eyes, might be their mother; but she looked on their fight with languid indifference, as if seeing, she saw it not. I spoke to her, and she shook her head in a mournful way, that told me she did not understand my language. Poor, forlorn wanderer! would I could place thee and thy beautiful boys under shelter of sun-ripened vines, surrounded by the music of thy mother-land! Pence I will give thee, though political economy reprove the deed. They can but appease the hunger of the body; they cannot soothe the hunger of thy heart; that I obey the kindly impulse may make the world none the better—perchance some iota the worse; yet I must needs follow it—I cannot otherwise.

I raised my eyes above the woman's weather-beaten head, and saw, behind the window of clear, plate glass, large vases of gold and silver, curiously wrought. They spoke significantly of the sad contrasts in this disordered world; and excited in my mind whole volumes, not of political, but of angelic economy. 'Truly,' said I, 'if the Law of Love prevailed, vases of gold and silver might even more abound—but no homeless outcast would sit shivering beneath their glittering mockery. All would be richer, and no man the poorer. When will the mighty discord come into heavenly harmony?' I looked at the huge stone structures of commercial wealth, and they gave an answer that chilled my heart. Weary of city walks, I would have turned homeward; but nature, ever true and harmonious, beckoned to me from the Battery, and the glowing twilight gave me friendly welcome. It seemed as if the dancing Spring Hours had thrown their rosy mantles on old silvery winter in the lavishness of youthful love.

I opened my heart to the gladsome influence, and forgot that earth was not a mirror of the heavens. It was but for a moment; for there, under the leafless trees, lay two ragged little boys, asleep in each other's arms. I remembered having read in the police reports, the day before, that two little children, thus found, had been taken up as vagabonds. They told, with simple pathos, how both their mothers had been dead for months; how they had formed an intimate friendship, had begged together, ate together, hungered together, and together slept uncovered beneath the steel-cold stars.

The twilight seemed no longer warm; and brushing away a tear, I walked hastily homeward. As I turned into the street where God has provided me with a friendly shelter, something lay across my path. It was a woman, apparently dead; with garments all draggled in New-York gutters, blacker than waves of the infernal rivers. Those who gathered around, said she had fallen in intoxication, and was rendered senseless by the force of the blow. They carried her to the watch-house, and the doctor promised she should be well attended. But, alas, for watch-house charities to a breaking heart! I could not bring myself to think otherwise than that hers *was* a breaking heart! Could she but give a full revelation of early emotions checked in their full and kindly flow, of affections repressed, of hopes blighted, and energies misemployed through ignorance, the heart would kindle and melt, as it does when genius stirs its deepest recesses.

It seemed as if the voice of human wo[e] was destined to follow me through the whole of that unblest day. Late in the night I heard the sound of voices in the street, and raising the window, saw a poor, staggering woman in the hands of a watchman. My ear caught the words, 'Thank you kindly, sir. I should *like* to go home.' The sad and humble accents in which the simple phrase was uttered, the dreary image of the watch-house, which that poor wretch dreamed was her *home*, proved too much for my overloaded sympathies. I hid my face in the pillow, and wept; for 'my heart was almost breaking with the misery of my kind.'

I thought, then, that I would walk no more abroad, till the fields were green. But my mind and body grow alike impatient of being inclosed with walls; both ask for the free breeze, and the wide, blue dome that overarches and embraces *all*. Again I rambled forth under the February sun, as mild and genial as the breath of June. Heart, mind, and frame grew glad and strong, as we wandered on, past the old Stuyvesant church, which a few years agone was surrounded by fields and Dutch farm-houses, but now stands in the midst of peopled streets;—and past the trim, new houses, with their green verandahs, in the airy suburbs. Following the railroad, which lay far beneath our feet, as we wound our way over the hills, we came to the burying-ground of the poor. Weeds and brambles grew along the sides, and the stubble of last year's grass waved over it, like dreary memories of the past; but the sun smiled on it, like God's love on the desolate soul. It was inexpressibly touching to see the frail memorials of affection, placed there by hearts crushed under the weight of poverty. In one place was a small rude cross of wood, with the initials J. S. cut with a penknife, and apparently filled with ink. In another a small hoop had been bent into the form of a heart, painted green, and nailed on a stick at the head of the grave. On one upright shingle was painted only 'MUTTER;' the German word for Mother. On another was scrawled, as if with charcoal, *'So ruhe wohl, du unser liebes kind.'* (Rest well, our beloved child.) One recorded life's brief history thus: 'H. G. born in Bavaria; died in New-York.' Another short epitaph, in French, told that the sleeper came from the banks of the Seine.

The predominance of foreign epitaphs affected me deeply. Who could now tell with what high hopes those departed ones had left the heart-homes of Germany, the sunny hills of Spain, the laughing skies of Italy, or the wild beauty of Switzerland? Would not the friends they had left in their childhood's home, weep scalding tears to find them in a pauper's grave, with their initials rudely carved on a fragile shingle? Some had not even these frail memorials. It seemed there was none to care whether they lived or died. A wide, deep trench was open; and there I could see piles of unpainted coffins heaped one upon the other, left uncovered with earth, till the yawning cavity was filled with its hundred tenants.

Returning homeward, we passed a Catholic burying-ground. It belonged to the upper classes, and was filled with marble monuments, covered with long inscriptions. But none of them touched my heart like that rude shingle, with the simple word 'Mutter' inscribed thereon. The gate was open, and hundreds of Irish, in their best Sunday clothes, were stepping reverently among the graves, and kissing the very sods. Tenderness for the dead is one of the loveliest features of their nation and their church.

The evening was closing in, as we returned, thoughtful, but not gloomy. Bright lights shone through crimson, blue, and green, in the apothecaries' windows, and were reflected in prismatic beauty from the dirty pools in the street. It was like poetic thoughts in the minds of the poor and ignorant; like the memory of pure aspirations in the vicious; like a rainbow of promise, that God's spirit never leaves even the most degraded soul. I smiled, as my spirit gratefully accepted this love-token from the outward; and I thanked our heavenly Father for a world beyond this.

LETTER XXXIII

December 8, 1842

At the present time, indications are numerous that the human mind is tired out in the gymnasium of controversy, and asks earnestly for repose, protection, mystery, and undoubting faith. This tendency betrays itself in the rainbow mysticism of Coleridge, the patriarchal tenderness of Wordsworth, the infinite aspiration of Beethoven. The reverential habit of mind varies its forms, according to temperament and character. In some minds, it shows itself in a superstitious fondness for all *old* forms of belief; the Church which is proved to their minds to resemble the apostolic, in its ritual, as well as its creed, is therefore the true Church. . . .

Episcopacy rebukes, and dissenters argue; but that which ministers to the sentiment of reverence, will have power over many souls, who hunt in vain for truth through the mazes of argument. To the ear that loves music, and sits listening intently for the voice that speaks while the dove descends from heaven, how discordant, how altogether unprofitable, is this hammering of sects!—this coopering and heading up of empty barrels, so industriously carried on in theological schools! When I am stunned by the loud, and many-tongued jargon of sect, I no longer wonder that men are ready to fall down and worship Romish absurdities, dressed up in purple robes and golden crown; the marvel rather is, that they have not returned to the worship of the ancient graces, the sun, the moon, the stars, or even the element of fire. . . .

Meanwhile, let us hope and trust; and respect sincere devotion, wheresoever found. A wise mind never despises aught that flows from a feeling heart. Nothing would tempt me to disturb, even by the rustle of my garments, the Irish servant girl, kneeling in the crowded aisle. Blessed be any power, which, even for a moment, brings the human soul to the foot of the cross, conscious of its weakness and its ignorance, its errors and its sins! We may call it superstition if we will, but the zealous faith of the Catholic is everywhere conspicuous above that of the Protestant. . . .

I love the Irish. Blessings on their warm hearts, and their leaping fancies! Clarkson records that while opposition met him in almost every form, not a single Irish member of the British Parliament ever voted against the abolition of the slave-trade; and how is the heart of that generous island now throbbing with sympathy for the American slave!

Creatures of impulse and imagination, their very speech is poetry. 'What are you going to kill?' said I to one of the most stupid of Irish serving-maids, who seemed in great haste to crush some object in the corner of the room. 'A black *boog*, ma'am,' she replied. 'That is a cricket,' said I. 'It does no harm, but makes a friendly chirping on the hearth stone.' 'Och, and is it a cricket it is? And when the night is abroad, will it be *spaking*? Sure I'll not be after killing it, at all.'

The most faithful and warm-hearted of Irish labourers, (and the good among them are the best on earth) urged me last spring not to fail, by any means, to rise before the sun on Easter morning. 'The Easter sun always dances when

it rises,' said he. Assuredly he saw no mockery in my countenance, but perhaps he saw incredulity; for he added, with
pleading earnestness, 'And why should it *not* dance, by reason of rejoicement?' In his believing ignorance, he had small
cause to envy me the superiority of my reason; at least I felt
so for the moment. Beautiful is the superstition that makes
all nature hail the holy; that sees the cattle all kneel at the
hour Christ was born, and the sun dance, 'by reason of rejoicement,' on the morning of his resurrection; that believes
the dark Cross, actually found on the back of every ass, was
first placed there when Jesus rode into Jerusalem with palm-
branches strewed before him.

Not in vain is Ireland pouring itself all over the earth.
Divine Providence has a mission for her children to fulfil;
though a mission unrecognised by political economists. There
is ever a moral balance preserved in the universe, like the
vibrations of the pendulum. The Irish, with their glowing
hearts and reverent credulity, are needed in this cold age of
intellect and scepticism.

Africa furnishes another class, in whom the heart ever takes
guidance of the head; and all over the world the way is opening for them among the nations. Hayti and the British West
Indies; Algiers, settled by the French; British colonies,
spreading over the west and south of Africa; and emancipation urged throughout the civilized world.

Women, too, on whose intellect ever rests the warm light
of the affections, are obviously coming into a wider and wider
field of action.

All these things prophesy of physical force yielding to
moral sentiment; and they are all agents to fulfil what they
prophesy. God speed the hour.

LETTER XXXIV

January 1843

You ask what are my opinions about 'Women's Rights.' I
confess, a strong distaste to the subject, as it has been generally treated. On no other theme probably has there been

uttered so much of false, mawkish sentiment, shallow philosophy, and sputtering, farthing-candle wit. If the style of its advocates has often been offensive to taste, and unacceptable to reason, assuredly that of its opponents have been still more so. College boys have amused themselves with writing dreams, in which they saw women in hotels, with their feet hoisted, and chairs tilted back, or growling and bickering at each other in legislative halls, or fighting at the polls, with eyes blackened by fisticuffs. But it never seems to have occurred to these facetious writers, that the proceedings which appear so ludicrous and improper in *women*, are also ridiculous and disgraceful in *men*. It were well that *men* should learn not to hoist their feet above their heads, and tilt their chairs backward, nor to growl and snap in the halls of legislation, nor give each other black eyes at the polls.

Maria Edgeworth says, 'We are disgusted when we see a woman's mind overwhelmed with a torrent of learning: that the tide of literature has passed over it should be betrayed only by its fertility.' This is beautiful and true; but is it not likewise applicable to man? The truly great never seek to display themselves. If they carry their heads high above the crowd, it is only made manifest to others by accidental revelations of their extended vision. 'Human duties and proprieties do not lie so very far apart,' said Harriet Martineau; 'if they did, there would be two gospels and two teachers, one for man and another for woman.'

It would seem indeed, as if men were willing to give women the exclusive benefit of gospel-teaching. '*Women* should be gentle,' say the advocates of subordination: but when Christ said, 'Blessed are the meek,' did he preach to women only? '*Girls* should be modest,' is the language of common teaching, continually uttered in words and customs. Would it not be an improvement for men also to be scrupulously pure in manners, conversation and life? Books addressed to young married people abound with advice to the *wife*, to control her temper, and never to utter wearisome complaints, or vexatious words when the husband comes home fretful and unreasonable from his out-of-door conflicts with the world. Would not the advice be as excellent and appropriate, if the husband were advised to conquer *his* fretfulness, and forbear *his* complaints, in consideration of his wife's ill-health, fatiguing cares, and the thousand disheartening influences of domestic routine? In short, whatsoever can be named as loveliest, best, and most graceful in woman, would likewise be good and graceful in man. You will perhaps remind me of courage. If you use the word in its highest signification, I answer, that woman, above others, has abundant need of it in her pilgrimage: and the true woman wears it with a quiet grace. If you mean mere animal courage, *that* is not mentioned in the Sermon on the Mount, among those qualities which enable us to inherit the earth, or become the children of God. That the feminine ideal approaches much nearer to the gospel standard, than the prevalent idea of manhood, is shown by the universal tendency to represent the Saviour and his most beloved disciple with mild, meek expression, and feminine beauty. None speak of the bravery, the might, or the intellect of Jesus; but the devil is always imagined as a being of acute intellect, political cunning, and the fiercest courage. These universal and instinctive tendencies of the human mind reveal much.

That the present position of women in society is the result of physical force, is obvious enough; whosoever doubts it, let her reflect why she is afraid to go out in the evening without the protection of a man. What constitutes the danger of aggression? Superior physical strength, uncontrolled by the moral sentiments. If physical strength were in complete subjection to moral influence, there would be no need of outward protection. That animal instinct and brute force now govern the world, is painfully apparent in the condition of women everywhere; from the Morduan Tartars, whose ceremony of marriage consists in placing the bride on a mat, and consigning her to the bridegroom, with the words, 'Here, wolf, take thy lamb,'—to the German remark, that 'stiff ale, stinging tobacco, and a girl in her smart dress, are the best things.' The same thing, softened by the refinements of civilization, peeps out in Stephens's remark, that 'woman never looks so interesting, as when leaning on the arm of a soldier;' and in Hazlitt's complaint that 'it is not easy to keep up a conversation with women in company. It is thought a piece of rudeness to differ from them; it is not quite fair to ask them a *reason* for what they say.'

This sort of politeness to women is what men call gallantry; an odious word to every sensible woman, because she sees that it is merely the flimsy veil which foppery throws over sensuality, to conceal its grossness. So far is it from indicating sincere esteem and affection for women, that the profligacy of a nation may, in general, be fairly measured by its gallantry. This taking away *rights,* and *condescending* to grant *privileges,* is an old trick of the physical-force principle; and with the immense majority, who only look on the surface of things, this mask effectually disguises an ugliness, which would otherwise be abhorred. The most inveterate slave-holders are probably those who take most pride in dressing their household servants handsomely, and who would be most ashamed to have the name of being *unnecessarily* cruel. And profligates, who form the lowest and most sensual estimate of women, are the very ones to treat them with an excess of outward deference.

There are few books which I can read through, without feeling insulted as a woman; but this insult is almost universally conveyed through that which was intended for praise. Just imagine, for a moment, what impression it would make on men, if women authors should write about *their* 'rosy lips,' and 'melting eyes,' and 'voluptuous forms,' as they write about *us!* That women in general do not feel this kind of flattery to be an insult, I readily admit; for, in the first place, they do not perceive the gross chattel-principle, of which it is the utterance; moreover, they have, from long habit, become accustomed to consider themselves as household conveniences, or gilded toys. Hence, they consider it feminine and pretty to abjure all such use of their faculties, as would make them co-workers with man in the advancement of those great principles, on which the progress of society depends. 'There is perhaps no *animal,*' says Hannah

More, 'so much indebted to subordination, for its good behaviour, as woman.' Alas, for the animal age, in which such utterance could be tolerated by public sentiment!

Martha More, sister of Hannah, describing a very impressive scene at the funeral of one of her Charity School teachers, says: 'The spirit within seemed struggling to speak, and I was in a sort of agony; but I recollected that I had heard, somewhere, a woman must not speak in the *church*. Oh, had she been buried in the church-*yard*, a messenger from Mr. Pitt himself should not have restrained me; for I seemed to have received a message from a higher Master within.'

This application of theological teaching carries its own commentary.

I have said enough to show that I consider prevalent opinions and customs highly unfavourable to the moral and intellectual development of women: and I need not say, that, in proportion to their true culture, women will be more useful and happy, and domestic life more perfected. True culture, in them, as in men, consists in the full and free development of individual character, regulated by their *own* perceptions of what is true, and their *own* love of what is good.

This individual responsibility is rarely acknowledged, even by the most refined, as necessary to the spiritual progress of women. I once heard a very beautiful lecture from R. W. Emerson, on Being and Seeming. In the course of many remarks, as true as they were graceful, he urged women to *be*, rather than *seem*. He told them that all their laboured education of forms, strict observance of genteel etiquette, tasteful arrangement of the toilette, &c., all this *seeming* would not *gain hearts* like *being* truly what God made them; that earnest simplicity, the sincerity of nature, would kindle the eye, light up the countenance, and give an inexpressible charm to the plainest features.

The advice was excellent, but the motive, by which it was urged, brought a flush of indignation over my face. *Men* were exhorted to *be*, rather than to *seem*, that they might fulfil the sacred mission for which their souls were embodied; that they might in God's freedom, grow up into the full stature of spiritual manhood, but *women* were urged to simplicity and truthfulness, that they might become more *pleasing*.

Are we not all immortal beings? Is not each one responsible for himself and herself? There is no measuring the mischief done by the prevailing tendency to teach women to be virtuous as a duty to *man* rather than to *God*—for the sake of pleasing the creature, rather than the Creator. 'God is thy law, *thou* mine,' said Eve to Adam. May Milton be forgiven for sending that thought 'out into everlasting time' in such a jewelled setting. What weakness, vanity, frivolity, infirmity of moral purpose, sinful flexibility of principle—in a word, what soul-stifling, has been the result of thus putting man in the place of God!

But while I see plainly that society is on a false foundation, and that prevailing views concerning women indicate the want of wisdom and purity, which they serve to perpetuate —still, I must acknowledge that much of the talk about Women's Rights offends both my reason and my taste. I am not of those who maintain there is no sex in souls; nor do I like the results deducible from that doctrine. Kinmont, in his admirable book, called the Natural History of Man, speaking of the warlike courage of the ancient German women, and of their being respectfully consulted on important public affairs, says: 'You ask me if I consider all this right, and deserving of approbation? or that women were here engaged in their appropriate tasks? I answer, yes; it is just as right that they should take this interest in the honour of their country, as the other sex. Of course, I do not think that women were *made* for war and battle; neither do I believe that *men* were. But since the fashion of the times had made it so, and settled it that war was a necessary element of greatness, and that no safety was to be procured without it, I argue that it shows a healthful state of feeling in other respects, that the feelings of both sexes were *equally* enlisted in the cause: that there was no *division* in the house, or the state; and that the serious pursuits and objects of the one were also the serious pursuits and objects of the other.'

The nearer society approaches to divine order, the less

separation will there be in the characters, duties, and pursuits of men and women. Women will not become less gentle and graceful, but men will become more so. Women will not neglect the care and education of their children, but men will find themselves ennobled and refined by sharing those duties with them; and will receive, in return, co-operation and sympathy in the discharge of various other duties, now deemed inappropriate to women. The more women become rational companions, partners in business and in thought, as well as in affection and amusement, the more highly will men appreciate *home*—that blessed word, which opens to the human heart the most perfect glimpse of Heaven, and helps to carry it thither, as on an angel's wings.

> 'Domestic bliss,
> That can, the world eluding, be itself
> A world enjoyed; that wants no witnesses
> But its own sharers and approving heaven;
> That, like a flower deep hid in rocky cleft,
> Smiles, though 'tis looking only at the sky.'

Alas, for these days of Astor houses and Tremonts, and Albions! where families exchange comfort for costliness, fireside retirement for flirtation and flaunting, and the simple, healthful, cozy meal, for gravies and gout, dainties and dyspepsia. There is no characteristic of my countrymen, which I regret so deeply as their slight degree of adhesiveness to home. Closely intertwined with this instinct, is the religion of a nation. The Home and the Church bear a near relation to each other. The French have no such word as home in their language, and I believe they are the least reverential and religious of all the Christian nations. A Frenchman had been in the habit of visiting a lady constantly for several years, and being alarmed at a report that she was sought in marriage, he was asked why he did not marry her himself. '*Marry* her!' exclaimed he,—'Good heavens! *where should I spend my evenings?*' The idea of domestic happiness was altogether a foreign idea to his soul, like a word that

conveyed no meaning. Religious sentiment in France leads
the same roving life as the domestic affections; breakfasting
at one restaurateur's and supping at another's. When some
wag in Boston reported that Louis Philippe had sent over
for Dr. Channing to manufacture a religion for the French
people, the witty significance of the joke was generally appreciated.

There is a deep spiritual reason why all that relates to
the domestic affections should ever be found in close proxim-
ity with religious faith. The age of chivalry was likewise one
of unquestioning veneration, which led to the crusade for
the holy sepulchre. The French revolution, which tore down
churches, and voted that there was no God, likewise annulled
marriage; and the doctrine, that there is no sex in souls, has
usually been urged by those of infidel tendencies. Carlyle
says, 'But what feeling it was in the ancient, devout, deep
soul, which of marriage made a *sacrament,* this, of all things
in the world, is what Diderot will think of for aeons without
discovering; unless perhaps it were to increase the *vestry
fees.*'

The conviction that woman's present position in society is
a false one, and therefore re-acts disastrously on the happiness and improvement of man, is pressing by slow degrees
on the common consciousness, through all the obstacles of
bigotry, sensuality, and selfishness. As man approaches to the
truest life, he will perceive more and more that there is no
separation or discord in their mutual duties. They will be one;
but it will be as affection and thought are one; the treble
and bass of the same harmonious tune.

LETTER XXXI*

December 31, 1844

Rapid approximation to the European style of living is
more and more observable in this city. The number of serv-

* This is the thirty-first letter in the second volume of Mrs.
Child's *Letters.* The preceding letters were taken from Volume I.

ants in livery visibly increases every season. Foreign artistic upholsterers assert that there will soon be more houses in New-York furnished according to the fortune and taste of noblemen, than there are either in Paris or London; and this prophecy may well be believed, when the fact is considered that it is already not very uncommon to order furniture for a single room, at the cost of ten thousand dollars. There would be no reason to regret this lavishness, if the convenience and beauty of social environment were really increased in proportion to the expenditure, and if there were a progressive tendency to equality in the distribution. But, alas, a few moments' walk from saloons superbly furnished in the style of Louis 14th, brings us to Loafers' Hall, a dreary desolate apartment, where shivering little urchins pay a cent apiece, for the privilege of keeping out of watchmen's hands, by sleeping on boards ranged in tiers.

But the effects of a luxurious and artificial life are sad enough on those who indulge in it, without seeking for painful contrast among the wretchedly poor. Sallow complexions, feeble steps, and crooked spines, already show an obvious deterioration in beauty, grace, and vigour. Spiritual bloom and elasticity are still more injured by modes of life untrue to nature. The characters of women suffer more than those of men, because their resources are fewer. Very many things are considered unfeminine to be done, and of those duties which are feminine by universal consent, few are deemed genteel by the upper classes. It is not genteel for mothers to wash and dress their own children, or make their clothing, or teach them, or romp with them in the open air. Thus the most beautiful and blessed of all human relations performs but half its healthy and renovating mission. The full, free, joyful growth of heart and soul is everywhere impeded by artificial constraint, and nature has her fountains covered by vanity and pride. Some human souls, finding themselves fenced within such narrow limits by false relations, seek fashionable distinction, or the excitement of gossip, flirtation, and perpetual change, because they can find no other unforbidden outlets for the irrepressible activity of mind and heart.

A very few, of nature's noblest and strongest, quietly throw off the weight that presses on them, and lead a comparatively true life in the midst of shams, which they reprove only by example. Those who can do this, without complaint or noise, and attempt no defence of their peculiar course, except the daily beauty of their actions, will work out their freedom at last, in the most artificial society that was ever constructed; but the power to do this requires a rare combination of natural qualities. For the few who do accomplish this difficult task, I feel even more respect than I do for those who struggle upward under the heavy burden of early poverty. "For wealth bears heavier on talent, than poverty. Under gold mountains and thrones, who knows how many a spiritual giant may lie crushed down and buried?" I once saw a burdock shoot up so vigorously, that it threw off a piece of board in the platform, which covered it from light and air. I had great respect for the brave plant, and even carried my sympathy so far, as to reproach myself for not having lifted the board it was trying so hard to raise, instead of watching it curiously, to see how much it *could* do. The pressure of artificial life, I cannot take off from souls that are born in the midst of it; and few have within themselves such uplifting life as the burdock.

It is one of the saddest sights to see a young girl, born of wealthy and worldly parents, full of heart and soul, her kindly impulses continually checked by etiquette, her noble energies repressed by genteel limitations. She must not presume to love anybody, till father and mother find a suitable match; she must not laugh loud, because it is vulgar; she must not walk fast, because it is ungenteel; she must not work in the garden, for fear the sun and wind may injure her complexion; she must sew nothing but gossamer, lest it mar the delicacy of her hands; she must not study, because gentlemen do not admire literary ladies. Thus left without ennobling objects of interest, the feelings and energies are usually concentrated on frivolous and unsatisfactory pursuits, and woman becomes a by-word and a jest, for her giddy vanity, her love of dress and beaux.

Others, of a deeper nature, but without sufficient clearness of perception, or energy of will, to find their way into freedom, become inert and sad. They acquire a certain amount of accomplishments, because society requires it, and it is less tedious than doing nothing. They walk languidly through the routine of genteel amusements, until they become necessary as a habit, though they impart little pleasure. I have heard such persons open their hearts, and confess a painful consciousness of being good for nothing, of living without purpose or aim. But as active usefulness is the only mode of satisfying the human soul, and as usefulness is ungenteel, there was no help for them, except through modes that would rouse the opposition of relatives. And so they moved on, in their daily automaton revolutions, with a vague, half-smothered hope that life had something in store for them, more interesting than the past had been. Thus the crew of the Benedict Arnold, when they approached the shore of New-England, dismantled, in a dark cold night, danced in a circle, to keep themselves from freezing, till the light should dawn. But unless light is within, there come no clear directions from outward circumstances; and the chance is that these half-stifled souls will enter into some uncongenial marriage, merely for the sake of novelty and change of scene.

Not unfrequently, have I heard women, who were surrounded by all the advantages that outward wealth can give, say, with sad and timid self-reproach, "I ought to be happy. It is my own fault that I am not. But, I know not how it is, I cannot get up an interest in anything." When I remind them that Richter said, "I have fire-proof perennial enjoyments, called employments," few have faith in such a cure for the inanity of life. But the only certain way to attain habitual content and cheerfulness, is by the active use of our faculties and feelings. Mrs. Somerville finds too much excitement and pleasure in her astronomical investigations, to need the poor stimulus of extravagant expenditure, or gossiping about her neighbours. Yet the astronomer discharges all womanly duties with beautiful propriety. She takes nothing from her family. She merely gives to science those hours which many women in the same station waste in idleness or dissipation.

What can be more charming than the example of Mrs. Huber, devoting herself to the study of Natural History, to assist her blind husband in his observations? Or Mrs. Blake, making graceful drawings in her husband's studio, working off the impressions of his plates, and colouring them beautifully with her own hand? Compare a mere leader of ton[e] with the noble German Countess Julie Von Egloffstein, who dared to follow her genius for Art, though all the prejudices of people in her own rank were strongly arrayed against it. Mrs. Jameson says, "When I have looked at the Countess Julie in her painting room, surrounded by her drawings, models, casts—all the powers of her exuberant, enthusiastic mind, flowing free in their natural direction, I have felt at once pleasure, admiration, and respect." The same writer says, "In general, the conscious power of maintaining themselves, habits of attention and manual industry in women, the application of our feminine superfluity of sensibility and imagination to a tangible result, have produced fine characters."

That woman is slowly making her way into freer life is evinced by the fact that, in a few highly cultivated countries, literature is no longer deemed a disparagement to woman, and even professed authorship does not involve loss of caste in society. Maria Edgeworth, Mary Howitt, Frederika Bremer, our own admirable and excellent Catherine Sedgwick, and many others widely known as writers, were placed in the genteel ranks of society by birth; but they are universally regarded with increased respect, because they have enlarged their bounds of usefulness, to strengthen and refresh thousands of minds.

Dorothea L. Dix, when she retired from school teaching, because the occupation disagreed with her health, had a competence that precluded the necessity of further exertion. "Now she has nothing to do, but to be a lady and enjoy herself," said an acquaintance. But Miss Dix, though characterized by a most womanly sense of propriety, did not think it ladylike to be useless, or enjoyment to be indolent. "In a world where there is so much to be done," said she, "I felt strongly impressed that there must be something for me to do." Circumstances attracted her attention to the insane inmates of prisons and almshouses; and for several years, she has been to them a missionary of mercy, soothing them by her gentle influence, guiding them by her counsel, and greatly ameliorating their condition by earnest representations to selectmen and legislators. Her health has improved wonderfully under this continual activity of body, mind, and heart.

Frederika Bremer, in her delightful book called Home, tells of one of the unmarried daughters of a large family who evinced similar wisdom. She obtained from her father the sum that would have been her marriage portion, established a neat household for herself, and adopted two friendless orphan girls to educate.

"Thou mayest own the world, with health
And unslumbering powers;
Industry alone is wealth,
What we do is ours."

Use is the highest law of our being, and it cannot be disobeyed with impunity. The more alive and earnest the soul is by nature, the more does its vitality need active use, and its earnestness an adequate motive. It will go well with society, when it practically illustrates Coleridge's beautiful definition: "Labour should be the pleasant exercise of sane minds in healthy bodies. . . ."

Angelina Grimké Weld was born in 1805 in Charleston, South Carolina, the daughter of a wealthy slaveowner and judge. Dissatisfied with the frivolities of upper-class southern girlhood, she early sought a more meaningful life through religion. Raised a high-church Episcopalian, she initially was converted to Presbyterianism, and then, to Quakerism, largely under the influence of an older sister, Sarah Grimké. But Angelina Grimké soon found the Quaker faith a dead end, for instead of liberating her energies by sanctioning the promptings of her conscience, the authoritarian Society of Friends in Philadelphia (where she had moved in 1829 to be with her sister) deplored any contact between their members and radical causes.

Thwarted by the Society in her hopes to go to Hartford, Connecticut, to learn how to teach from Catharine Beecher, she became increasingly drawn to the abolitionist cause. And finally, in 1835, after unsuccessfully attempting to get influential Friends to support her in her efforts to spread the message of immediate emancipation among Quakers, she broke with the faith and, with her sister, became an agent for the new National Female Anti-Slavery Society in New York.

In 1836 Angelina Grimké wrote her "Appeal to Southern Women" while Sarah Grimké was working on a series of letters on the province of her sex. The Grimkés believed that abolition and women's rights were inextricably connected, for they saw that their own effectiveness as lecturers was undermined by the widespread prejudice against women's speaking in public. However, many prominent abolitionists, including John Greenleaf Whittier and Theodore Weld, feared that the emancipation of the slaves would be delayed if the two reform movements became confused in the popular mind, and prevailed upon the Grimkés to argue women's rights in practice but not in theory.

In 1838 Angelina Grimké married Weld and lived with him, and Sarah, for the rest of her life. She gave her last public address only three days after her marriage, and from that time on confined herself to teaching, nursing, and writing. Her sudden retirement has been explained in terms of a nervous affliction which incapacitated her for the excitements of public life, but it is impossible not to wonder if Theodore Weld's own inability to go on lecturing because of a persistent throat irritation did not have something to do with her abrupt disappearance from the platform.

The Welds had three children and became increasingly liberal in their religious beliefs in later years, casting off all doctrinal structures in favor of "loving and following Jesus." Angelina Weld died in 1879 after several years of ill health that can be dated from her discovery that one of her brothers, a slaveowner to his death, had fathered three illegitimate sons whom he had never acknowledged, much less emancipated.

Appeal to the Christian Women of the South, Angelina Grimké Weld*

"Then Mordecai commanded to answer Esther, Think not within thyself that thou shalt escape in the king's house more than all the Jews. For if thou altogether holdest thy peace at this time, then shall there enlargement and deliverance arise to the Jews from another place: but thou and thy father's house shall be destroyed: and who knoweth whether thou art come to the kingdom for such a time as this. And Esther bade them return Mordecai this answer:—and so will I go in unto the king, which is not according to law, and if I perish, I perish." Esther IV. 13–16.

Respected Friends,

It is because I feel a deep and tender interest in your present and eternal welfare that I am willing thus publicly to address you. Some of you have loved me as a relative, and some have felt bound to me in Christian sympathy, and Gospel fellowship; and even when compelled by a strong sense of duty, to break those outward bonds of union which bound us together as members of the same community, and members of the same religious denomination, you were generous enough to give me credit, for sincerity as a Christian, though you believed I had been most strangely deceived. I thanked you then for your kindness, and I ask you *now*, for the sake of former confidence, and former friendship, to read the following pages in the spirit of calm investigation and fervent prayer. It is because you have known me, that I write thus unto you.

* Mrs. Weld's "Appeal" was first published in pamphlet form in New York in 1836.

But there are other Christian women scattered over the Southern States, and these, a very large number of whom have never seen me, and never heard my name, and who feel *no* interest whatever in *me*. But I feel an interest in *you*, as branches of the same vine from whose root I daily draw the principle of spiritual vitality—Yes! Sisters in Christ I feel an interest in *you*, and often has the secret prayer arisen on your behalf, Lord "open thou their eyes that they may see wondrous things out of thy Law"—It is then, because I *do feel* and *do pray* for you, that I thus address you upon a subject about which of all others, perhaps you would rather not hear any thing; but, "would to God ye could bear with me a little in my folly, and indeed bear with me, for I am jealous over you with godly jealousy." Be not afraid then to read my appeal; it is *not* written in the heat of passion or prejudice, but in that solemn calmness which is the result of conviction and duty. It is true, I am going to tell you unwelcome truths, but I mean to speak those *truths in love*, and remember Solomon says, "faithful are the *wounds* of a friend." I do not believe the time has yet come when *Christian women* "will not endure sound doctrine," even on the subject of Slavery, if it is spoken to them in tenderness and love, therefore I now address *you*.

To all of you then, known or unknown, relatives or strangers, (for you are all *one* in Christ,) I would speak. I have felt for you at this time, when unwelcome light is pouring in upon the world on the subject of slavery; light which even Christians would exclude, if they could, from our country, or at any rate from the southern portion of it, saying, as its rays strike the rock bound coasts of New England and scatter their warmth and radiance over her hills and valleys, and from thence travel onward over the Palisades of the Hudson, and down the soft flowing waters of the Delaware and gild the waves of the Potomac, "hitherto shalt thou come and no further;" I know that even professors of His name who has been emphatically called the "Light of the world" would, if they could, build a wall of adamant around the Southern States whose top might reach unto heaven, in order to shut out the light which is bounding from mountain to mountain and from the hills to the plains and valleys beneath, through the vast extent of our Northern States. But believe me, when I tell you, their attempts will be as utterly fruitless as were the efforts of the builders of Babel; and why? Because moral, like natural light, is so extremely subtle in its nature as to overleap all human barriers, and laugh at the puny efforts of man to control it. All the excuses and palliations of this system must inevitably be swept away, just as other "refuges of lies" have been, by the irresistible torrent of a rectified public opinion. "The *supporters* of the slave system," says Jonathan Dymond in his admirable work on the Principles of Morality, "will *hereafter* be regarded with the same public feeling, as he who was an advocate for the slave trade *now is*." It will be, and that very soon, clearly perceived and fully acknowledged by all the virtuous and the candid, that in *principle* it is as sinful to hold a human being in bondage who has been born in Carolina, as one who has been born in Africa. All that sophistry of argument which has been employed to prove, that although it is sinful to send to Africa to procure men and women as slaves, who have never been in slavery, that still, it is not sinful to keep those in bondage who have come down by inheritance, will be utterly overthrown. We must come back to the good old doctrine of our forefathers who declared to the world, "this self evident truth that *all* men are created equal, and that they have certain *inalienable* rights among which are life, *liberty*, and the pursuit of happiness." It is even a greater absurdity to suppose a man can be legally born a slave under *our free Republican* Government, than under the petty despotisms of barbarian Africa. If then, we have no right to enslave an African, surely we can have none to enslave an American; if it is a self evident truth that *all* men, every where and of every color are born equal, and have an *inalienable right to liberty*, then it is equally true that *no* man can be born a slave, and no man can ever *rightfully* be reduced to *involuntary* bondage and held as a slave, however fair may be the claim of his master or mistress through wills and title-deeds.

But after all, it may be said, our fathers were certainly mistaken, for the Bible sanctions Slavery, and that is the highest authority. Now the Bible is my ultimate appeal in all matters of faith and practice, and it is to *this test* I am anxious to bring the subject at issue between us. Let us then begin with Adam and examine the charter of privileges which was given to him. "Have dominion over the fish of the sea, and over the fowl of the air, and over every living thing that moveth upon the earth." In the eighth Psalm we have a still fuller description of this charter which through Adam was given to all mankind. "Thou madest him to have dominion over the works of thy hands; thou hast put all things under his feet. All sheep and oxen, yea, and the beasts of the field, the fowl of the air, the fish of the sea, and whatsoever passeth through the paths of the seas." And after the flood when this charter of human rights was renewed, we find *no additional* power vested in man. "And the fear of you and the dread of you shall be upon every beast of the earth, and every fowl of the air, and upon all that moveth upon the earth, and upon all the fishes of the sea, into your hand are they delivered." In this charter, although the different kinds of *irrational* beings are so particularly enumerated, and supreme dominion over *all of them* is granted, yet *man* is *never* vested with this dominion *over his fellow man;* he was never told that any of the human species were put *under his feet;* it was only *all things,* and man, who was created in the image of his Maker, *never* can properly be termed a *thing,* though the laws of Slave States do call him "a chattel personal;" *Man* then, I assert *never* was put *under the feet of man,* by that first charter of human rights which was given by God, to the Fathers of the Antediluvian and Postdiluvian worlds, therefore this doctrine of equality is based on the Bible.

But it may be argued, that in the very chapter of Genesis from which I have last quoted, will be found the curse pronounced upon Canaan, by which his posterity was consigned to servitude under his brothers Shem and Japheth. I know this prophecy was uttered, and was most fearfully and wonderfully fulfilled, through the immediate descendants of

Canaan, i.e. the Canaanites, and I do not know but it has been through all the children of Ham, but I do know that prophecy does *not* tell us what *ought to be*, but what actually does take place, ages after it has been delivered, and that if we justify America for enslaving the children of Africa, we must also justify Egypt for reducing the children of Israel to bondage, for the latter was foretold as explicitly as the former. I am well aware that prophecy has often been urged as an excuse for Slavery, but be not deceived, the fulfilment of prophecy will *not cover one sin* in the awful day of account. Hear what our Saviour says on this subject; "it must needs be that offences come, but *woe unto that man through whom they come*"—Witness some fulfilment of this declaration in the tremendous destruction of Jerusalem, occasioned by that most nefarious of all crimes the crucifixion of the Son of God. Did the fact of that event having been foretold, exculpate the Jews from sin in perpetrating it; No—for hear what the Apostle Peter says to them on this subject, "Him being delivered by the determinate counsel and foreknowledge of God, *ye* have taken, and by *wicked* hands have crucified and slain." Other striking instances might be adduced, but these will suffice.

But it has been urged that the patriarchs held slaves, and therefore, slavery is right. Do you really believe that patriarchal servitude was like American slavery? Can you believe it? If so, read the history of these primitive fathers of the church and be undeceived. Look at Abraham, though so great a man, going to the herd himself and fetching a calf from thence and serving it up with his own hands, for the entertainment of his guests. Look at Sarah, that princess as her name signifies, baking cakes upon the hearth. If the servants they had were like Southern slaves, would they have performed such comparatively menial offices for themselves? Hear too the plaintive lamentation of Abraham when he feared he should have no son to bear his name down to posterity. "Behold thou hast given me no seed, &c, one born in my house *is mine* heir." From this it appears that one of his *servants* was to inherit his immense estate. Is this like

Southern slavery? I leave it to your own good sense and candor to decide. Besides, such was the footing upon which Abraham was with *his* servants, that he trusted them with arms. Are slaveholders willing to put swords and pistols into the hands of their slaves? He was as a father among his servants; what are planters and masters generally among theirs? When the institution of circumcision was established, Abraham was commanded thus; "He that is eight days old shall be circumcised among you, *every* man-child in your generations; he that is born in the house, or bought with money of any stranger which is not of thy seed." And to render this command with regard to his *servants* still more impressive it is repeated in the very next verse; and herein we may perceive the great care which was taken by God to guard the *rights of servants* even under this "dark dispensation." What too was the testimony given to the faithfulness of this eminent patriarch. "For I know him that he will command his children and his *household* after him, and they shall keep the way of the Lord to do justice and judgment." Now my dear friends many of you believe that circumcision has been superseded by baptism in the Church; *Are you* careful to have *all* that are born in your house or bought with money of any stranger, baptized? Are *you* as faithful as Abraham to command *your household to keep the way of the Lord?* I leave it to your own consciences to decide. Was patriarchal servitude then like American Slavery?

But I shall be told, God sanctioned Slavery, yea commanded Slavery under the Jewish Dispensation. Let us examine this subject calmly and prayerfully. I admit that a species of *servitude* was permitted to the Jews, but in studying the subject I have been struck with wonder and admiration at perceiving how carefully the servant was guarded from violence, injustice and wrong. I will first inform you how these servants became servants, for I think this a very important part of our subject. From consulting Horne, Calmet and the Bible, I find there were six different ways by which the Hebrews became servants legally.

1. If reduced to extreme poverty, a Hebrew might sell

himself, i.e. his services, for six years, in which case *he* received the purchase money *himself*. Lev. xxv, 39.

2. A father might sell his children as servants, i.e. his *daughters*, in which circumstance it was understood the daughter was to be the wife or daughter-in-law of the man who bought her, and the *father* received the price. In other words, Jewish women were sold as *white women* were in the first settlement of Virginia—as *wives, not* as slaves. Ex. xxi, 7.

3. Insolvent debtors might be delivered to their creditors as servants. 2 Kings iv, 1.

4. Thieves not able to make restitution for their thefts, were sold for the benefit of the injured person. Ex. xxii, 3.

5. They might be born in servitude. Ex. xxi, 4.

6. If a Hebrew had sold himself to a rich Gentile, he might be redeemed by one of his brethren at any time the money was offered; and he who redeemed him, was *not* to take advantage of the favor thus conferred, and rule over him with rigor. Lev. xxv, 47–55.

Before going into an examination of the laws by which these servants were protected, I would just ask whether American slaves have become slaves in any of the ways in which the Hebrews became servants. Did they sell themselves into slavery and receive the purchase money into their own hands? No! Did they become insolvent, and by their own imprudence subject themselves to be sold as slaves? No! Did they steal the property of another, and were they sold to make restitution for their crimes? No! Did their present masters, as an act of kindness, redeem them from some heathen tyrant to whom *they had sold themselves* in the dark hour of adversity? No! Were they born in slavery? No! No! not according to *Jewish Law*, for the servants who were born in servitude among them, were born of parents who had *sold themselves* for six years: Ex. xxi, 4. Were the female slaves of the South sold by their fathers? How shall I answer this question? Thousands and tens of thousands never were, *their* fathers *never* have received the poor compensation of silver or gold for the tears and toils, the suffering, and anguish, and hopeless bondage of *their* daughters. They labor day by day, and year by year, side by side, in the same field, if haply their daughters are permitted to remain on the same plantation with them, instead of being as they often are, separated from their parents and sold into distant states, never again to meet on earth. But do the *fathers of the South ever sell their daughters?* My heart beats, and my hand trembles, as I write the awful affirmative, Yes! The fathers of this Christian land often sell their daughters, *not* as Jewish parents did, to be the wives and daughters-in-law of the man who buys them, but to be the abject slaves of petty tyrants and irresponsible masters. Is it not so, my friends? I leave it to your own candor to corroborate my assertion: Southern slaves then have *not* become slaves in any of the six different ways in which Hebrews became servants, and I hesitate not to say that American masters *cannot* according to *Jewish law* substantiate their claim to the men, women, or children they now hold in bondage. . . .

I will next proceed to an examination of those laws which were enacted in order to protect the Hebrew and the Heathen servant; for I wish you to understand that both are protected by Him, of whom it is said "his mercies are over *all* his works." I will first speak of those which secured the rights of Hebrew servants. This code was headed thus:

1. Thou shalt *not* rule over him with *rigor*, but shalt fear thy God.

2. If thou buy a Hebrew servant, six years shall he serve, and in the seventh year he shall go out free for nothing. Ex. xx, 2.*

3. If he come in by himself, he shall go out by himself; if he were married, then his wife shall go out with him.

4. If his master have given him a wife and she have borne

---

* And when thou sendest him out free from thee, thou shalt not let him go away empty: Thou shalt furnish him *liberally* out of thy flock and out of thy floor, and out of thy wine-press: of that wherewith the Lord thy God hath blessed thee, shalt thou give unto him. Deut. xv, 13, 14.

him sons and daughters, the wife and her children shall be his master's, and he shall go out by himself.

5. If the servant shall plainly say, I love my master, my wife, and my children; I will not go out free; then his master shall bring him unto the Judges, and he shall bring him to the door, or unto the door-post, and his master shall bore his ear through with an awl, and he shall serve him *forever*. Ex. xxi, 3–6.

6. If a man smite the eye of his servant, or the eye of his maid, that it perish, he shall let him go *free* for his eye's sake. And if he smite out his man servant's tooth or his maid servant's tooth, he shall let him go *free* for his tooth's sake. Ex. xxi, 26, 27.

7. On the Sabbath rest was secured to servants by the fourth commandment. Ex. xx, 10.

8. Servants were permitted to unite with their masters three times in every year in celebrating the Passover, the feast of Pentecost, and the feast of Tabernacles; every male throughout the land was to appear before the Lord at Jerusalem with a gift; here the bond and the free stood on common ground. Deut. xvi.

9. If a man smite his servant or his maid with a rod, and he die under his hand, he shall be surely punished. Notwithstanding, if he continue a day or two, he shall not be punished, for he is his money. Ex. xxi, 20, 21.

From these laws we learn that Hebrew men servants were bound to serve their masters *only six* years, unless their attachment to their employers, their wives and children, should induce them to wish to remain in servitude, in which case, in order to prevent the possibility of deception on the part of the master, the servant was first taken before the magistrate, where he openly declared his intention of continuing in his master's service, (probably a public register was kept of such) he was then conducted to the door of the house, (in warm climates doors are thrown open,) and *there* his ear was *publicly* bored, and by submitting to this operation he testified his willingness to serve him *forever*, i.e. during his life, for Jewish Rabbins who must have understood Jewish *slavery*, (as it is called,) "affirm that servants were set free at the death of their masters and did *not* descend to their heirs;" or that he was to serve him until the year of Jubilee, when all servants were set at liberty. To protect servants from violence, it was ordained that if a master struck out the tooth or destroyed the eye of a servant, that servant immediately became *free*, for such an act of violence evidently showed he was unfit to possess the power of a master, and therefore that power was taken from him. All servants enjoyed the rest of the Sabbath and partook of the privileges and festivities of the three great Jewish Feasts; and if a servant died under the infliction of chastisement, his master was surely to be punished. As a tooth for a tooth and life for life was the Jewish law, of course he was punished with death. I know that great stress has been laid upon the following verse: "Notwithstanding, if he continue a day or two, he shall not be punished, for he is his money."

Slaveholders, and the apologists of slavery, have eagerly seized upon this little passage of scripture, and held it up as the masters' Magna Charta, by which they were liscensed by God himself to commit the greatest outrages upon the defenceless victims of their oppression. But, my friends, was it designed to be so? If our Heavenly Father would protect by law the eye and the tooth of a Hebrew servant, can we for a moment believe that he would abandon that same servant to the brutal rage of a master who would destroy even life itself. Do we not rather see in this, the only law which protected masters, and was it not right that in case of the death of a servant, one or two days after chastisement was inflicted, to which other circumstances might have contributed, that the master should be protected when, in all probability, he never intended to produce so fatal a result? But the phrase "he is his money" has been adduced to show that Hebrew servants were regarded as mere *things*, "chattels personal;" if so, why were so many laws made to *secure their rights as men,* and to ensure their rising into equality and freedom? If they were mere *things*, why were they regarded as responsible beings, and one law made for them as well as for their masters? But I pass on now to the consideration of how the *female* Jewish servants were protected by *law*.

1. If she please not her master, who hath betrothed her to himself, then shall he let her be redeemed: to sell her unto another nation he shall have no power, seeing he hath dealt deceitfully with her.

2. If he have betrothed her unto his son, he shall deal with her after the manner of daughters.

3. If he take him another wife, her food, her raiment, and her duty of marriage, shall he not diminish.

4. If he do not these three unto her, then shall she go out *free* without money.

On these laws I will give you Calmet's remarks; "A father could not sell his daughter as a slave, according to the Rabbins, until she was at the age of puberty, and unless he were reduced to the utmost indigence. Besides, when a master bought an Israelitish girl, it was *always* with the presumption that he would take her to wife. Hence Moses adds, 'if she please not her master, and he does not think to marry her, he shall set her at liberty,' or according to the Hebrew, 'he shall let her be redeemed.' 'To sell her to another nation he shall have no power, seeing he hath dealt deceitfully with her;' as to the engagement implied, at least of taking her to wife. 'If he have betrothed her unto his son, he shall deal with her after the manner of daughters, i.e. he shall take care that his son uses her as his wife, that he does not despise or maltreat her. If he make his son marry another wife, he shall give her her dowry, her clothes and compensation for her virginity; if he does none of these three, she shall *go out free* without money." Thus were the *rights of female servants carefully secured by law* under the Jewish Dispensation; and now I would ask, are the rights of female slaves at the South thus secured? Are *they* sold only as wives and daughters-in-law, and when not treated as such, are they allowed to go out free? No! They have all not only been illegally obtained as servants according to Hebrew law, but they are thus illegally *held* in bondage. Masters at the South and West have all forfeited their claims, (*if they ever had any,*) to their female slaves. . . .

There are however two other laws which I have not yet noticed. The one effectually prevented *all involuntary* servitude, and the other completely abolished Jewish servitude every fifty years. They were equally operative upon the Heathen and the Hebrew.

1. "Thou shall *not* deliver unto his master the servant that is escaped from his master unto thee. He shall dwell with thee, even among you, in that place which he shall choose, in one of thy gates where it liketh him best: thou shall *not* oppress him." Deut. xxxiii, 13, 16.

2. "And ye shall hallow the fiftieth year, and proclaim *Liberty* throughout *all* the land, unto *all* the inhabitants thereof: it shall be a jubilee unto you." Deut. xxv, 10.

Here, then, we see that by this first law, the *door of Freedom was opened wide to every servant* who had any cause whatever for complaint; if he was unhappy with his master, all he had to do was to leave him, and *no man* had a right to deliver him back to him again, and not only so, but the absconded servant was to *choose* where he should live, and no Jew was permitted to oppress him. He left his master just as our Northern servants leave us; we have no power to compel them to remain with us, and no man has any right to oppress them; they go and dwell in that place where it chooseth them, and live just where they like. Is it so at the South? Is the poor runaway slave protected *by law* from the violence of that master whose oppression and cruelty has driven him from his plantation or his house? No! no! Even the free states of the North are compelled to deliver unto his master the servant that is escaped from his master into them. By *human* law, under the *Christian Dispensation,* in the *nineteenth century we* are commanded to do, what God more than *three thousand years* ago, under the *Mosaic Dispensation, positively commanded* the Jews *not* to do. In the wide domain even of our free states, there is not *one* city of refuge for the poor runaway fugitive; not one spot upon

which he can stand and say, I am a free man—I am protected in my rights as a *man*, by the strong arm of the law;
no! *not one*. How long the North will thus shake hands with
the South in sin, I know not. How long she will stand by like
the persecutor Saul, *consenting* unto the death of Stephen,
and keeping the raiment of them that slew him. I know not;
but one thing I do know, the *guilt of the North* is increasing in a tremendous ratio as light is pouring in upon her on
the subject and the sin of slavery. As the sun of righteousness climbs higher and higher in the moral heavens, she will
stand still more and more abashed as the query is thundered
down into her ear, "*Who* hath required *this* at thy hand?" It
will be found *no* excuse then that the Constitution of our
country required that *persons bound to service* escaping from
their masters should be delivered up; no more excuse than
was the reason which Adam assigned for eating the forbidden fruit. *He* was *condemned and punished because* he
hearkened to the voice of *his wife*, rather than to the command of his Maker; and *we* will assuredly be condemned
and punished for obeying *Man* rather than *God,* if we do not
speedily repent and bring forth fruits meet for repentance.
Yea, are we not receiving chastisement even *now?*

But by the second of these laws a still more astonishing
fact is disclosed. If the first effectually prevented *all involuntary servitude,* the last absolutely forbade even *voluntary
servitude being perpetual.* On the great day of atonement
every fiftieth year the Jubilee trumpet was sounded throughout the land of Judea, and *Liberty* was proclaimed to *all* the
inhabitants thereof. I will not say that the servants' *chains*
fell off and their *manacles* were burst, for there is no evidence that Jewish servants *ever* felt the weight of iron chains,
and collars, and handcuffs; but I do say that even the man
who had voluntarily sold himself and the *heathen* who had
been sold to a Hebrew master, were set free, the one as well
as the other. This law was evidently designed to prevent the
oppression of the poor, and the possibility of such a thing as
perpetual servitude existing among them.

Where, then, I would ask, is the warrant, the justification,

or the palliation of American Slavery from Hebrew servitude?
How many of the southern slaves would now be in bondage
according to the laws of Moses; Not one. You may observe
that I have carefully avoided using the term *slavery* when
speaking of Jewish servitude; and simply for this reason, that
no such thing existed among that people; the word translated
servant does *not* mean *slave*, it is the same that is applied
to Abraham, to Moses, to Elisha and the prophets generally.
Slavery then *never* existed under the Jewish Dispensation at
all, and I cannot but regard it as an aspersion on the character of Him who is "glorious in Holiness" for any one to assert
that "*God sanctioned, yea commanded slavery* under the old
dispensation." I would fain lift my feeble voice to vindicate
Jehovah's character from so foul a slander. If slaveholders
are determined to hold slaves as long as they can, let them
not dare to say that the God of mercy and of truth *ever*
sanctioned such a system of cruelty and wrong. It is blas-
phemy against Him.

We have seen that the code of laws framed by Moses with
regard to servants was designed to *protect them* as *men and
women*, to secure to them their *rights* as *human beings*,
to guard them from oppression and defend them from violence of every kind. Let us now turn to the Slave laws of the
South and West and examine them too. I will give you the
substance only, because I fear I shall tresspass too much on
your time, were I to quote them at length.

1. *Slavery* is hereditary and perpetual, to the last moment
of the slave's earthly existence, and to all his descendants to
the latest posterity.

2. The labor of the slave is compulsory and uncompen-
sated; while the kind of labor, the amount of toil, the time
allowed for rest, are dictated solely by the master. No bargain is made, no wages given. A pure despotism governs the
human brute; and even his covering and provender, both as
to quantity and quality, depend entirely on the master's discretion.

3. The slave being considered a personal chattel may be
sold or pledged, or leased at the will of his master. He may

be exchanged for marketable commodities, or taken in execution for the debts or taxes either of a living or dead master. Sold at auction, either individually, or in lots to suit the purchaser, he may remain with his family, or be separated from them for ever.

4. Slaves can make no contracts and have no *legal* right to any property, real or personal. Their own honest earnings and the legacies of friends belong in point of law to their masters.

5. Neither a slave nor a free colored person can be a witness against any *white,* or free person, in a court of justice, however atrocious may have been the crimes they have seen him commit, if such testimony would be for the benefit of a *slave;* but they may give testimony *against a fellow slave,* or free colored man, even in cases affecting life, if the *master* is to reap the advantage of it.

6. The slave may be punished at his master's discretion—without trial—without any means of legal redress; whether his offence be real or imaginary; and the master can transfer the same despotic power to any person or persons, he may choose to appoint.

7. The slave is not allowed to resist any free man under *any* circumstances, *his* only safety consists in the fact that his *owner* may bring suit and recover the price of his body, in case his life is taken, or his limbs rendered unfit for labor.

8. Slaves cannot redeem themselves, or obtain a change of masters, though cruel treatment may have rendered such a change necessary for their personal safety.

9. The slave is entirely unprotected in his domestic relations.

10. The laws greatly obstruct the manumission of slaves, even where the master is willing to enfranchise them.

11. The operation of the laws tends to deprive slaves of religious instruction and consolation.

12. The whole power of the laws is exerted to keep slaves in a state of the lowest ignorance.

13. There is in this country a monstrous inequality of law and right. What is a trifling fault in the *white* man, is con-

sidered highly criminal in the *slave;* the same offences which cost a white man a few dollars only, are punished in the negro with death.

14. The laws operate most oppressively upon free people of color.

Shall I ask you now my friends, to draw the *parallel* between Jewish *servitude* and American *slavery?* No! For there is *no likeness* in the two systems; I ask you rather to mark the contrast. The laws of Moses *protected servants* in their *rights* as *men and women,* guarded them from oppression and defended them from wrong. The Code Noir of the South *robs the slave of all his rights* as a *man,* reduces him to a chattel personal, and defends the *master* in the exercise of the most unnatural and unwarantable power over his slave. They each bear the impress of the hand which formed them. The attributes of justice and mercy are shadowed out in the Hebrew code; those of injustice and cruelty, in the Code Noir of America. Truly it was wise in the slaveholders of the South to declare their slaves to be "chattels personal;" for before they could be robbed of wages, wives, children, and friends, it was absolutely necessary to deny they were human beings. It is wise in them, to keep them in abject ignorance, for the strong man armed must be bound before we can spoil his house—the powerful intellect of man must be bound down with the iron chains of nescience before we can rob him of his rights as a man; we must reduce him to a *thing* before we can claim the right to set our feet upon his neck, because it was only *all things* which were originally *put under the feet of man* by the Almighty and Beneficent Father of all, who has declared himself to be *no respecter* of persons, whether red, white or black.

But some have even said that Jesus Christ did not condemn slavery. To this I reply that our Holy Redeemer lived and preached among the Jews only. The laws which Moses had enacted fifteen hundred years previous to his appearance among them, had never been annulled, and these laws protected every servant in Palestine. If then He did not condemn Jewish servitude this does not prove that he would not have condemned such a monstrous system as that of American *slavery*, if that had existed among them. But did not Jesus condemn slavery? Let us examine some of his precepts. *"Whatsoever* ye would that men should do to you, do *ye even so to them,"* Let every slaveholder apply these queries to his own heart; Am I willing to be a slave—Am I willing to see *my* wife the slave of another—Am I willing to see my mother a slave, or my father, my sister or my brother? If *not,* then in holding others as slaves, I am doing what I would *not* wish to be done to me or any relative I have; and thus have I broken this golden rule which was given *me* to walk by.

But some slaveholders have said, "we were never in bondage to any man," and therefore the yoke of bondage would be insufferable to us, but slaves are accustomed to it, their backs are fitted to the burden. Well, I am willing to admit that you who have lived in freedom would find slavery even more oppressive than the poor slave does, but then you may try this question in another form—Am I willing to reduce *my little child* to slavery? You know that *if it is brought up a slave* it will never know any contrast, between freedom and bondage, its back will become fitted to the burden just as the negro child's does—*not by nature*—but by daily, violent pressure, in the same way that the head of the Indian child becomes flattened by the boards in which it is bound. It has been justly remarked that *"God never made a slave,"* he made man upright; his back was *not* made to carry burdens, nor his neck to wear a yoke, and the *man* must be crushed within him, before *his* back can be *fitted* to the burden of perpetual slavery; and that his back is *not* fitted to it, is manifest by the insurrections that so often disturb the peace and security of slaveholding countries. Who ever heard of a rebellion of the beasts of the field; and why not? simply because *they* were all placed *under the feet of man,* into whose hand they were delivered; it was originally designed that they should serve him, therefore their necks have been formed for the yoke, and their backs for the burden; but *not so with man,* intellectual, immortal man! I appeal to you, my friends, as mothers; Are you willing to enslave *your* children? You start back with horror and indignation at such a question. But why, if slavery is *no wrong* to those upon whom it is imposed? why, if as has often been said, slaves are. happier than their masters, free from the cares and perplexities of providing for themselves and their families? why not place *your children* in the way of being supported without your having the trouble to provide for them, or they for themselves? Do you not perceive that as soon as this golden rule of action is applied to *yourselves* that you involuntarily shrink from the test; as soon as *your* actions are weighed in *this* balance of the sanctuary that *you are found wanting?* Try yourselves by another of the Divine precepts, "Thou shalt love thy neighbor as thyself." Can we love a man *as* we love *ourselves* if we do, and continue to do unto him, what we would not wish any one to do to us? Look too, at Christ's example, what does he say of himself, "I came *not* to be ministered unto, but to minister." Can you for a moment imagine the meek, and lowly, and compassionate Saviour, *a slaveholder?* do you not shudder at this thought as much as at that of his being *a warrior?* But why, if slavery is not sinful? . . .

There is no difference in *principle*, in *Christian ethics*, between the despised slavedealer and the *Christian* who buys slaves from, or sells slaves to him; indeed, if slaves were not wanted by the respectable, the wealthy, and the religious in a community, there would be no slaves in that community, and of course no *slavedealers*. It is then the *Christians* and the *honorable men* and *women* of the South, who are the *main pillars* of this grand temple built to Mammon and to Moloch. It is the *most enlightened* in every country who are *most* to blame when any public sin is supported by public opinion, hence Isaiah says, "*When* the Lord hath performed his whole work upon mount *Zion* and on *Jerusalem,* (then) I will punish the fruit of the stout heart of the king of Assyria, and the glory of his high looks." And was it not so? Open the historical records of that age, was not Israel carried into captivity B.C. 606, Judah B.C. 588, and the stout heart of the heathen monarchy not punished until B.C. 536, fifty-two years *after* Judah's, and seventy years *after* Israel's captivity, when it was overthrown by Cyrus, king of Persia? Hence, too, the apostle Peter says, "judgment must *begin at the house of God.*" Surely this would not be the case, if the *professors of religion* were not *most worthy* of blame.

But it may be asked, why are *they* most culpable? I will tell you, my friends. It is because sin is imputed to us just in proportion to the spiritual light we receive. Thus the prophet Amos says, in the name of Jehovah, "*You only* have I known of all the families of the earth: *therefore* I will punish *you* for all your iniquities." Hear too the doctrine of our Lord on this important subject; "The servant who *knew* his Lord's will and *prepared not* himself, neither did according to his will, shall be beaten with *many* stripes:" and why? "For unto whomsoever *much* is given, *of him* shall *much* be required; and to whom men have committed *much*, of *him* they will ask the *more.*" Oh! then that the *Christians* of the south would ponder these things in their hearts, and awake to the vast responsibilities which rest *upon them* at this important crisis.

I have thus, I think, clearly proved to you seven propositions, viz.: First, that slavery is contrary to the declaration of our independence. Second, that it is contrary to the first charter of human rights given to Adam, and renewed to Noah. Third, that the fact of slavery having been the subject of prophecy, furnishes *no* excuse whatever to slavedealers. Fourth, that no such system existed under the patriarchal dispensation. Fifth, that *slavery never* existed under the Jewish dispensation; but so far otherwise, that every servant was placed under the *protection of law*, and care taken not only to prevent all *involuntary* servitude, but all *voluntary perpetual* bondage. Sixth, that slavery in America reduces a *man* to a *thing*, a "chattel personal," *robs him* of *all* his rights as a *human being*, fetters both his mind and body, and protects the *master* in the most unnatural and unreasonable power, whilst it *throws him out* of the protection of law.

Seventh, that slavery is contrary to the example and precepts of our holy and merciful Redeemer, and of his apostles.

But perhaps you will be ready to query, why appeal to *women* on this subject? *We* do not make the laws which perpetuate slavery. *No* legislative power is vested in *us; we* can do nothing to overthrow the system, even if we wished to do so. To this I reply, I know you do not make the laws, but I also know that *you are the wives and mothers, the sisters and daughters of those who do;* and if you really suppose *you* can do nothing to overthrow slavery, you are greatly mistaken. You can do much in every way: four things I will name. 1st. You can read on this subject. 2d. You can pray over this subject. 3d. You can speak on this subject. 4th. You can *act* on this subject. I have not placed reading before praying because I regard it more important, but because, in order to pray aright, we must understand what we are praying for; it is only then we can "pray with the understanding and the spirit also."

1. Read then on the subject of slavery. Search the Scriptures daily, whether the things I have told you are true. Other books and papers might be a great help to you in this investigation, but they are not necessary, and it is hardly probable that your Committees of Vigilance will allow you to have any other. The *Bible* then is the book I want you to read in the spirit of inquiry, and the spirit of prayer. Even the enemies of Abolitionists, acknowledge that their doctrines are drawn from it. In the great mob in Boston, last autumn, when the books and papers of the Anti-Slavery Society, were thrown out of the windows of their office, one individual laid hold of the Bible and was about tossing it out to the ground, when another reminded him that it was the Bible he had in his hand. *"O! 'tis all one,"* he replied, and out went the sacred volume, along with the rest. We thank him for the acknowledgment. Yes, *"it is all one,"* for our books and papers are mostly commentaries on the Bible, and the Declaration. Read the *Bible* then, it contains the words of Jesus, and they are spirit and life. Judge for your-

selves whether *he sanctioned* such a system of oppression
and crime.

2. Pray over this subject. When you have entered into
your closets, and shut to the doors, then pray to your father,
who seeth in secret, that he would open your eyes to see
whether slavery is *sinful*, and if it is, that he would enable
you to bear a faithful, open and unshrinking testimony against
it, and to do whatsoever your hands find to do, leaving the
consequences entirely to him, who still says to us whenever
we try to reason away duty from the fear of consequences,
"What is that to thee, follow thou me." Pray also for that
poor slave, that he may be kept patient and submissive under
his hard lot, until God is pleased to open the door of freedom
to him without violence or bloodshed. Pray too for the master
that his heart may be softened, and he made willing to
acknowledge, as Joseph's brethren did, "Verily we are guilty
concerning our brother," before he will be compelled to add
in consequence of Divine judgment, "therefore is all this
evil come upon us." Pray also for all your brethren and sisters who are laboring in the righteous cause of Emancipation in the Northern States, England and the world. There
is great encouragement for prayer in these words of our
Lord. "Whatsoever ye shall ask the Father *in my name,*
he *will give* it to you"—Pray then without ceasing, in the
closet and the social circle.

3. Speak on this subject. It is through the tongue, the pen,
and the press, that truth is principally propagated. Speak
then to your relatives, your friends, your acquaintances on
the subject of slavery; be not afraid if you are conscientiously convinced it is *sinful*, to say so openly, but calmly,
and to let your sentiments be known. If you are served by
the slaves of others, try to ameliorate their condition as much
as possible; never aggravate their faults, and thus add fuel
to the fire of anger already kindled, in a master and mistress's
bosom; remember their extreme ignorance, and consider
them as your Heavenly Father does the *less* culpable on
this account, even when they do wrong things. Discounte-
nance *all* cruelty to them, all starvation, all corporal chas-

tisement; these may brutalize and *break* their spirits, but will never bend them to willing, cheerful obedience. If possible, see that they are comfortably and *seasonably* fed, whether in the house or the field; it is unreasonable and cruel to expect slaves to wait for their breakfast until eleven o'clock, when they rise at five or six. Do all you can, to induce their owners to clothe them well, and to allow them many little indulgences which would contribute to their comfort. Above all, try to persuade your husband, father, brothers and sons, that *slavery is a crime against God and man,* and that it is a great sin to keep *human beings* in such abject ignorance; to deny them the privilege of learning to read and write. The Catholics are universally condemned, for denying the Bible to the common people, but, *slaveholders must not* blame them, for *they* are doing the *very same thing,* and for the very same reason, neither of these systems can bear the light which bursts from the pages of that Holy Book. And lastly, endeavour to inculcate submission on the part of the slaves, but whilst doing this be faithful in pleading the cause of the oppressed.

> "Will *you* behold unheeding,
> Life's holiest feelings crushed,
> Where *woman's* heart is bleeding,
> Shall *woman's* voice be hushed?"

4. Act on this subject. Some of you *own* slaves yourselves. If you believe slavery is *sinful,* set them at liberty, "undo the heavy burdens and let the oppressed go free." If they wish to remain with you, pay them wages, if not let them leave you. Should they remain teach them, and have them taught the common branches of an English education; they have minds and those minds, *ought to be improved.* So precious a talent as intellect, never was given to be wrapt in a napkin and buried in the earth. It is the *duty* of all, as far as they can, to improve their own mental faculties, because we are commanded to love God with *all our minds,* as well as with all our hearts, and we commit a great sin, if we

forbid or prevent that cultivation of the mind in others, which would enable them to perform this duty. Teach your servants then to read &c, and encourage them to believe it is their *duty* to learn, if it were only that they might read the Bible.

But some of you will say, we can neither free our slaves nor teach them to read, for the laws of our state forbid it. Be not surprised when I say such wicked laws *ought to be no barrier* in the way of your duty, and I appeal to the Bible to prove this position. What was the conduct of Shiphrah and Puah, when the king of Egypt issued his cruel mandate, with regard to the Hebrew children? "*They* feared *God*, and did *not* as the King of Egypt commanded them, but saved the men children alive." Did these *women* do right in disobeying that monarch? "*Therefore* (says the sacred text,) *God dealt well* with them, and made them houses" Ex. I. What was the conduct of Shadrach, Meshach, and Abednego, when Nebuchadnezzar set up a golden image in the plain of Dura, and commanded all people, nations, and languages, to fall down and worship it? "Be it known, unto thee, (said these faithful *Jews*) O king, that *we will not* serve thy gods, nor worship the image which thou hast set up." Did these men *do right in disobeying the law* of their sovereign? Let their miraculous deliverance from the burning fiery furnace, answer; Dan. iii. What was the conduct of Daniel, when Darius made a firm decree that no one should ask a petition of any man or God for thirty days? Did the prophet cease to pray? No! "When Daniel *knew that the writing was signed*, he went into his house, and his windows being *open* towards Jerusalem, he kneeled upon his knees three times a day, and prayed and gave thanks before his God, as he did aforetime." Did Daniel do right thus to *break* the law of his king? Let his wonderful deliverance out of the mouths of the lions answer; Dan. vii. Look, too, at the Apostles Peter and John. When the rulers of the Jews, "*commanded them not* to speak at all, nor teach in the name of Jesus," what did they say? "Whether it be right in the sight of God, to hearken unto you more than unto God, judge ye." And what did they do? "They spake the word of God with boldness, and with great power gave the Apostles witness of the *resurrection* of the Lord Jesus;" although *this* was the very doctrine, for the preaching of which, they had just been cast into prison, and further threatened. Did these men do right? I leave *you* to answer, who now enjoy the benefits of their labors and sufferings, in that Gospel they dared to preach when positively commanded *not to teach any more* in the name of Jesus; Acts iv.

But some of you may say, if we do free our slaves, they will be taken up and sold, therefore there will be no use in doing it. Peter and John might just as well have said, we will not preach the gospel, for if we do, we shall be taken up and put in prison, therefore there will be no use in our preaching. *Consequences*, my friends, belong no more to *you*, than they did to these apostles. Duty is ours and events are God's. If you think slavery is sinful, all *you* have to do is to set your slaves at liberty, do all you can to protect them, and in humble faith and fervent prayer, commend them to your common Father. He can take care of them; but if for wise purposes he sees fit to allow them to be sold, this will afford you an opportunity of testifying openly, wherever you go, against the crime of *manstealing*. Such an act will be *clear robbery*, and if exposed, might, under the Divine direction, do the cause of Emancipation more good, than any thing that could happen, for, "He makes even the wrath of man to praise him, and the remainder of wrath he will restrain."

I know that this doctrine of obeying *God*, rather than man, will be considered as dangerous, and heretical by many, but I am not afraid openly to avow it, because it is the doctrine of the Bible; but I would not be understood to advocate resistance to any law however oppressive, if, in obeying it, I was not obliged to commit *sin*. If for instance, there was a law, which imposed imprisonment or a fine upon me if I manumitted a slave, I would on no account resist that law, I would set the slave free, and then go to prison or pay the fine. If a law commands me to *sin I will break it;* if it calls me to *suffer*, I will let it take its course *unresistingly*. The doctrine of blind obedience and unqualified submission to *any human* power, whether civil or ecclesiastical, is the doctrine of despotism, and ought to have no place among Republicans and Christians.

But you will perhaps say, such a course of conduct would inevitably expose us to great suffering. Yes! my christian friends, I believe it would, but this will *not* excuse you or any one else for the neglect of *duty*. If Prophets and Apostles, Martyrs, and Reformers had not been willing to suffer for the truth's sake, where would the world have been now? If they had said, we cannot speak the truth, we cannot do what we believe is right, because the *laws of our country or public opinion are against us,* where would our holy religion have been now? The Prophets were stoned, imprisoned, and killed by the Jews. And why? Because they exposed and openly rebuked public sins; they opposed public opinion; had they held their peace, they all might have lived in ease and died in favor with a wicked generation. Why were the Apostles persecuted from city to city, stoned, incarcerated, beaten, and crucified? Because they dared to *speak the truth;* to tell the Jews, boldly and fearlessly, that *they* were the *murderers* of the Lord of Glory, and that, however great a stumbling-block the Cross might be to them, there was no other name given under heaven by which men could be saved, but the name of Jesus. Because they declared, even at Athens, the seat of learning and refinement, the self-evident truth, that "they be no gods that are made with men's hands," and exposed to the Grecians the foolishness of worldly wisdom, and the impossibility of salvation but through Christ, whom they despised on account of the ignominious death he died. Because at Rome, the proud mistress of the world, they thundered out the terrors of the law upon that idolatrous, war-making, and slave-holding community. Why were the martyrs stretched upon the rack, gibbetted and burnt, the scorn and diversion of a Nero, whilst their tarred and burning bodies sent up a light which illuminated the Roman capital? Why were the Waldenses hunted like wild beasts upon the mountains of Piedmont, and slain with the sword of the Duke of Savoy and the proud monarch of France? Why were the Presbyterians chased like the partridge over the highlands

of Scotland—the Methodists pumped, and stoned, and pelted
with rotten eggs—the Quakers incarcerated in filthy prisons,
beaten, whipped at the cart's tail, banished and hung? Because they dared to *speak* the *truth*, to *break* the unright-
eous *laws* of their country, and chose rather to suffer affliction with the people of God, "not accepting deliverance,"
even under the gallows. Why were Luther and Calvin persecuted and excommunicated, Crammer, Ridley, and Latimer
burnt? Because they fearlessly proclaimed the truth, though
that truth was contrary to public opinion, and the authority
of Ecclesiastical councils and conventions. Now all this vast
amount of human suffering might have been saved. All these
Prophets and Apostles, Martyrs, and Reformers, might have
lived and died in peace with all men, but following the example of their great pattern, "they despised the shame, endured
the cross, and are now set down on the right hand of the
throne of God," having received the glorious welcome of "well
done good and faithful servants, enter ye into the joy of your
Lord."

But you may say we are *women*, how can *our* hearts endure persecution? And why not? Have not *women* stood
up in all the dignity and strength of moral courage to be the
leaders of the people, and to bear a faithful testimony for
the truth whenever the providence of God has called them
to do so? Are there no *women* in that noble army of martyrs
who are now singing the song of Moses and the Lamb? Who
led out the women of Israel from the house of bondage, striking the timbrel, and singing the song of deliverance on the
banks of that sea whose waters stood up like walls of crystal
to open a passage for their escape? It was a *woman;* Miriam,
the prophetess, the sister of Moses and Aaron. Who went up
with Barak to Kadesh to fight against Jabin, King of Canaan,
into whose hand Israel had been sold because of their iniquities? It was a *woman!* Deborah the wife of Lapidoth, the
judge, as well as the prophetess of that backsliding people;
Judges iv, 9. Into whose hands was Sisera, the captain of
Jabin's host delivered? Into the hand of a *woman*. Jael the
wife of Heber! Judges vi, 21. Who dared to *speak the truth*

concerning those judgments which were coming upon Judea, when Josiah, alarmed at finding that his people "had not kept the word of the Lord to do after all that was written in the book of the Law," sent to enquire of the Lord concerning these things? It was a *woman*. Huldah the prophetess, the wife of Shallum; 2, Chron. xxxiv, 22. Who was chosen to deliver the whole Jewish nation from that murderous decree of Persia's King, which wicked Haman had obtained by calumny and fraud? It was a *woman;* Esther the Queen; yes, weak and trembling *woman* was the instrument appointed by God, to reverse the bloody mandate of the eastern monarch, and save the *whole visible church* from destruction. What human voice first proclaimed to Mary that she should be the mother of our Lord? It was a *woman!* Elizabeth, the wife of Zacharias; Luke i, 42, 43. Who united with the good old Simeon in giving thanks publicly in the temple, when the child, Jesus, was presented there by his parents, "and spake of him to all them that looked for redemption in Jerusalem?" It was a *woman!* Anna the prophetess. Who first proclaimed Christ as the true Messiah in the streets of Samaria, once the capital of the ten tribes? It was a *woman!* Who ministered to the Son of God whilst on earth, a despised and persecuted Reformer, in the humble garb of a carpenter? They were *women!* Who followed the rejected King of Israel, as his fainting footsteps trod the road to Calvary? "A great company of people and of *women;*" and it is remarkable that to *them alone,* he turned and addressed the pathetic language, "Daughters of Jerusalem, weep not for me, but weep for yourselves and your children." Ah! who sent unto the Roman Governor when he was set down on the judgment seat, saying unto him, "Have thou nothing to do with that just man, for I have suffered many things this day in a dream because of him?" It was a *woman!* the wife of Pilate. Although *"he knew* that for envy the Jews had delivered Christ," yet *he* consented to surrender the Son of God into the hands of a brutal soldiery, after having himself scourged his naked body. Had the *wife* of Pilate sat upon that judgment seat, what would have been the result of the trial of this "just person?"

And who last hung round the cross of Jesus on the mountain of Golgotha? Who first visited the sepulchre early in the morning on the first day of the week, carrying sweet spices to embalm his precious body, not knowing that it was incorruptible and could not be holden by the bands of death? These were *women!* To whom did he first appear after his resurrection? It was to a *woman!* Mary Magdalene; Mark xvi, 9. Who gathered with the apostles to wait at Jerusalem, in prayer and supplication, for "the promise of the Father;" the spiritual blessing of the Great High Priest of his Church, who had entered, *not* into the splendid temple of Solomon, there to offer the blood of bulls, and of goats, and the smoking censer upon the golden altar, but into Heaven itself, there to present his intercessions, after having "given himself for us, an offering and a sacrifice to God for a sweet smelling savor?" *Women* were among that holy company; Acts i, 14. And did *women* wait in vain? Did those who had ministered to his necessities, followed in his train, and wept at his crucifixion, wait in vain? No! No! Did the cloven tongues of fire descend upon the heads of *women* as well as men? Yes, my friends, "it sat upon *each one of them;*" Acts ii, 3. *Women* as well as men were to be living stones in the temple of grace, and therefore *their* heads were consecrated by the descent of the Holy Ghost as well as those of men. Were *women* recognized as fellow laborers in the gospel field? They were! Paul says in his epistle to the Philippians, "help those *women* who labored with me, in the gospel;" Phil. iv, 3.

But this is not all. Roman *women* were burnt at the stake, *their* delicate limbs were torn joint from joint by the ferocious beasts of the Amphitheatre, and tossed by the wild bull in his fury, for the diversion of that idolatrous, warlike, and slaveholding people. Yes, *women* suffered under the ten persecutions of heathen Rome, with the most unshrinking constancy and fortitude; not all the entreaties of friends, nor the claims of new born infancy, nor the cruel threats of enemies could make *them* sprinkle one grain of incense upon the altars of Roman idols. Come now with me to the beautiful valleys of Piedmont. Whose blood stains the green sward, and decks the wild flowers with colors not their own, and smokes on the sword of persecuting France? It is *woman's*, as well as man's? Yes, *women* were accounted as sheep for the slaughter, and were cut down as the tender saplings of the wood.

But time would fail me, to tell of all those hundreds and thousands of *women*, who perished in the Low countries of Holland, when Alva's sword of vengeance was unsheathed against the Protestants, when the Catholic Inquisitions of Europe became the merciless executioners of vindictive wrath, upon those who dared to worship God, instead of bowing down in unholy adoration before "my Lord God the *Pope*," and when England, too, burnt her Ann Ascoes at the stake of martyrdom. Suffice it to say, that the Church, after having been driven from Judea to Rome, and from Rome to Piedmont, and from Piedmont to England, and from England to Holland, at last stretched her fainting wings over the dark bosom of the Atlantic, and found on the shores of a great wilderness, a refuge from tyranny and oppression—as she thought, but *even here,* (the warm blush of shame mantles my cheek as I write it,) *even here, woman* was beaten and banished, imprisoned, and hung upon the gallows, a trophy to the Cross.

And what, I would ask in conclusion, have *women* done for the great and glorious cause of Emancipation? Who wrote that pamphlet which moved the heart of Wilberforce to pray over the wrongs, and his tongue to plead the cause of the oppressed African? It was a *woman*, Elizabeth Heyrick. Who labored assiduously to keep the sufferings of the slave continually before the British public? They were *women*. And how did they do it? By their needles, paint brushes and pens, by speaking the truth, and petitioning Parliament for the abolition of slavery. And what was the effect of their labors? Read it in the Emancipation bill of Great Britain. Read it, in the present state of her West India Colonies. Read

it, in the impulse which has been given to the cause of
freedom, in the United States of America. Have English
women then done so much for the negro, and shall American
women do nothing? Oh no! Already are there sixty female
Anti-Slavery Societies in operation. These are doing just what
the English women did, telling the story of the colored man's
wrongs, praying for his deliverance, and presenting his kneeling image constantly before the public eye on bags and
needle-books, card-racks, pen-wipers, pin-cushions, &c. Even
the children of the north are inscribing on their handy work,
"May the points of our needles prick the slaveholder's conscience." Some of the reports of these Societies exhibit not
only considerable talent, but a deep sense of religious duty,
and a determination to persevere through evil as well as good
report, until every scourge, and every shackle, is buried under the feet of the manumitted slave.

The Ladies' Anti-Slavery Society of Boston was called last
fall, to a severe trial of their faith and constancy. They were
mobbed by "the gentlemen of property and standing," in that
city at their anniversary meeting, and their lives were
jeoparded by an infuriated crowd; but their conduct on that
occasion did credit to our sex, and affords a full assurance that
they will *never* abandon the cause of the slave. The pamphlet, Right and Wrong in Boston, issued by them in which
a particular account is given of that "mob of broad cloth in
broad day," does equal credit to the head and the heart of
her who wrote it. I wish my Southern sisters could read it;
they would then understand that the women of the North
have engaged in this work from a sense of *religious duty*,
and that nothing will ever induce them to take their hands
from it until it is fully accomplished. They feel no hostility
to you, no bitterness or wrath; they rather sympathize in
your trials and difficulties; but they well know that the first
thing to be done to help you, is to pour in the light of truth
on your minds, to urge you to reflect on, and pray over the
subject. This is all *they* can do for you, *you* must work out
your own deliverance with fear and trembling, and with the
direction and blessing of God, *you can do it*. Northern women

may labor to produce a correct public opinion at the North, but if Southern women sit down in listless indifference and criminal idleness, public opinion cannot be rectified and purified at the South. It is manifest to every reflecting mind, that slavery must be abolished; the era in which we live, and the light which is overspreading the whole world on this subject, clearly show that the time cannot be distant when it will be done. Now there are only two ways in which it can be effected, by moral power or physical force, and it is for *you* to choose which of these you prefer. Slavery always has, and always will produce insurrections wherever it exists, because it is a violation of the natural order of things, and no human power can much longer perpetuate it. The opposers of abolitionists fully believe this; one of them remarked to me not long since, there is no doubt there will be a most terrible overturning at the South in a few years, such cruelty and wrong, must be visited with Divine vengeance soon. Abolitionists believe, too, that this must inevitably be the case if you do not repent, and they are not willing to leave you to perish without entreating you, to save yourselves from destruction; well may they say with the apostle, "am I then your enemy because I tell you the truth," and warn you to flee from impending judgments.

But why, my dear friends, have I thus been endeavoring to lead you through the history of more than three thousand years, and to point you to that great cloud of witnesses who have gone before, "from works to rewards?" Have I been seeking to magnify the sufferings, and exalt the character of woman, that she "might have praise of men?" No! no! my object has been to arouse *you*, as the wives and mothers, the daughters and sisters, of the South, to a sense of your duty as *women*, and as Christian women, on that great subject, which has already shaken our country, from the St. Lawrence and the lakes, to the Gulf of Mexico, and from the Mississippi to the shores of the Atlantic; *and will continue mightily to shake it*, until the polluted temple of slavery fall and crumble into ruin. I would say unto each one of you, "what meanest thou, O sleeper! arise and call upon thy God,

if so be that God will think upon us that we perish not."
Perceive you not that dark cloud of vengeance which hangs
over our boasting Republic? Saw you not the lightnings of
Heaven's wrath, in the flame which leaped from the Indian's
torch to the roof of yonder dwelling, and lighted with its
horrid glare the darkness of midnight? Heard you not the
thunders of Divine anger, as the distant roar of the cannon
came rolling onward, from the Texian country, where Protestant American Rebels are fighting with Mexican Republicans—for what? For the re-establishment of *slavery;* yes!
of American slavery in the bosom of a Catholic Republic,
where that system of robbery, violence, and wrong, had been
legally abolished for twelve years. Yes! citizens of the United
States, after plundering Mexico of her land, are now engaged
in deadly conflict, for the privilege of fastening chains, and
collars, and manacles—upon whom? upon the subjects of some
foreign prince? No! upon native born American Republican
citizens, although the fathers of these very men declared to
the whole world, while struggling to free themselves from the
three penny taxes of an English king, that they believed it
to be a *self-evident* truth that *all men* were created equal,
and had an *unalienable right to liberty.*

Well may the poet exclaim in bitter sarcasm,

"The fustian flag that proudly waves
In solemn mockery o'er *a land of slaves.*"

Can you not, my friends, understand the signs of the times;
do you not see the sword of retributive justice hanging over
the South, or are you still slumbering at your posts?—Are
there no Shiphrahs, no Puahs among you, who will dare in
Christian firmness and Christian meekness, to refuse to obey
the *wicked laws* which require *woman to enslave, to degrade and to brutalize woman?* Are there no Miriams, who
would rejoice to lead out the captive daughters of the Southern States to liberty and light? Are there no Huldahs there
who will dare to *speak the truth* concerning the sins of the
people and those judgments, which it requires no prophet's

eye to see, must follow if repentance is not speedily sought? Is there no Esther among you who will plead for the poor devoted slave? Read the history of this Persian queen, it is full of instruction; she at first refused to plead for the Jews; but, hear the words of Mordecai, "Think not within thyself, that *thou* shalt escape in the king's house more than all the Jews, for *if thou altogether holdest thy peace at this time,* then shall their enlargement and deliverance arise to the Jews from another place: but *thou and thy father's house shall be destroyed.*" Listen, too, to her magnanimous reply to this powerful appeal; "*I will* go in unto the king, which is *not* according to law, and if I perish, I perish." Yes! if there were but *one* Esther at the South, she *might* save her country from ruin; but let the Christian women there arise, as the Christian women of Great Britain did, in the majesty of moral power, and that salvation is certain. Let them embody themselves in societies, and send petitions up to their different legislatures, entreating their husbands, fathers, brothers and sons, to abolish the institution of slavery; no longer to subject *woman* to the scourge and the chain, to mental darkness and moral degradation; no longer to tear husbands from their wives, and children from their parents; no longer to make men, women, and children, work *without wages;* no longer to make their lives bitter in hard bondage; no longer to reduce *American citizens* to the abject condition of *slaves,* of "chattels personal;" no longer to barter the *image of God* in human shambles for corruptible things such as silver and gold.

The *women of the South can overthrow* this horrible system of oppression and cruelty, licentiousness and wrong. Such appeals to your legislatures would be irresistible, for there is something in the heart of man which *will bend under moral suasion.* There is a swift witness for truth in his bosom, which *will respond to truth* when it is uttered with calmness and dignity. If you could obtain but six signatures to such a petition in only one state, I would say, send up that petition, and be not in the least discouraged by the scoffs and jeers of the heartless, or the resolution of the house to lay it on the table. It will be a great thing if the subject can be introduced into your legislatures in any way, even by *women*, and *they* will be the most likely to introduce it there in the best possible manner, as a matter of *morals* and *religion*, not of expediency or politics. You may petition, too, the different ecclesiastical bodies of the slave states. Slavery must be attacked with the whole power of truth and the sword of the spirit. You must take it up on *Christian* ground, and fight against it with Christian weapons, whilst your feet are shod with the preparation of the gospel of peace. And *you are now* loudly called upon by the cries of the widow and the orphan, to arise and gird yourselves for this great moral conflict, with the whole armour of righteousness upon the right hand and on the left.

There is every encouragement for you to labor and pray, my friends, because the abolition of slavery as well as its existence, has been the theme of prophecy. "Ethiopia (says the Psalmist) shall stretch forth her hands unto God." And is she not now doing so? Are not the Christian negroes of the south lifting their hands in prayer for deliverance, just as the Israelites did when their redemption was drawing nigh? Are they not sighing and crying by reason of the hard bondage? And think you, that He, of whom it was said, "and God heard their groaning, and their cry came up unto him by reason of the hard bondage," think you that his ear is heavy that he cannot *now* hear the cries of his suffering children? Or that He who raised up a Moses, an Aaron, and a Miriam, to bring them up out of the land of Egypt from the house of bondage, cannot now, with a high hand and a stretched out arm, rid the poor negroes out of the hands of their masters? Surely you believe that his arm is *not* shortened that he cannot save. And would not such a work of mercy redound to his glory? But another string of the harp of prophecy vibrates to the song of deliverance: "But they shall sit every man under his vine, and under his fig-tree, and *none shall make them afraid;* for the mouth of the Lord of Hosts hath spoken it." The *slave* never can do this as long as he is a *slave;* whilst he is a "chattel personal" he can own *no* property;

but the time *is to come* when *every* man is to sit under *his own* vine and *his own* fig-tree, and no domineering driver, or irresponsible master, or irascible mistress, shall make him afraid of the chain or the whip. Hear, too, the sweet tones of another string: "Many shall run to and fro, and *knowledge* shall be increased." Slavery is an insurmountable barrier to the increase of knowledge in every community where it exists; *slavery, then, must be abolished before* this prediction can be fulfiled. The last chord I shall touch, will be this, "They shall *not* hurt nor destroy in all my holy mountain."

Slavery, then, must be overthrown before the prophecies can be accomplished, but how are they to be fulfiled? Will the wheels of the millennial car be rolled onward by miraculous power? No! God designs to confer this holy privilege upon *man;* it is through *his* instrumentality that the great and glorious work of reforming the world is to be done. And see you not how the mighty engine of *moral power* is dragging in its rear the Bible and peace societies, anti-slavery and temperance, sabbath schools, moral reform, and missions? or to adopt another figure, do not these seven philanthropic associations compose the beautiful tints in that bow of promise which spans the arch of our moral heaven? Who does not believe, that if these societies were broken up, their constitutions burnt, and the vast machinery with which they are laboring to regenerate mankind was stopped, that the black clouds of vengeance would soon burst over our world, and every city would witness the fate of the devoted cities of the plain? Each one of these societies is walking abroad through the earth scattering the seeds of truth over the wide field of our world, not with the hundred hands of a Briareus, but with a hundred thousand.

Another encouragement for you to labor, my friends, is, that you will have the prayers and co-operation of English and Northern philanthropists. You will never bend your knees in supplication at the throne of grace for the overthrow of slavery, without meeting there the spirits of other Christians, who will mingle their voices with yours, as the morning or evening sacrifice ascends to God. Yet, the spirit of prayer and of supplication has been poured out upon many, many hearts; there are wrestling Jacobs who will not let go of the prophetic promises of deliverance for the captive, and the opening of prison doors to them that are bound. There are Pauls who are saying, in reference to this subject, "Lord, what wilt thou have me to do?" There are Marys sitting in the house now, who are ready to arise and go forth in this work as soon as the message is brought, "the master is come and calleth for thee." And there are Marthas, too, who have already gone out to meet Jesus, as he bends his footsteps to their brother's grave, and weeps, *not* over the lifeless body of Lazarus bound hand and foot in grave-clothes, but over the politically and intellectually lifeless slave, bound hand and foot in the iron chains of oppression and ignorance. Some may be ready to say, as Martha did, who seemed to expect nothing but sympathy from Jesus, "Lord, by this time he stinketh, for he hath been dead four days." She thought it useless to remove the stone and expose the loathesome body of her brother; she could not believe so great a miracle could be wrought, as to raise *that putrefied body* into life; but "Jesus said, take *ye* away the stone;" and when *they* had taken away the stone where the dead was laid, and uncovered the body of Lazarus, then it was that "Jesus lifted up his eyes and said, Father, I thank thee that thou hast heard me," &c. "And when he had thus spoken, he cried with a loud voice, Lazarus, come forth." Yes, some may be ready to say of the colored race, how can *they* ever be raised politically and intellectually, they have been dead four hundred years? But *we* have *nothing* to do with *how* this is to be done; *our business* is to take away the stone which has covered up the dead body of our brother, to expose the putrid carcass, to show *how* that body has been bound with the grave-clothes of heathen ignorance, and his face with the napkin of prejudice, and having done all it was our duty to do, to stand by the negro's grave, in humble faith and holy hope, waiting to hear the life-giving command of "Lazarus, come forth." This is just what Anti-Slavery Societies are doing; they are taking away the stone from the mouth of the tomb of slavery, where lies the putrid carcass of our brother. They want the pure light of heaven to shine into that dark and gloomy cave; they want all men to see *how* that dead body has been bound, *how* that face has been wrapped in the *napkin of prejudice;* and shall they wait beside that grave in vain? Is not Jesus still the resurrection and the life? Did He come to proclaim liberty to the captive, and the opening of prison doors to them that are bound, in vain? Did He promise to give beauty for ashes, the oil of joy for mourning, and the garment of praise for the spirit of heaviness unto them that mourn in Zion, and will He refuse to beautify the mind, anoint the head, and throw around the captive negro the mantle of praise for that spirit of heaviness which has so long bound him down to the ground? Or shall we not rather say with the prophet, "the zeal of the Lord of Hosts *will* perform this?" Yes, his promises are sure, and amen in Christ Jesus, that he will assemble her that halteth, and gather her that is driven out, and her that is afflicted.

But I will now say a few words on the subject of Abolitionism. Doubtless you have all heard Anti-Slavery Societies denounced as insurrectionary and mischievous, fanatical and dangerous. It has been said they publish the most abominable untruths, and that they are endeavoring to excite rebellions at the South. Have you believed these reports, my friends? have *you* also been deceived by these false assertions? Listen to me, then, whilst I endeavor to wipe from the fair character of Abolitionism such unfounded accusations. You know that I am a Southerner; you know that my dearest relatives are now in a slave State. Can you for a moment believe I would prove so recreant to the feelings of a daughter and a sister, as to join a society which was seeking to overthrow slavery by falsehood, bloodshed, and murder? I appeal to you who have known and loved me in days that are passed, can *you* believe it? No! my friends. As a Carolinian, I was peculiarly jealous of any movements on this subject; and before I would join an Anti-Slavery Society, I took the pre-

caution of becoming acquainted with some of the leading
Abolitionists, of reading their publications and attending
their meetings, at which I heard addresses both from colored
and white men; and it was not until I was fully convinced
that their principles were *entirely pacific,* and their efforts
only moral, that I gave my name as a member to the Female
Anti-Slavery Society of Philadelphia. Since that time, I have
regularly taken the Liberator, and read many Anti-Slavery
pamphlets and papers and books, and can assure you I *never*
have seen a single insurrectionary paragraph, and never
read any account of cruelty which I could not believe. South-
erners may deny the truth of these accounts, but why do
they not *prove* them to be false. Their violent expressions
of horror at such accounts being believed, *may* deceive some,
but they cannot deceive *me,* for I lived too long in the midst
of slavery, not to know what slavery is. When I speak of this
system, "I speak that I do know," and I am not at all afraid
to assert, that Anti-Slavery publications have *not* overdrawn
the monstrous features of slavery at all. And many a Southerner *knows* this as well as I do. A lady in North Carolina
remarked to a friend of mine, about eighteen months since,
"Northerners know nothing at all about slavery; they think
it is perpetual bondage only; but of the *depth of degradation* that word involves, they have no conception; if they
had, *they would never cease* their efforts until so *horrible* a
system was overthrown." She did not know how faithfully
some Northern men and Northern women had studied this
subject; how diligently they had searched out the cause of
"him who had none to help him," and how fearlessly they
had told the story of the negro's wrongs. Yes, Northerners
know *every* thing about slavery now. This monster of iniquity
has been unveiled to the world, her frightful features unmasked, and soon, very soon will she be regarded with no
more complacency by the American republic than is the idol
of Juggernaut, rolling its bloody wheels over the crushed
bodies of its prostrate victims. . . .

What can I say more, my friends, to induce *you* to set

your hands, and heads, and hearts, to this great work of justice and mercy. Perhaps you have feared the consequences of immediate Emancipation, and been frightened by all those dreadful prophecies of rebellion, bloodshed and murder, which have been uttered. "Let no man deceive you;" they are the predictions of that same "lying spirit" which spoke through the four thousand prophets of old, to Ahab king of Israel, urging him on to destruction. *Slavery* may produce these horrible scenes if it is continued five years longer, but Emancipation *never will*. . . .

Sisters in Christ, I have done. As a Southerner, I have felt it was my duty to address you. I have endeavoured to set before you the exceeding sinfulness of slavery, and to point you to the example of those noble women who have been raised up in the church to effect great revolutions, and to suffer for the truth's sake. I have appealed to your sympathies as women, to your sense of duty as *Christian women*. I have attempted to vindicate the Abolitionists, to prove the entire safety of immediate Emancipation, and to plead the cause of the poor and oppressed. I have done—I have sowed the seeds of truth, but I well know, that even if an Apollos [sic] were to follow in my steps to water them, *"God only* can give the increase." To Him then who is able to prosper the work of his servant's hand, I commend this Appeal in fervent prayer, that as he "hath *chosen the weak things of the world,* to confound the things which are mighty," so He may cause His blessing, to descend and carry conviction to the hearts of many Lydias through these speaking pages. Farewell—Count me not your "enemy because I have told you the truth," but believe me in unfeigned affection,

Your sympathizing Friend,

ANGELINA E. GRIMKÉ

The eldest of the four daughters of Lyman and Roxanna Beecher, **Catharine Esther Beecher** was born in 1800 and at the age of sixteen took over the responsibilities of a large family when her mother died. She later maintained that her early domestic duties had given her a higher education that compared favorably with the book learning of her brothers. Lyman Beecher, a Presbyterian minister, was famous for his defense of evangelical religion, although he was notably unsuccessful at converting his own children. His eldest daughter's rejection of the Calvinist model of religious life grew out of her grief over the death of her fiancé, a professor of mathematics at Yale, who was lost at sea four months after their engagement. Lyman Beecher insisted that Alexander Fisher's exemplary life was no guarantee of salvation, in fact, Beecher sincerely doubted that a man who had not undergone an identifiable spiritual crisis and been violently brought to grace in this world could hope for heaven in the next. Toward the end of her life Catharine Beecher became an Episcopalian, but while still a relatively young woman she had begun to argue in favor of a domesticated religious experience in which each child was gradually brought to Christ through the moral suasion of his family.

Catharine Beecher had begun to teach before her engagement, and, with the money Fisher left her in his will, she opened a school in 1825 with her sister Mary. Miss Beecher was highly critical of the curriculum of the typical female seminary, and early in her career tried to envision truly appropriate education for young women in which expert teachers, each with her own field, taught everything from domestic science to calisthenics. Lyman Beecher was serenely confident that Fisher's death showed that God meant Catharine to remain celibate and to devote her life to public service. His daughter got the message but not the serenity. In 1828 she felt her restlessness approached insanity; in 1835 she had what we would call a nervous breakdown. Her insistence on endowments for girls' schools can be read as nothing more than a natural reaction to the financial instability which marked her assorted educational enterprises, yet it also reflected her perennially unsatisfied need for a truly adequate outlet for her energies. Catharine Beecher's mature life was marked by a recurrent pattern, periods of intense activity—founding schools, lecturing on female education and teacher training, writing on religion and domestic economy—and periods of collapse. Before her death in 1878 she had visited no less than thirteen different health establishments, trying without success to find in water therapy and Swedish movement cures a lasting sense of well-being.

An Address to the Christian Women of America, Catharine Beecher*

My Dear and Honored Countrywomen:

When I wrote the first address in this volume, I had a very imperfect idea of the scope and magnitude of the questions which the women of this nation, who aim to be followers of Jesus Christ, will soon be called to investigate and to decide—questions which are the very foundation principles of both morals and religion—questions which every woman must settle for herself aided by common sense, the Bible and the Divine aid obtained by prayer.

To us Jesus Christ appears as the only one born into this world who lived to maturity, then died and then returned to life again; first to prove that death does not end our existence, and next to teach what awaits us in the invisible world to which we all are hastening.

Let those who have mused in lonely sorrow by the grave of the dearest friends and asked with infinite longings—where are they? is this the end? are we too to lie down in utter annihilation?—say how we could have these questions answered so as to best secure a comforting belief? Should we not say let our well known, well beloved friends, come forth from the tomb and live with us again—walk, talk, eat, sleep, and act, as in past times—and this for days and weeks and not alone with us, but with many others who had known them through life? Can we imagine anything to ask more satisfactory than this, to prove that death does not end our existence?

* From Miss Beecher's *Woman Suffrage and Woman's Profession* (Hartford, Connecticut, 1871).

Suppose that Abraham Lincoln, after his body had lain in state for three days, had risen from his coffin and for thirty days had been surrounded by his family, his cabinet, his personal friends, and by as many as three hundred persons who knew him well; can we conceive of anything more satisfactory to prove that death does not destroy the soul: And would not his honest teachings of what is to be experienced after death, be sought as the most reliable evidence possible of what awaits us all when we pass to the invisible world? This is exactly what the believers in the Christian religion claim was done for us when Jesus Christ came and dwelt on earth for thirty-three years, then was slain by enemies determined to prevent his predicted resurrection, and then arose from the dead, bringing life and immortality to light. And why did this good Being come and dwell on earth, then die, and then arise from the dead? It was to teach us not only that an immortal existence stretches before us after death, but that the happiness of that immortality depends on *the character which is formed by education here.*

What then is the character which we are to seek in order to attain immortal blessedness? The first sermon of our Lord has this very topic as its burden:

"Blessed are the poor in spirit,"—those who feel the need of knowledge, guidance, and help.

"Blessed are the meek,"—those that receive rebuke and instruction without anger.

"Blessed are they that do hunger and thirst after righteousness,"—those that long to know what is the right way, and to walk in it.

"Blessed are the happiness makers,"—those who make happiness the right way, as taught by the Master—"for they are the children of God,"—having His nature as the child has the father's nature, and they are to dwell with Him forever.

It is such who are to "rejoice and be exceeding glad" even when persecuted, hated, and reviled, for right words and actions. It is such who are to enter the kingdom of Heaven.

And what is this kingdom? It is one made up of the righteous, those who long to know what is right and to do it, who hunger and thirst after righteousness, and so are forever to be satisfied. And then the Master teaches that His kingdom is not of this world, but exactly the opposite. For the children of this world do not feel poor in spirit, but rather seek to be called Rabbi, and to teach others. They do not wish to be told of their ignorance, mistakes and sins, and are angry when it is done. They do not hunger and thirst to find the lowly way of righteousness, but rather the way of riches, honor, and power.

They do not seek to become true "happiness makers" as taught by the words and example of the Master, taking a humble place, going about and doing good, and working for others more than for self. Instead of this they work and plan for self, first, and then for those belonging to self and care little for the world that the Master came to save. They seek to be at the top and to have all below look up to them.

Now, the family state is instituted to educate our race to the Christian character,—to train the young to be followers of Christ. Woman is its chief minister, and the work to be done is the most difficult of all, requiring not only intellectual power but a moral training nowhere else so attainable as in the humble, laborious, daily duties of the family state.

Woman's great mission is to train immature, weak, and ignorant creatures, to obey the laws of God; the physical, the intellectual, the social, and the moral—first in the family, then in the school, then in the neighborhood, then in the nation, then in the world—that great family of God whom the Master came to teach and to save. And His most comprehensive rule is, "Thou shall love the Lord thy God with all thy heart," and "this is the love of God that ye keep His commandments." And next, "Thou shalt love thy neighbor as thyself." These two the Master teaches are the chief end of man including all taught by Moses and the prophets. This then is woman's work, to train the young in the family and the school *to obey God's laws* as learned partly by experience, partly by human teaching and example, and partly by revelations from God.

Now the Christian woman in the family and in the school is the most complete autocrat that is known, as the care of the helpless little ones, the guidance of their intellect, and the formation of all their habits, are given to her supreme control. Scarcely less is she mistress and autocrat over a husband, whose character, comfort, peace, and prosperity, are all in her power. In this responsible position is she to teach, by word and example, as did Jesus Christ? Is she to set an example to children and servants not only of that of a ruler, but also of obedience as a subordinate? In the civil state her sons will be subjects to rulers who are weak and wicked, just as she may be subject to a husband and father every way her inferior in ability and moral worth? Shall she teach her children and servants by her own example to be humble, obedient, meek, patient, forgiving, gentle, and loving, even to the evil and unthankful, or shall she form rebellious parties and carry her points by contest and discord? God has given man the physical power, the power of the purse, and the civil power, and woman must submit with Christian equinimity or contend. What is the answer of common sense, and what are the teachings of Christ and His Apostles?

Let every woman who is musing on these questions, take a reference Bible and examine all the New Testament directions on the duties of the family state, and she will have no difficulty in deciding what was the view of Christ and His Apostles as to woman's position and duties. She is *a subordinate* in the family state, just as her father, husband, brother, and sons are subordinates in the civil state. And the same rules that are to guide them are to guide her. She and they are to be obedient to "the higher powers"—those that can force obedience—except when their demands are contrary to the higher law of God, and in such a conflict they are "to obey God rather than man," and take the consequences whatever they may be. And a woman has no more difficulty in deciding when to obey God rather than man in the family state than her husband, father, and sons have, in the civil state. And obedience in the family to "the higher power" held by man, is no more a humiliation than is man's obedience to a civil ruler.

If this be so, then the doctrine of woman's subjugation is established and the opposing doctrine of Stuart Mills and his followers is in direct opposition to the teachings both of common sense and Christianity.

There is a moral power given to woman in the family state much more controlling and abiding than the inferior, physical power conferred on man. And the more men are trained to refinement, honor, and benevolence, the more this moral power of woman is increased. This is painfully illustrated in cases where an amiable and Christian man is bound for life to an unreasonable, selfish, and obstinate woman. With such a woman reasoning is useless, and physical force alone can conquer, and this such a man cannot employ. The only alternatives are ceaseless conflicts, at the sacrifice of conscience and self-respect, or hopeless submission to a daily and grinding tyranny.

The general principles to guide both men and women as to the duties of those in a subordinate station, have been made clear by discussions relating to civil government. But the corresponding duties of those invested with power and authority have not been so clearly set forth, especially those of the family state. While the duties of subordination, subjection, and obedience, have been abundantly enforced on woman the corresponding duties of man as head and ruler of the family state have not received equal attention either from the pulpit or the press. And this is not because they are not as difficult, as important and as clearly taught by the Master and the Apostles of Christianity.

St. Paul, who, while He dwelt in retirement in Arabia, received the direct instructions of Jesus Christ, claims to have full authority from the Master to instruct on this important and fundamental topic, and in His Epistle to the Ephesians we have His express and full teachings. In this most interesting passage we find that the family state is the emblem to represent Jesus Christ and the Church—the Church "which is the great company of faithful people" in all ages

and all lands—those who are appointed to guide and save
the world—the true educators of our race, who, by self-
denying labors are to train men for Heaven. Of this body the
Apostles teaches that Jesus Christ is the head—those whom
He has redeemed by His labor and sacrifice, and who are
to bring home to His eternal family all whom they can
rescue from ignorance and sin, by similar labor and sacrifice.

It is in this connection that He sets forth the duties of the
family state, Ephesians v: 22 to 33, "Wives submit yourselves unto your own husbands *as unto the Lord.* For the
husband is head of the wife, even as Christ is head of the
Church: Therefore, as the Church is subject to Christ so
let the wives be to their own husbands in everything."

"Husbands love your wives even as Christ also loved the
Church and gave Himself for it, that He might sanctify and
cleanse it with the washing of water by the word, that He
might present it to Himself, a glorious Church, not having
spot or wrinkle or any such thing, but that it should be holy
and without blemish. So ought men to love their wives as
their own bodies. He that loveth his wife loveth himself. For
no man ever yet hated his own flesh, but nourisheth and
cherisheth it even as the Lord the Church. For we are members of His body, of His flesh, and of His bones. For this
cause shall a man leave his father and mother and shall be
joined unto his wife, and they two shall be one flesh."

No wonder these directions close with "this is a great mystery"; for the most advanced followers of Christ have but
just begun to understand the solemn relations and duties of
the family state—man the head, protector, and provider—
woman the chief educator of immortal minds—man to labor
and suffer to train and elevate woman for her high calling,
woman to set an example of meekness, gentleness, obedience, and self-denying love, as she guides her children and
servants heavenward.

It is this comprehensive view of the family state as organized to train immortal minds for the eternal world that in-
dicates the reason for the stringency of the teachings of our

Lord as to the indissoluble union of man and wife in marriage.

"And he said unto them, Moses, *because of the hardness of your hearts,* suffered you to put away your wives; but from the beginning it was not so. And I say unto you, whosoever shall put away his wife, except it be for fornication, and shall marry another committeth adultery; and whosoever marrieth her that is put away doth commit adultery."

"Have ye not read that He which made them at the beginning made them male and female, and said, For this cause shall a man leave father and mother and shall cleave to his wife, and they twain shall be one flesh. What therefore God hath joined together let not man put asunder."

This then is "the higher law" which abrogates all contrary human Statutes and forbids to marry more than once, except when death or adultery breaks the bond. This statute brings all the advocates of free divorce in direct antagonism with the teachings of Jesus Christ. And it is a striking fact that the great body of those who advocate free divorce and free love, deny the authority of Jesus Christ as the authorized teacher of faith and morals.

In the discussions as to woman's rights and wrongs, it is assumed on one side that she is not to take a subordinate position either in the family or the State. And the apparent plausibility of the claim is owing to a want of logical clearness in the use of words. When it is said that "all men are created free and equal and equally entitled to life, liberty, and the pursuit of happiness," and that women as much as men are included, it is true in one use of terms and false in another. It is true in this sense, that woman's happiness and usefulness are equal in value to man's and ought to be so treated. But it is not true that women are and should be treated as the equals of men in *every* respect. They certainly are not his equals in physical power, which is the final resort in *government* of both the family and the State. And it is owing to this fact that she is placed as a subordinate both in the family and the State. At the same time it is required of man who is holding "the higher powers" so to administer that woman shall have equal advantages with man for usefulness and happiness.

Hitherto the laws relating to women in the civil state have been formed on the assumption that society is a combination of families, in each of which the husband and father is the representative head, and the one who, it is supposed, will secure all that is just and proper for the protection and well being of wife and daughters. And if the teachings of Christianity were dominant, and every man loved his wife as himself, and was ready to sacrifice himself and suffer for her elevation and improvement, even as Christ suffered to redeem and purify the Church, there would be no trouble.

But both men and women have been selfish and sinful, neither party having attained the high ideal of Christianity, and very many have not even understood it so as to aim at it. But it is woman's mission as the educator of the race to remedy the evil, not by giving up the ideal but by striving more and more to conform herself and all under her care to its blessed outlines. And in past times those families have been the most peaceful and prosperous where the wife and mother has most faithfully aimed to obey the teachings of Christ and His Apostles, in this as in every other direction.

The agitation at the present time in regard to woman's right[s] and wrongs is greatly owing to the fact that, from various causes, large multitudes of women are without the love and protection secured by marriage. And yet the laws and customs of society are framed on the general rule that every man is to be head of a family and every woman a wife. But war, emigration, vicious indulgencies, and many other causes have rendered marriage impossible to multitudes of women; counting by tens of thousands in each of the older States, and by hundreds of thousands in our nation. A large portion of these women must earn their own independence, while those who are provided with a support are embarrassed by false customs or unjust laws. In regard to the multitudes of women who flock to our cities, and such direful temptations it is often said, why do they not become servants in families? Let any woman who has a young daughter ponder this question as one that may reach her own family. Does not almost every woman feel, more or less, the bondage of *caste* and shrink from taking the *lowest place,* even though the Lord of Glory set the example?

And is it not the chief attraction toward our pitying Saviour that He loves and tenderly cares for the weak, the wandering and the lost? And are we not walking in His steps when we try to help the weak and foolish who will not take care of themselves?

That there is an emergency which demands changes in our customs and laws, all well informed and benevolent persons will concede. But the main question is, what should be the nature of these changes and how shall they be secured?

There are certain customs of society which are based on the assumption that all women are to marry and be supported by husbands, and that all men are to provide for the support of a family. It is on this assumption that in cases where men and women do the same work and do it equally well men receive much larger wages than women. As one example of injustice, it is granted by all who superintend public schools, that women are as good and often better teachers than men, and yet they are unjustly denied equal compensation. In many other directions the same unjust custom prevails. Still more unjust is the custom which gives superior advantages to men for the scientific and practical training for a profession by which an honorable independence may be secured and almost none at all are provided for women. So also in the distribution of public offices of trust and emolument which secure an income from the civil state, there are several in which woman can perform the duties as well or better then men, especially in the care of schools, hospitals, jails, and all public institutions of benevolence.

Almost all persons of intelligence will concede that justice and mercy call for changes and improvement in these particulars. The main question is what is the best method for securing such improvement?

The party of men and women who are demanding woman suffrage claim that this is the only sure and effective remedy for these and all other wrongs that oppress women both in the family and in the civil state. The party is organized and led by intelligent, energetic, and benevolent women; they have well-conducted periodicals to urge their views and to excite sympathy by details of the various ways in which women suffer from unjust customs and laws; and they are sustained by the approval and co-operation of many gentlemen of talents and benevolence.

But the great majority of intelligent and benevolent men and women are opposed to this measure, first, on account of the probable evils involved and next because the good aimed at may be secured by a safer, more speedy, and more appropriate method.

In enumerating the evils that would result from introducing woman to the responsibilities and excitements of political life, the most prominent is her increased withdrawal from the more humble, but more important offices of the family state. At the present time, the services of the seamstress and the mantau-maker are imperfectly supplied, and when obtained it is often from those who are poorly trained. An economical, trustworthy, and competent cook, is a treasure growing more and more rare, which often the highest wages cannot procure. A kind, intelligent, and affectionate woman, to aid a mother in the cares of the nursery, is still more rare.

If the good mothers and grandmothers, who have trained their own offspring, would take pity on the young mothers all over the land who are suffering for want of just such sympathy and help as only such women can bestow, they would soon find, especially in the poorer classes, a field of usefulness far more in keeping with the tender spirit of Christian love and humility than any offices that political action would provide.

Again, the demand for well trained governesses and family teachers is unsupplied, while multitudes of children all over the nation have no teachers and no schools of any kind. To open avenues to political place and power for all classes of women would cause these humble labors of the family and school to be still more undervalued and shunned.

Another evil to be apprehended from introducing women into political life is increasing the temptations to draw them from the humble, self-sacrificing Christian labor among the ignorant and neglected, which now is so imperfectly supplied. To be a member of the Legislature, a member of Congress, a Judge, a Governor, or a President, are temptations heretofore unknown to women. Who shall say what would be the result should every woman of *every class in society* be stimulated by such temptations?

Another danger to be feared, is the introducing into political strifes the distinctive power of sex, an element as yet untried in our form of government. In some short experiments that have been made we have seen how pure and intelligent women can be deceived and misled by the baser sort, their very innocence and inexperience making them credulous and the helpless tools of the guilty and bold.

Another danger from universal woman suffrage would result from the course that would be taken by many of the most virtuous and intelligent women. Of those who would regard this measure as an act of injustice and oppression, forcing duties on their sex unsuited to their character and circumstances, many would refuse to assume any such responsibilities. Thus a large number of the most intelligent and conscientious women would be withdrawn from the polls, increasing the relative proportion of the ignorant and incompetent voters, a class that already brings doubt on the success of republican institutions. On the other hand, another portion would be forced to the polls by conscientious motives, and there meet the lowest and vilest of their sex as those who are to appoint their rulers and decide their laws. How would it be possible for such women to honor the rulers and respect the laws instituted by such agencies?

The final objection to universal woman suffrage is that there is another safer, surer and more speedy method at command which would secure all the benefits aimed at without any of these dangers.

This method is based on the general principle that in seeking either favors or rights it is a wise policy to assume the good character and good intentions of those who have the power to give or withold. The law making power is now in the hands of men, and the advocates of women suffrage practically are saying, "you men are so selfish and unjust that you cannot be trusted with the interests of your wives, daughters and sisters; therefore give them the lawmaking power that they may take care of themselves."

As a mere matter of policy, to say nothing of justice, how much wiser it would be to assume that men are ready and willing to change unjust laws and customs whenever the better way is made clear and then to ask to have all evils that laws can remedy removed. Whenever this course has been practiced it has always been successful and therefore should first be tried. For any men who would give up the law making power to women in order to remedy existing evils, would surely be those most ready to enact the needful laws themselves.

The woman suffrage party is so extensively organized, with such energetic and persistent leaders and such ably conducted papers and tracts, that those of our sex who are opposed to this measure begin to feel disturbed and anxious lest it should finally be consummated. Instead of meeting this danger by ridicule and obloquy I would suggest that a practical method be instituted in which conservative men and women can unite, and which the most radical will approve and aid.

This volume will be sent to clergymen of all denominations in the State of Connecticut, with the request that their wives or some lady of their parish take measures to aid in establishing and endowing a Connecticut Woman's University, in some one or all of these methods.

First, by promoting the sale of this little volume, and also of the work on Domestic Science mentioned it; all the author's profits being pledged toward such an endowment.

Secondly, by using their influence to secure the introduction of the work on Domestic Science in, as a text book, in schools for young women, as another mode of raising an endowment.

Thirdly, by obtaining signatures of both men and women all over the States to the following petition for an endowment for the Health Department of a Women's University, for restoring women teachers to health, and also for training pupils to become health keepers in families, schools, and communities.

The importance of this last measure will appear in the following extract from a public address of a regularly educated American physician:

It is much to be deplored that we have no chair devoted to *Hygiene* in any of our medical colleges. During four courses of Lectures, that I attended, one of them in Paris, I never heard a single lecture upon the Laws of Health; and when on one occasion I asked one of our Professors if he would not devote one or more of his course to this subject, he replied, that he ought to, but feared he would not find time; and then jokingly remarked, that we would find it more to our interests to learn how to cure people than to keep them well; that we would get gratitude and money for healing the sick, but neither the one nor the other for preserving the health of the people, however well we might do it.

I have since found that there was more truth in the remark then [sic] I was then willing to admit. Still, I cannot help thinking that we should have such Lectures in every medical school, if for no other purpose but to enable its graduates to heal the sick—confident that more can be gained in this way by a thorough knowledge of Hygiene, than by any other means whatever. No drug or medicine is as powerful for good in disease as a wise advantage of Nature's laws.

We spent in one Session over three weeks in the study of Mercury, its different preparations, effects, etc.; not one hour in learning the value of Light, Air, Sleep, Food, and Clothing. The result was we know much about Calomel, and literally nothing about the Laws of Health; so we sat, something over four hundred students, for five or six hours daily, in a room—an amphitheatre—the seats extending from the floor to the ceiling—so small, that another hundred could not possibly be packed into it—and not a window opened all winter—no ventilation whatever—a regular "black hole of Calcutta"—the air heavy, foul, offensive with bad breaths—the odors of tobacco, liquor, onions—poisonous in the extreme—not a fresh cheek among the four hundred. Many of the students drank; most of them used tobacco, coffee, sausages, pork, in short lived like Barbarians. A large proportion of them were ill all the time, and some died before the session closed, others soon after, and many since. The professors themselves were often ailing—not very healthy men. If any of my readers will step into any of the medical lectures in any of the colleges of this city, some winter afternoon, he will be able to verify the truth of this description. Their presiding genius seems to have no respect for fresh air, sunlight—in short for the laws of health. How then shall these schools inspire respect for these laws in others? How can they teach them when they know so little of them?

Dr. Willard Parker, of New York, in a recent public address also has lamented the fact that a Woman's Medical College should be the first one sustaining a Chair for instructing in Hygiene, as if it were a conceded fact that it is not the business of physicians to *prevent* disease in a community, but only to cure their patients with medicines.

Is it not a proper time and measure for the women of our country to ask for benefactions, both private and legislative, to secure equal advantage for their professional duty as health-keepers, such as have so long and so liberally been bestowed on men to train them for their professions?

Believing that such a measure would meet the approval and co-operation of a large number of the citizens of Connecticut the following form of petition is drawn up, which has already secured the approval of the Governor of the State and of the Trustees of the Hartford Female Seminary, and other citizens of Hartford.

To the honorable members of the Senate and House
of Representatives of the State of Connecticut:

We the undersigned, ladies of the State of Connecticut

and gentlemen citizens of the same, respectfully petition that an appropriation be made to endow one department of a *Connecticut Woman's University* under charge of the Trustees of the Hartford Female Seminary; the object of which shall be to train school-teachers and house-keepers in all that relates to health in schools and families, and that this endowment be made equal to what has been or may be given to endow the Sheffield Scientific School for Young Men; and also that this be given on condition that the citizens of Hartford give an equal sum to promote the scientific and practical training of women for their distinctive professions.

Note A. Mrs. Livermore, in her address which followed this, expressed the wish that I had noticed more directly the main point (i.e.) woman's natural, as well as constitutional right to the ballot. This I will briefly attempt here.

It will be conceded by all, that neither man or woman has any right to anything which is contrary to the *best* good of society. The question then is, does the best good of society demand a *division of responsibilities,* so that man shall take those out of the family, and woman those in it? In other words, shall man take the responsibilities of nursery and kitchen in addition to his outside business, and shall women take charge of government, war, and the work men must do in addition to her home duties? Past laws and customs demand the division, and it is probable that it will be retained.

As to the constitution of the United States, and the 14th and 15th amendments, the question all turns on the use of the terms *citizen* and *people*. Both these words, (as the dictionaries show,) have two uses, a wide, and a limited. In the widest sense they include men, women and children. In the limited sense they include only a portion of society with certain qualifications which the *best* good of society requires. It is not probable that any court will ever decide that the framers of the constitution, or of the two amendments used these terms in the widest sense, thus including not only women, but children.

If the best good of society requires women to be lawmakers, judges and juries, she has a right to these offices; if it does not, she has no right to them. As to taxation, it is probable that the best good of society *does* require that *women holding property* shall have the ballot, for this would increase the proportion of responsible and intelligent voters, and not add a mass of irresponsible and ignorant ones, as would universal woman suffrage.

It is owing to this that in Europe the statesmen are aiming to give suffrage, not to all women as demanded here, but only to those who hold property and pay taxes; for this, in reality, is a method of increasing the proportion of intelligent voters. And if this measure were adopted here it probably would add to the safety of our institutions.

It is worthy of notice that a large portion of those who demand woman suffrage are persons who have not been trained to reason, and are chiefly guided by their generous sensibilities. Such do not seem to be aware that all *reasoning* consists in the presentation of evidence to prove that a given proposition is included in a more general one already believed and granted, and also that in this process there must be definitions of the sense in which terms are used that have several meaning.

Instead of this, they write and talk as if *reasoning* were *any kind* of writing or talking which tends to convince people that some doctrine or measure is true and right. And so they deal abundantly in exciting narratives and rhetorical declamations, and employ words in all manner of deceptive senses.

For example, when Mrs. Livermore pleads that women should have equal rights with men before law, everybody grants it in *some* sense. But the question is in what sense is she to be made equal? All will allow that law should be so framed that woman's highest usefulness and happiness shall be treated as equal in value to that of man's. But this is not relevant to the question whether laws be framed by fathers, husbands, and brothers, or by women. Most women believe that it is for their best good that the responsibility of making and enforcing laws be taken by men and not by women.

But however clearly these distinctions are urged, Mrs. Livermore and her party will keep on saying that women should be made equal with men before the law, without stating in what sense she uses these terms. So also they will insist that all "citizens" and all the "people" have a right to vote, without stating what they mean by "a right," or in which sense they use the words "people" and "citizens."

Statistics of Female Health, Catharine Beecher*

During my extensive tours in all portions of the Free States, I was brought into most intimate communion, not only with my widely-diffused circle of relatives, but with very many of my former pupils who had become wives and mothers. From such, I learned the secret domestic history both of those I visited and of many of their intimate friends. And oh! what heartaches were the result of these years of quiet observation of the experience of my sex in domestic life. How many young hearts have revealed the fact, that what they had been trained to imagine the highest earthly felicity, was but the beginning of care, disappointment, and sorrow, and often led to the extremity of mental and physical suffering. Why was it that I was so often told that "young girls little imagined what was before them when they entered married life?" Why did I so often find those united to the most congenial and most devoted husbands expressing the hope that their daughters would never marry? For years these were my quiet, painful conjectures.

But the more I traveled, and the more I resided in health establishments, the more the conviction was pressed on my attention that there was a terrible decay of female health all over the land, and that this evil was bringing with it an incredible extent of individual, domestic, and social suffering, that was increasing in a most alarming ratio. At last, certain developments led me to take decided measures to obtain some reliable statistics on the subject. During my travels the last year I have sought all practicable methods of obtaining

* From Miss Beecher's *Woman Suffrage and Woman's Profession* (Hartford, Connecticut, 1871).

information, and finally adopted this course with most of the married ladies whom I met, either on my journeys or at the various health establishments at which I stopped.

I requested each lady first to write the *initials* of *ten* of the married ladies with whom she was best acquainted in her place of residence. Then she was requested to write at each name, her impressions as to the health of each lady. In this way, during the past year, I obtained statistics from about two hundred different places in almost all the Free States.

Before giving any of these, I will state some facts to show how far they are reliable: In the first place, the *standard of health* among American women is so low that few have a correct idea of *what a healthy woman is.* I have again and again been told by ladies that they were "perfectly healthy," who yet, on close inquiry, would allow that they were subject to frequent attacks of neuralgia, or to periodic nervous headaches, or to local ailments, to which they had become so accustomed, that they were counted as "nothing at all." A woman who has tolerable health finds herself so much above the great mass of her friends in this respect, that she feels herself a prodigy of good health.

In the next place, I have found that women who enjoy universal health are seldom well informed as to the infirmities of their friends. Repeatedly I have taken accounts from such persons, that seemed singularly favorable, when, on more particular inquiry, it was found that the greater part, who were set down as perfectly healthy women, were habitual sufferers from serious ailments. The delicate and infirm go for sympathy, not to the well and buoyant, but to those who have suffered like themselves.

This will account for some very favorable statements, given by certain ladies, that have not been inserted, because more accurate information showed their impressions to be false. As a general fact, it has been found that the more minute the inquiry, the greater the relative increase of ill health in all these investigations.

Again, I have found that ladies were predisposed usually to give the *most favorable* view of the case; for all persons like to feel that they are living in "a healthy place" rather than the reverse.

Again, I have found that almost every person in the result obtained, found that the case was worse than had been supposed, the proportion of sick or delicate to the strong and healthy being so small.

It must be remembered, that in regard to those marked as "sickly," "delicate," or "feeble," there can be no mistake, the knowledge being in all cases *positive*, while those marked as "well" may have ailments that are not known. For multitudes of American women, with their strict notions of propriety, and their patient and energetic spirit, often are performing every duty entirely silent as to any suffering or infirmities they may be enduring.

As to the terms used in these statements, in all cases there was a previous statement made as to the sense in which they were to be employed.

A "perfectly healthy" or "a vigorous and healthy woman" is one of whom there are *specimens* remaining in almost every place; such as used to *abound* when all worked, and *worked in pure air*.

Such a woman is one who can through the whole day be actively employed on her feet in all kinds of domestic duties without injury, and constantly and habitually has a feeling of perfect health and perfect freedom from pain. Not that she never has a fit of sickness, or takes a cold that interrupts the feeling of health, but that these are out of her ordinary experience.

A woman is marked "well" who usually has good health, but can not bear exposures, or long and great fatigue, without consequent illness.

A woman is marked "delicate" who, though she may be about and attend to most of her domestic employments, has a frail constitution that either has been undermined by ill health, or which easily and frequently yields to fatigue, or exposure, or excitement.

In the statements that follow, I shall place first those which are *most reliable*, inasmuch as in each case personal inquiries were made and the specific ailments were noted, to show that nothing was stated without full knowledge. As a matter of delicacy, the *initials* are changed, so that no individual can thus be identified.

MOST RELIABLE STATISTICS

Milwaukee, Wis. Mrs. A. frequent sick headaches. Mrs. B. very feeble. Mrs. S. well, except chills. Mrs. L. poor health constantly. Mrs. D. subject to frequent headaches. Mrs. B. very poor health. Mrs. C. consumption. Mrs. A. pelvic displacements and weakness. Mrs. H. pelvic disorders and a cough. Mrs. B. always sick. Do not know one perfectly healthy woman in the place.

Essex, Vt. Mrs. S. very feeble. Mrs. D. slender and delicate. Mrs. S. feeble. Mrs. S. not well. Mrs. G. quite feeble. Mrs. C. quite feeble. Mrs. B. quite feeble. Mrs. S. quite slender. Mrs. B. quite feeble. Mrs. F. very feeble. Knows but one perfectly healthy woman in town.

Peru, N.Y. Mrs. C. not healthy. Mrs. H. not healthy. Mrs. E. healthy. Mrs. B. pretty well. Mrs. K. delicate. Mrs. B. not strong and healthy. Mrs. S. healthy and vigorous. Mrs. L. pretty well. Mrs. L. pretty well.

Canton, Penn. Mrs. R. feeble. Mrs. B. bad headaches. Mrs. D. bad headaches. Mrs. V. feeble. Mrs. S. erysipelas. Mrs. K. headaches, but tolerably well. Mrs. R. miserably sick and nervous. Mrs. G. poor health. Mrs. L. invalid. Mrs. C. invalid.

Oberlin, Ohio. Mrs. A. usually well, but subject to neuralgia. Mrs. D. poor health. Mrs. K. well, but subject to nervous headaches. Mrs. M. poor health. Mrs. C. not in good health. Mrs. P. not in good health. Mrs. P. delicate. Mrs. F. not in good health. Mrs. F. not in good health.

Wilmington, Del. Mrs. ——, scrofula. Mrs. B. in good health. Mrs. D. delicate. Mrs. H. delicate. Mrs. S. healthy. Mrs. P. healthy. Mrs. G. delicate. Mrs. O. delicate. Mrs. T. very delicate. Mrs. S. headaches.

New Bedford, Mass. Mrs. B. pelvic diseases, and every way out of order. Mrs. J. W. pelvic disorders. Mrs. W. B. well, except in one respect. Mrs. C. sickly. Mrs. C. rather delicate. Mrs. P. not healthy. Mrs. C. unwell at times. Mrs. L. delicate. Mrs. B. subject to spasms. Mrs. H. very feeble. Can not think of but one perfectly healthy woman in the place.

Paxton, Vt. Mrs. T. diseased in liver and back. Mrs. H. stomach and back diseased. Mrs. W. sickly. Mrs. S. very delicate. Mrs. C. sick headaches, sickly. Mrs. W. bilious complaints. Mrs. T. very delicate. Mrs. T. back complaint. Mrs. C. bilious sometimes, well most of the time. Do not know a perfectly healthy woman in the place. Many of these are the wives of wealthy farmers, who *overwork* when there is no need of it.

Crown Point, N.Y. Mrs. H. bronchitis. Mrs. K. very delicate. Mrs. A. very delicate. Mrs. A. diseased in back and stomach. Mrs. S. consumption. Mrs. A. dropsy. Mrs. M. delicate. Mrs. M. G. delicate. Mrs. P. delicate. Mrs. C. consumption. Do not know one perfectly healthy woman in the place.

Batavia, Illinois. Mrs. H. an invalid. Mrs. G. scrofula. Mrs. W. liver complaint. Mrs. K. pelvic disorders. Mrs. S. pelvic diseases. Mrs. B. pelvic diseases very badly. Mrs. B. not healthy. Mrs. T. very feeble. Mrs. G. cancer. Mrs. N. liver complaint. Do not know one healthy woman in the place.

Oneida, N.Y. Mrs. C. delicate. Mrs. P. scrofula. Mrs. S. not well. Mrs. L. very delicate and nervous. Mrs. L. invalid. Mrs. L. tolerably well. Mrs. A. invalid. Mrs. W. broken down. Mrs. D. feeble. Mrs. W. pale but pretty well.

North Adams, Mass. Mrs. R. scrofula and liver complaint. Mrs. R. consumption. Mrs. C. consumption. Mrs. B. liver complaint. Mrs. B. consumption. Mrs. B. general debility. Mrs. F. consumption. Mrs. W. paralytic. Mrs. W. confined always to her bed. Mrs. R. scrofula.

Charlotte, Vt. Mrs. W. spinal complaint. Mrs. D. spinal complaint. Mrs. N. spinal complaint. Mrs. R. bilious and paralytic. Mrs. R. pelvic disorders. Mrs. H. heart disease and dropsy. Mrs. B. dropsical. Mrs. H. pelvic disease and palsy. Mrs. H. scrofula and consumption. Mrs. S. quite delicate. Knows but one perfectly healthy woman in the place.

Maria, N.Y. Mrs. H. consumption. Mrs. E. dyspepsia. Mrs. T. dyspepsia. Mrs. D. consumption. Mrs. P. dyspepsia. Mrs. R. sickly. Mrs. M. sickly. Mrs. R. delicate. Mrs. S. sickly. Mrs. R. consumption. Knows not one perfectly healthy woman in the place.

Vergennes, Vt. Mrs. L. delicate. Mrs. H. consumption. Mrs. H. consumption. Mrs. C. sickly. Mrs. S. liver complaint. Mrs. S. asthma. Mrs. S. sickly. Mrs. B. bronchitis. Mrs. S. consumptive. Mrs. B. delicate. Does not know a perfectly healthy woman in the place.

Brooklyn, N.Y. Mrs. B. very delicate. Mrs. G. scrofulous. Mrs. R. pelvic displacements. Mrs. I. nervous headaches. Mrs. A. pelvic diseases. Mrs. W. heart disease. Mrs. S. organic disease. Mrs. B. well but delicate. Mrs. L. well but delicate. Mrs. C. delicate.

Berlin, Conn. Mrs. A. dyspepsia. Mrs. B. quite delicate. Mrs. C. nervous headaches. Mrs. G. pelvic disorders. Mrs. M. weak lungs. Mrs. F. not sound. Mrs. C. delicate. Mrs. N. vigorous and healthy. Mrs. C. well. Mrs. A. delicate.

Whitestown, N.Y. Mrs. A. consumptive. Mrs. P. well but delicate. Mrs. M. well but delicate. Mrs. S. pelvic disorders. Mrs. R. dropsy. Mrs. B. pelvic disorders. Mrs. H. sick headaches. Mrs. K. organic disorder. Mrs. B. well but delicate. Mrs. T. bronchitis.

Proctorville, Vt. Mrs. B. well. Mrs. H. well. Mrs. S. pelvic and stomach disorders. Mrs. S. not healthy. Mrs. F. not healthy. Mrs. B. sickly. Mrs. C. not healthy. Mrs. W. not healthy. Mrs. A. vigorous and usually well. Knows no other strong and healthy woman.

Saratoga, N.Y. Mrs. M. pelvic disorders. Mrs. H. pelvic disorders. Mrs. A. pelvic disorders. Mrs. C. well. Mrs. C. neuralgia. Mrs. P. well. Mrs. T. consumptive. Mrs. J. tolerably well. Mrs. B. consumptive. Mrs. B. not well.

Knows only one more well one among her acquaintance.

Saratoga, N.Y. (by another resident). Mrs. T. pelvic disorder. Mrs. C. pelvic disease. Mrs. H. not well. Mrs. S. well and strong. Mrs. B. tolerably well. Mrs. M. usually well. Mrs. O. headaches. Mrs. H. O. well. Mrs. S. delicate. Mrs. P. not well.

Canandaigua, N.Y. Mrs. A. well. Mrs. B. an invalid. Mrs. C. delicate. Mrs. H. delicate. Mrs. H. an invalid. Mrs. J. well. Mrs. P. delicate. Mrs. A. well. Mrs. C. an invalid. Mrs. W. well.

Livonia, N.Y. Mrs. H. rheumatic. Mrs. R. healthy and vigorous. Mrs. S. well. Mrs. R. good health. Mrs. P. very poor health. Mrs. B. well. Mrs. G. an invalid. Mrs. S. delicate. Mrs. T. poor health. Mrs. ——. pelvic disorders.

Turkhannock, Penn. Mrs. P. delicate and sickly. Mrs. L. delicate and well. Mrs. R. well and vigorous. Mrs. S. tolerably well. Mrs. C. well. Mrs. S. healthy. Mrs. T. consumption. Mrs. M. healthy. Mrs. R. well. Mrs. ——. pelvic disorders.

Bath, N.Y. Mrs. H. an invalid. Mrs. H. rheumatic. Mrs. H. healthy and vigorous. Mrs. S. vigorous. Mrs. K. delicate. Mrs. K. very healthy. Mrs. W. broken down. Mrs. W. tolerably well. Mrs. W. an invalid. Mrs. H. poor health.

Castleton, N.Y. Mrs. S. sickly. Mrs. W. healthy. Mrs. S. very delicate. Mrs. H. delicate. Mrs. H. delicate. Mrs. B. delicate. Mrs. W. not healthy. Mrs. H. not healthy. Mrs. D. not healthy.

The following were furnished by ladies who simply arranged the names of the ten married ladies best known to them in the place of their residence, in three classes, as marked over the several columns:

Residence	Strong and perfectly Healthy	Delicate or Diseased	Habitual Invalids
Hudson, Michigan	2	4	4
Castleton, Vermont	Not one.	9	1
Bridgeport, "	4	4	2

Residence	Strong and Healthy	Delicate or Diseased	Invalids
Dorset, "	Not one.	1	9
South Royalston, Mass.	4	2	4
Townsend, Vermont	4	3	3
Greenbush, New York	2	5	3
Southington, Connecticut	3	5	2
Newark, New Jersey	2	3	5
New York City	2	4	4
Oneida, New York	3	2	5
Milwaukee, Wisconsin	1	3	6
Rochester, New York	2	6	2
Plainfield, New Jersey	2	4	4
New York City	3	6	1
Lennox, Massachusetts	4	3	3
Union Vale, New York	2	5	3
Albany, "	2	3	5
Hartford, Conn.	1	5	4
Cincinnati, Ohio	1	4	5
Andover, Mass.	2	5	3
Brunswick, Maine	2	5	3

Residence	Strong and Healthy	Delicate or Diseased	Invalids
Southington, Connecticut	3	5	2
Rochester, New York	2	6	2
Albany, "	2	4	4
Milwaukee, Wisconsin	1	3	6
Plainfield, New Jersey	2	4	4
New York City	3	6	1
New York City	2	4	4
Worcester, Massachusetts	1	6	2
Newark, New Jersey	2	3	5
Bonhomme, Missouri	3	5	2
Painted Post, New York	1	3	6
Wilkins, "	2	3	5
Johnsburg, "	3	6	1
Burdett, "	4	3	3
Horse Heads, "	3	2	5
Pompey, "	4	4	2
Tioga, Pennsylvania	3	4	3
Lodi, New York	2	5	3
Seymour, Connecticut	3	7	0
Williamsville, New York	4	2	4
Herkimer, "	3	2	5
Hudson, Michigan	2	4	4
Kalamazoo, "	3	6	1

The following are those not so reliable as the preceding, as the papers were some of them not clear, and some uncertainty about others for want of personal inquiry:

Cattskill, N.Y. Three vigorous, two well, three delicate, two sickly.

Batavia, N.Y. One vigorous, two well, three delicate, one sickly.

Ogden, N.Y. Three well, five well but delicate, two sickly.

Utica, N.Y. Nine well but not vigorous, one invalid.

Rhinebeck, N.Y. One vigorous, six well but not vigorous, one delicate, one invalid.

Cooperstown, N.Y. Two vigorous, five well, two delicate, two sickly.

Lime, N.Y. Five well, three delicate, two sickly.

Rockaway, N.Y. Two vigorous, five well, one delicate, two sickly.

Brockport, N.Y. Three vigorous, six well, one delicate, one sickly.

Buffalo, N.Y. Five well, five delicate.

Potsdam, N.Y. Eight tolerably well, two sickly.

Rome, N.Y. Two well, seven tolerably well, one sickly.

Rochester, N.Y. Four well, three delicate, three sickly.

Princeton, N.J. Four well, five well but delicate, three sickly.

Muncy, Penn. Two vigorous, six well but delicate, two sickly.

The remainder of accounts furnished being less reliable, for want of opportunities of definite inquiry on my part, and will therefore be omitted. But they do not essentially differ from these presented.

I will now add my own personal observation. First, in my own family connection: I have nine married sisters and sisters-in-law, all of them either delicate or invalids, except two. I have fourteen married female cousins, and not one of them but is either delicate, often ailing, or an invalid. In my wide circle of friends and acquaintance all over the land out of my family circle, the same impression is made. In Boston I can not remember but one married female friend who is perfectly healthy. In Hartford, Conn., I can think of only one. In New Haven, but one. In Brooklyn, N.Y., but one. In New

York city, but one. In Cincinnati, but one. In Buffalo, Cleveland, Chicago, Milwaukee, Detroit, those whom I have visited are either delicate or invalids. I am not able to recall, in my immense circle of friends and acquaintance all over the Union, so many as *ten* married ladies born in this century and country, who are perfectly sound, healthy, and vigorous. Not that I believe there are not more than this among the friends with whom I have associated, but among all whom I can bring to mind of whose health I have any accurate knowledge, I can not find this number of entirely sound and healthy women.

Another thing has greatly added to the impression of my own observations, and that is the manner in which my inquiries have been met. In a majority of cases, when I have asked for the number of perfectly healthy women in a given place, the first impulsive answer has been "not one." In other cases, when the reply has been more favorable, and I have asked for specifics, the result has always been such as to diminish the number calculated, rather than to increase it. With a few exceptions the persons I have asked, who had not directed their thoughts to the subject, and took a favorable view of it, have expressed surprise at the painful result obtained in their own immediate circle.

But the thing which has pained and surprised me the most is the result of inquiries among the country-towns and industrial classes in our country. I had supposed that there would be a great contrast between the statements gained from persons from such places, and those furnished from the wealthy circles, and especially from cities. But such has not been the case. It will be seen that the larger portion of the accounts inserted in the preceding pages are from country-towns, while a large portion of the worst accounts were taken from the industrial classes.

In another index of the state of health among the industrial classes may be mentioned these facts: During the past year I made my usual inquiry of the wife of a Methodist clergyman, who resided in a small country-town in New York. Her reply was, "There are no healthy women where I live, and my husband says he would travel a great many miles for the pleasure of finding one."

In another case I conversed with a Baptist clergyman and his wife, in Ohio, and their united testimony gave this result in three places where his parishioners were chiefly of the industrial class. They selected at random ten families best known in each place:

Worcester, Ohio. Women in perfect health, two. In medium health, one. *Invalids, seven.*

Norwalk, Ohio. Women perfectly healthy, one, but doubtfully so. Medium, none. *Invalids, nine.*

Cleveland, Ohio. Women in perfect health, one. Medium health, two. *Invalids, seven.*

In traveling at the West the past winter, I repeatedly conversed with drivers and others among the laboring class on this subject, and always heard such remarks as these: "Well! it is strange how sickly the women are getting!" "Our women-folks don't have such health as they used to do!"

One case was very striking. An old lady from New England told me her mother had twelve children; eleven grew up healthy, and raised families. Her father's mother had fifteen children, and raised them all; and all but one, who was drowned, lived to a good old age. This lady stated that she could not remember that there was a single "weakly woman" in the town where she lived when she was young.

This lady had two daughters with her, both either delicate or diseased, and a sick niece from that same town, once so healthy when the old lady was young. This niece told me she could not think of even one really robust, strong, and perfectly healthy woman in that place! The husband of this old lady told me that in his youth he also did not know of any sickly women in the place where he was reared.

A similar account was given me by two ladies, residents of Goshen, Litchfield Co., Connecticut.

The elder lady gave the following account of her married acquaintance some forty years ago in that place:

Mrs. L. strong and perfectly healthy. Mrs. A. healthy and strong as a horse. Mrs. N. perfectly well always. Mrs. H.

strong and well. Mrs. B. strong and generally healthy, but sometimes ailing a little. Mrs. R. always well. Mrs. W. strong and well. Mrs. G. strong and hearty. Mrs. H. strong and healthy. Mrs. L. strong and healthy

All the above persons performed their own family work.

The following account was given by the daughter of the lady mentioned above, and the list is chiefly made up of the daughters of the above healthy women living at this time in the same town:

Mrs. C. constitution broken by pelvic disorders. Mrs. P. very delicate. Mrs. L. delicate and feeble. Mrs. R. feeble and nervous. Mrs. S. bad scrofulous humors. Mrs. D. very feeble, head disordered. Mrs. R. delicate and sickly. Mrs. G. healthy. Mrs. D. healthy. Mrs. W. well.

These last three were the only healthy married women she knew in the place.

I have received statements from more than a hundred other places besides those recorded here. The larger portion of these were taken by others, or else by myself in such circumstances that I could not make the inquiries needed to render them reliable, and some I have lost. The general impression made, even by these alone, would bring out very nearly the same result. The proportion of the sick and delicate to those who were strong and well was, in the majority of cases, a melancholy story. But among them were a few cases in which a very favorable statement was verified by close examination. In several such cases, however, most of the healthy women proved to be either English, Irish, or Scotch. In one case, a lady from a country-town, not far from Philadelphia, gave an account, showing eight out of ten perfectly healthy, and the other two were not very much out of health. On inquiry, I found that this was a Quaker settlement, and most of the healthy ones were Quakers.

In one town of Massachusetts, the lady giving the information said all the ten she gave were healthy, but two. Her associates were all women who were in easy circumstances, and did their own family work. These two places, however, are the *only* instances I have found, where, on close inquiry, the majority was on the side of good health.

There is no doubt that there are many places like these two, of which some resident would report that a majority of their acquaintance were healthy women; but out of about two hundred towns and cities, located in most of the Free States, only two have as yet presented so favorable a case in the line of my inquiries during the year in which they have been prosecuted.

Let these considerations now be taken into account. The generation represented in these statistics, by universal consent, is a feebler one than that which immediately preceded. Knowing the changes in habits of living, in habits of activity, and in respect to *pure air*, we properly infer that it must be so, while universal testimony corroborates the inference.

The present generation of parents, then, have given their children, so far as the mother has hereditary influence, feebler constitutions than the former generation received, so that most of our young girls have started in life with a more delicate organization than their mothers. Add to this the sad picture given in a former letter of all the abuses of health suffered by the young during their early education, and what are the present prospects of the young women who are not entering married life?

This view of the case, in connection with some dreadful developments which will soon be indicated, proved so oppressive and exciting that it has been too painful and exhausting to attempt any investigation as to the state of health among young girls. But every where I go, mothers are constantly saying, "What shall I do? As soon as my little girl begins school she has the headache." Or this—"I sent my daughter to such a boarding-school, but had to take her away on account of her health."

The public schools of our towns and cities, where the great mass of the people are to be educated, are the special subject of remark and complaint in this respect.

Consider also that "man that is born of a woman" depends on her not only for the constitutional stamina with which he starts in life, but for all he receives during the developments of infancy and the training of childhood, and what are we to infer of the condition and prospects of the other sex now in the period of education?

Harriet Beecher Stowe was born in Hartford, Connecticut, in 1811. She was only four when her mother died and had a series of surrogate mothers, including her sister Catharine and her father's half-sister, Aunt Esther. It was Aunt Esther whom Mrs. Stowe had in mind when she later described the spinster saint in "The Cathedral," a learned and meticulous yet secretly passionate woman who sacrificed her own desire for a larger life to support that sacred institution, the family. Aunt Esther, in fact, had introduced Harriet Beecher to the writings of Byron, lending her niece her own copy of *The Corsair*. One introduction eventually led to another, and in the 1850s, on a triumphal tour of England after the publication of *Uncle Tom's Cabin,* Mrs. Stowe met Lady Byron, who had heard of the American woman's girlhood infatuation with her husband, and had sought her advice as one who would "understand." Counting on Mrs. Stowe's sympathy, Lady Byron proceeded to tell her the story of her husband's incestuous relations with his half-sister.

Apparently only the horror expressed by Mary Beecher Perkins, Harriet Stowe's sister and traveling companion (and the grandmother of Charlotte Perkins Gilman), kept Mrs. Stowe from advising Lady Byron to tell all immediately and thus save herself from going down in literary history as the cold and mercenary female who drove Lord Byron into exile —and death. But in 1869, after the publication of just such an interpretation of the Byron's brief marriage, Mrs. Stowe herself could keep quiet no longer and published in *The Atlantic Monthly* "The True Story of Lady Byron's Life" which was soon expanded into a book, *Lady Byron Vindicated* (1870). The furor which followed this revelation nearly destroyed *The Atlantic,* and it was widely assumed that Harriet Beecher Stowe was finished as a popular writer. Some went so far as to accuse her of resorting to pornography to bolster a sagging career.

Within two years, the success of *My Wife and I* squelched these prophecies of literary doom. Still it is hard to know exactly what motivated Mrs. Stowe to get involved in the potentially suicidal defense of a rather distant friend. It is tempting to see in her gesture her own Byronism—Harriet Stowe was being recklessly gallant where, for once, Lord Byron had been a cad. However, it is unlikely that she would have gone so far if she had not at the same time identified with Lady Byron, the embodiment of selfless womanhood, modest and pure, entangled in circumstance, the slave to convention and her own sense of self-sacrificing duty.

The uncanny power of *Uncle Tom's Cabin* clearly owed a great deal to Harriet Beecher Stowe's ability to identify with the plight of the slave, an ability that sprang from her own sense of entrapment as the wife of Calvin Stowe, an impoverished biblical scholar and confirmed hypochondriac, and as the mother of six living children. In 1832 Lyman Beecher had moved to Cincinnati to take the presidency of Lane Theological Seminary, and there, four years later, Harriet Beecher had met and married one of the professors, Calvin Stowe. During the first decade of their marriage, Mrs. Stowe was too burdened by her growing family to do more than write an occasional short story, but the end of her domestic confinement was in sight.

In 1849 her sixth child died of cholera while Calvin Stowe was in Brattleboro, Vermont, taking the water cure. In 1850, she single-handedly moved the entire family back East where her husband had been appointed to a professorship at Bowdoin. In 1852 the Stowes moved again, this time to Massachusetts, where Calvin Stowe took another job at Andover Theological Seminary. In between 1850 and 1852 Mrs. Stowe wrote *Uncle Tom's Cabin*. Within a year of its publication in book form the novel sold 300,000 copies. In the years before the Civil War Mrs. Stowe made three triumphant tours of England and the Continent, and managed to write *A Key to Uncle Tom's Cabin*, *Dred*, and *The Minister's Wooing*, in which she put together her sister's experience of losing an unconverted fiancé at sea, her own grief at having lost a son by drowning, and a great deal of theological debate in which she came out once and for all in favor of a God of Love.

Mrs. Stowe's major writings after 1860 include *The Pearl of Orr's Island* (1862), *Oldtown Folks* (1869), and *Poganuc People* (1878). Never financially secure despite her enormous popularity, she continued to write children's stories, religious poems, and brief biographies of the famous, and even resorted to reading from *Uncle Tom's Cabin* on lyceum platforms to support her real estate investments. Harriet Beecher Stowe lived until 1896, although in later years she withdrew more and more into herself, stopped writing, and rarely answered when spoken to.

The Lady Who Does Her Own Work, Harriet Beecher Stowe[*]

"My dear Chris," said my wife, "isn't it time to be writing the next 'House and Home Paper'?"

I was lying back in my study-chair, with my heels luxuriously propped on an ottoman, reading for the two-hundredth time Hawthorne's "Mosses from an Old Manse," or his "Twice-Told Tales," I forget which,—I only know that these books constitute my cloud-land, where I love to sail away in dreamy quietude, forgetting the war, the price of coal and flour, the rates of exchange, and the rise and fall of gold. What do all these things matter, as seen from those enchanted gardens in Padua where the weird Rappaccini tends his enchanted plants, and his gorgeous daughter fills us with the light and magic of her presence, and saddens us with the shadowy allegoric mystery of her preternatural destiny? But my wife represents the positive forces of time, place, and number in our family, and, having also a chronological head, she knows the day of the month, and therefore gently reminded me that by inevitable dates the time drew near for preparing my—which is it, now, May or June number?

"Well, my dear, you are right," I said, as by an exertion I came head-uppermost, and laid down the fascinating volume. "Let me see, what was I to write about?"

"Why, you remember you were to answer that letter from the lady who does her own work."

[*] Originally published in *The Atlantic Monthly* in 1864, "The Lady Who Does Her Own Work" was later collected in volume VIII of *The Writings of Harriet Beecher Stowe* entitled *Household Papers and Stories* (Cambridge, Massachusetts, 1896).

"Enough!" said I, seizing the pen with alacrity; "you have hit the exact phrase:—

"'The *lady* who *does her own work.*'"

America is the only country where such a title is possible, —the only country where there is a class of women who may be described as *ladies* who do their own work. By a lady we mean a woman of education, cultivation, and refinement, of liberal tastes and ideas, who, without any very material additions or changes, would be recognized as a lady in any circle of the Old World or the New.

What I have said is, that the existence of such a class is a fact peculiar to American society, a clear, plain result of the new principles involved in the doctrine of universal equality.

When the colonists first came to this country, of however mixed ingredients their ranks might have been composed, and however imbued with the spirit of feudal and aristocratic ideas, the discipline of the wilderness soon brought them to a democratic level; the gentleman felled the wood for his log-cabin side by side with the ploughman, and thews and sinews rose in the market. "A man was deemed honorable in proportion as he lifted his hand upon the high trees of the forest." So in the interior domestic circle. Mistress and maid, living in a log-cabin together, became companions, and sometimes the maid, as the more accomplished and stronger, took precedence of the mistress. It became natural and unavoidable that children should begin to work as early as they were capable of it. The result was a generation of intelligent people brought up to labor from necessity, but turning on the problem of labor the acuteness of a disciplined brain. The mistress, outdone in sinews and muscles by her maid, kept her superiority by skill and contrivance. If she could not lift a pail of water she could invent methods which made lifting the pail unnecessary; if she could not take a hundred steps without weariness, she could make twenty answer the purpose of a hundred.

Slavery, it is true, was to some extent introduced into New

England, but it never suited the genius of the people, never struck deep root, or spread so as to choke the good seed of self-helpfulness. Many were opposed to it from conscientious principle,—many from far-sighted thrift, and from a love of thoroughness and well-doing which despised the rude, unskilled work of barbarians. People, having once felt the thorough neatness and beauty of execution which came of free, educated, and thoughtful labor, could not tolerate the clumsiness of slavery. Thus it came to pass that for many years the rural population of New England, as a general rule, did their own work, both out doors and in. If there were a black man or black woman or bound girl, they were emphatically only the *helps,* following humbly the steps of master and mistress, and used by them as instruments of lightening certain portions of their toil. The master and mistress with their children were the head workers.

Great merriment has been excited in the Old Country because years ago the first English travelers found that the class of persons by them denominated servants were in America denominated help or helpers. But the term was the very best exponent of the state of society. There were few servants in the European sense of the work; there was a society of educated workers, where all were practically equal, and where, if there was a deficiency in one family and an excess in another, a *helper,* not a servant, was hired. Mrs. Brown, who has six sons and no daughters, enters into agreement with Mrs. Jones, who has six daughters and no sons. She borrows a daughter, and pays her good wages to help in her domestic toil, and sends a son to help the labors of Mr. Jones. These two young people go into the families in which they are to be employed in all respects as equals and companions, and so the work of the community is equalized. Hence arose, and for many years continued, a state of society more nearly solving than any other ever did the problem of combining the highest culture of the mind with the highest culture of the muscles and the physical faculties.

Then were to be seen families of daughters, handsome, strong females, rising each day to their indoor work with cheerful alertness,—one to sweep the room, another to make the fire, while a third prepared the breakfast for the father and brothers who were going out to manly labor; and they chatted meanwhile of books, studies, embroidery, discussed the last new poem, or some historical topic started by graver reading, or perhaps a rural ball that was to come off the next week. They spun with the book tied to the distaff; they wove; they did all manner of fine needlework; they made lace, painted flowers, and, in short, in the boundless consciousness of activity, invention, and perfect health, set themselves to any work they had ever read or thought of. A bride in those days was married with sheets and tablecloths of her own weaving, with counterpanes and toilet-covers wrought in divers embroidery by her own and her sisters' hands. The amount of fancy work done in our days by girls who have nothing else to do will not equal what was done by these, who performed besides, among them, the whole work of the family.

For many years these habits of life characterized the majority of our rural towns. They still exist among a class respectable in numbers and position, though perhaps not as happy in perfect self-satisfaction and a conviction of the dignity and desirableness of its lot as in former days. Human nature is above all things—lazy. Every one confesses in the abstract that exertion which brings out all the powers of body and mind is the best thing for us all; but practically most people do all they can to get rid of it, and as a general rule nobody does much more than circumstances drive him to do. Even I would not write this article were not the publication-day hard on my heels. I should read Hawthorne and Emerson and Holmes, and dream in my armchair, and project in the clouds those lovely unwritten stories that curl and veer and change like mist-wreaths in the sun. So also, however dignified, however invigorating, however really desirable, are habits of life involving daily physical toil, there is a constant evil demon at every one's elbow, seducing him to evade it, or to bear its weight with sullen, discontented murmurs.

I will venture to say that there are at least, to speak very moderately, a hundred houses where these humble lines will be read and discussed, where there are no servants except the ladies of the household. I will venture to say, also, that these households, many of them, are not inferior in the air of cultivation and refined elegance to many which are conducted by the ministration of domestics. I will venture to assert furthermore that these same ladies who live thus find quite as much time for reading, letter-writing, drawing, embroidery, and fancy work as the women of families otherwise arranged. I am quite certain that they would be found on an average to be in the enjoyment of better health, and more of that sense of capability and vitality which gives one confidence in one's ability to look into life and meet it with cheerful courage, than three quarters of the women who keep servants; and that, on the whole, their domestic establishment is regulated more exactly to their mind, their food prepared and served more to their taste. And yet, with all this, I will *not* venture to assert that they are satisfied with this way of living, and that they would not change it forthwith if they could. They have a secret feeling all the while that they are being abused, that they are working harder than they ought to, and that women who live in their houses like boarders, who have only to speak and it is done, are the truly enviable ones. One after another of their associates, as opportunity offers and means increase, deserts the ranks, and commits her domestic affairs to the hands of hired servants. Self-respect takes the alarm. Is it altogether genteel to live as we do? To be sure, we are accustomed to it; we have it all systematized and arranged; the work of our own hands suits us better than any we can hire; in fact, when we do hire, we are discontented and uncomfortable, for who will do for us what we will do for ourselves? But when we have company! there's the rub, to get out all our best things and put them back,—to cook the meals and wash the dishes ingloriously,—and to make all appear as if we didn't do it, and had servants like other people. . . .

I fancy you now, my friends, whom I have in my eye. You are three happy women together. You are all so well that you know not how it feels to be sick. You are used to early rising, and would not lie in bed if you could. Long years of practice have made you familiar with the shortest, neatest, most expeditious method of doing every household office, so that really, for the greater part of the time in your house, there seems to a looker-on to be nothing to do. You rise in the morning and dispatch your husband, father, and brothers to the farm or wood-lot; you go sociably about chatting with each other, while you skim the milk, make the butter, turn the cheeses. The forenoon is long; it's ten to one that all the so-called morning work is over, and you have leisure for an hour's sewing or reading before it is time to start the dinner preparations. By two o'clock your housework is done, and you have the long afternoon for books, needlework, or drawing,—for perhaps there is among you one with a gift at her pencil. Perhaps one of you reads aloud while the others sew, and you manage in that way to keep up with a great deal of reading. I see on your bookshelves Prescott, Macaulay, Irving, besides the lighter fry of poems and novels, and, if I mistake not, the friendly covers of the "Atlantic." When you have company, you invite Mrs. Smith or Brown or Jones to tea: you have no trouble—they come early, with their knitting or sewing; your particular crony sits with you by your polished stove while you watch the baking of those light biscuits and tea rusks for which you are so famous, and Mrs. Somebodyelse chats with your sister, who is spreading the table with your best china in the best room. When tea is over, there is plenty of volunteering to help you wash your pretty India teacups, and get them back into the cupboard. There is no special fatigue or exertion in all this, though you have taken down the best things and put them back, because you have done all without anxiety or effort, among those who would do precisely the same if you were their visitors.

But now comes down pretty Mrs. Simmons and her pretty daughter to spend a week with you, and forthwith you are troubled. Your youngest, Fanny, visited them in New York last fall, and tells you of their cook and chambermaid, and the servant in white gloves that waits on the table. You say in your soul, "What shall we do? they never can be contented to live as we do; how shall we manage?" And now you long for servants.

This is the very time that you should know that Mrs. Simmons is tired to death of her fine establishment, and weighed down with the task of keeping the peace among her servants. She is a quiet soul, dearly loving her ease and hating strife; and yet last week she had five quarrels to settle between her invaluable cook and the other members of her staff, because invaluable cook, on the strength of knowing how to get up state dinners and to manage all sorts of mysteries which her mistress knows nothing about, asserts the usual right of spoiled favorites to insult all her neighbors with impunity, and rule with a rod of iron over the whole house. Anything that is not in the least like her own home and ways of living will be a blessed relief and change to Mrs. Simmons. Your clean, quiet house, your delicate cookery, your cheerful morning tasks, if you will let her follow you about, and sit and talk with you while you are at your work, will all seem a pleasant contrast to her own life. Of course, if it came to the case of offering to change lots in life, she would not do it; but very likely she *thinks* she would, and sighs over and pities herself, and thinks sentimentally how fortunate you are, how snugly and securely you live, and wishes she were as untrammeled and independent as you. And she is more than half right; for, with her helpless habits, her utter ignorance of the simplest facts concerning the reciprocal relations of milk, eggs, butter, saleratus, soda, and yeast, she is completely the victim and slave of the person she pretends to rule. . . .

Having written thus far on my article I laid it aside till evening, when, as usual, I was saluted by the inquiry, "Has papa been writing anything to-day?" and then followed loud petitions to hear it; and so I read as far, reader, as you have.

"Well, papa," said Jenny, "what are you meaning to make out there? Do you really think it would be best for us all to try to go back to that old style of living you describe? After all, you have shown only the dark side of an establishment with servants, and the bright side of the other way of living. Mamma does not have such trouble with her servants; matters have always gone smoothly in our family; and, if we are not such wonderful girls as those you describe, yet we may make pretty good housekeepers on the modern system, after all."

"You don't know all the troubles your mamma has had in your day," said my wife. "I have often, in the course of my family history, seen the day when I have heartily wished for the strength and ability to manage my household matters as my grandmother of notable memory managed hers. But I fear that those remarkable women of the olden times are like the ancient painted glass,—the art of making them is lost; my mother was less than her mother, and I am less than my mother."

"And Marianne and I come out entirely at the little end of the horn," said Jenny, laughing; "yet I wash the breakfast cups and dust the parlors, and have always fancied myself a notable housekeeper."

"It is just as I told you," I said. "Human nature is always the same. Nobody ever is or does more than circumstances force him to be and do. Those remarkable women of old were made by circumstances. There were, comparatively speaking, no servants to be had, and so children were trained to habits of industry and mechanical adroitness from the cradle, and every household process was reduced to the very minimum of labor. Every step required in a process was counted, every movement calculated; and she who took ten steps, when one would do, lost her reputation for 'faculty.' Certainly such an early drill was of use in developing the health and the bodily powers, as well as in giving precision to the practical mental faculties. All household economies were arranged with equal niceness in those thoughtful minds. A trained housekeeper knew just how many sticks of hickory of a certain size were required to heat her oven, and how many of each different kind of wood. She knew by a sort of intuition just what kind of food would yield the most palatable nutriment with the least outlay of accessories in cooking. She knew to a minute the time when each article must go into and be withdrawn from her oven; and, if she could only lie in her chamber and direct, she could guide an intelligent child through the processes with mathematical certainty. It is impossible, however, that anything but early training and long experience can produce these results, and it is earnestly to be wished that the grandmothers of New England had only written down their experiences for our children; they would have been a mine of maxims and traditions, better than any other traditions of the elders which we know of."

"One thing I know," said Marianne, "and that is, I wish I had been brought up so, and knew all that I should, and had all the strength and adroitness that those women had. I should not dread to begin housekeeping, as I now do. I should feel myself independent. I should feel that I knew how to direct my servants, and what it was reasonable and proper to expect of them; and then, as you say, I shouldn't be dependent on all their whims and caprices of temper. I dread those household storms, of all things."

Silently pondering these anxieties of the young expectant housekeeper, I resumed my pen, and concluded my paper as follows:—

In this country, our democratic institutions have removed the superincumbent pressure which in the Old World confines the servants to a regular orbit. They come here feeling that this is somehow a land of liberty, and with very dim and confused notions of what liberty is. They are for the most part the raw, untrained Irish peasantry, and the wonder is, that, with all the unreasoning heats and prejudices of the Celtic blood, all the necessary ignorance and rawness, there should be the measure of comfort and success there is in our domestic arrangements. But, so long as things are so, there will be constant changes and interruptions in every domestic establishment, and constantly recurring interregnums when the mistress must put her own hand to the work, whether the hand be a trained or, an untrained one. As matters now are, the young housekeeper takes life at the hardest. She has very little strength,—no experience to teach her how to save her strength. She knows nothing experimentally of the simplest processes necessary to keep her family comfortably fed and clothed; and she has a way of looking at all these things which makes them particularly hard and distasteful to her. She does not escape being obliged to do housework at intervals, but she does it in a weak, blundering, confused way, that makes it twice as hard and disagreeable as it need be.

Now what I have to say is, that, if every young woman learned to do housework and cultivated her practical faculties in early life, she would, in the first place, be much more likely to keep her servants, and, in the second place, if she lost them temporarily, would avoid all that wear and tear of the nervous system which comes from constant ill-success in those departments on which family health and temper mainly depend. This is one of the peculiarities of our American life which require a peculiar training. Why not face it sensibly?

The second thing I have to say is, that our land is now full of motorpathic institutions to which women are sent at great expense to have hired operators stretch and exercise their inactive muscles. They lie for hours to have their feet twigged, their arms flexed, and all the different muscles of the body worked for them, because they are so flaccid and torpid that the powers of life do not go on. Would it not be quite as cheerful and less expensive a process if young girls from early life developed the muscles in sweeping, dusting, ironing, rubbing furniture, and all the multiplied domestic processes which our grandmothers knew of? A woman who did all these, and diversified the intervals with spinning on the great and little wheel, never came to need the gymnastics of Dio Lewis or of the Swedish motorpathist, which really are

a necessity now. Does it not seem poor economy to pay servants for letting our muscles grow feeble, and then to pay
operators to exercise them for us? I will venture to say that
our grandmothers in a week went over every movement that
any gymnast has invented, and went over them to some productive purpose, too.

Lastly, my paper will not have been in vain if those ladies
who have learned and practice the invaluable accomplishment of doing their own work will know their own happiness
and dignity, and properly value their great acquisition, even
though it may have been forced upon them by circumstances.

Servants, Harriet Beecher Stowe*

"Don't you think, mamma," said Marianne, "that there has been a sort of reaction against woman's work in our day? So much has been said of the higher sphere of woman, and so much has been done to find some better work for her, that insensibly, I think, almost everybody begins to feel that it is rather degrading for a woman in good society to be much tied down to family affairs."

"Especially," said my wife, "since in these Woman's Rights Conventions there is so much indignation expressed at those who would confine her ideas to the kitchen and nursery."

"There is reason in all things," said I. "Woman's Rights Conventions are a protest against many former absurd, unreasonable ideas,—the mere physical and culinary idea of womanhood as connected only with puddings and shirt-buttons, the unjust and unequal burdens which the laws of harsher ages had cast upon the sex. Many of the women connected with these movements are as superior in everything properly womanly as they are in exceptional talent and culture. There is no manner of doubt that the sphere of woman is properly to be enlarged, and that republican governments in particular are to be saved from corruption and failure only by allowing to woman this enlarged sphere. Every woman has rights as a human being first, which belong to no sex, and ought to be as freely conceded to her as if she were a man,—and, first and foremost, the great right of doing anything which God and Nature evidently have fitted her

* Originally published in *The Atlantic Monthly* in 1864, "Servants" was later collected in volume VIII of *The Writings of Harriet Beecher Stowe* entitled *Household Papers and Stories* (Cambridge, Massachusetts, 1896).

to excel in. If she be made a natural orator, like Miss Dickinson, or an astronomer, like Mrs. Somerville, or a singer, like Grisi, let not the technical rules of womanhood be thrown in the way of her free use of her powers. Nor can there be any reason shown why a woman's vote in the state should not be received with as much respect as in the family. A state is but an association of families, and laws relate to the rights and immunities which touch woman's most private and immediate wants and dearest hopes; and there is no reason why sister, wife, and mother should be more powerless in the state than in the home. Nor does it make a woman unwomanly to express an opinion by dropping a slip of paper into a box, more than to express that same opinion by conversation. In fact, there is no doubt that, in all matters relating to the interests of education, temperance, and religion, the state would be a material gainer by receiving the votes of women.

"But, having said all this, I must admit, *per contra*, not only a great deal of crude, disagreeable talk in these conventions, but a too great tendency of the age to make the education of women anti-domestic. It seems as if the world never could advance except like ships under a head wind, tacking and going too far, now in this direction and now in the opposite. Our common-school system now rejects sewing from the education of girls, which very properly used to occupy many hours daily in school a generation ago. The daughters of laborers and artisans are put through algebra, geometry, trigonometry, and the higher mathematics, to the entire neglect of that learning which belongs distinctively to woman. A girl cannot keep pace with her class if she gives any time to domestic matters, and accordingly she is excused from them all during the whole term of her education. The boy of a family, at an early age, is put to a trade, or the labors of a farm; the father becomes impatient of his support, and requires of him to care for himself. Hence an interrupted education,—learning coming by snatches in the winter months, or in the intervals of work. As the result, the females in our country towns are commonly, in mental culture, vastly in advance of the males of the same household; but with this comes a physical delicacy, the result of an exclusive use of the brain and a neglect of the muscular system, with great inefficiency in practical domestic duties. The race of strong, hardy, cheerful girls, that used to grow up in country places, and made the bright, neat, New England kitchens of old times,—the girls that could wash, iron, brew, bake, harness a horse and drive him, no less than braid straw, embroider, draw, paint, and read innumerable books,—this race of women, pride of olden time, is daily lessening; and in their stead come the fragile, easily fatigued, languid girls of a modern age, drilled in book-learning, ignorant of common things. The great danger of all this, and of the evils that come from it, is that society by and by will turn as blindly against female intellectual culture as it now advocates it, and, having worked disproportionately one way, will work disproportionately in the opposite direction." . . .

Dress, or Who Makes the Fashions, Harriet Beecher Stowe[*]

"We have just come through a great struggle, in which our women have borne an heroic part,—have shown themselves capable of any kind of endurance and self-sacrifice; and now we are in that reconstructive state which makes it of the greatest consequence to ourselves and the world that we understand our own institutions and position, and learn that, instead of following the corrupt and worn-out ways of the Old World, we are called on to set the example of a new state of society,—noble, simple, pure, and religious; and women can do more towards this even than men, for women are the real architects of society.

"Viewed in this light, even the small, frittering cares of women's life—the attention to buttons, trimmings, thread, and sewing-silk—may be an expression of their patriotism and their religion. A noble-hearted woman puts a noble meaning into even the commonplace details of life. The woman of America can, if they choose, hold back their country from following in the wake of old, corrupt, worn-out, effeminate European society, and make America the leader of the world in all that is good."

"I'm sure," said Humming Bird, "we all would like to be noble and heroic. During the war, I did so long to be a man! I felt so poor and insignificant because I was nothing but a girl!"

[*] Originally published in *The Atlantic Monthly* in 1864, "Dress" was later collected in volume VIII of *The Writings of Harriet Beecher Stowe* entitled *Household Papers and Stories* (Cambridge, Massachusetts, 1896).

"Ah, well," said Pheasant, "but then one wants to do something worth doing, if one is going to do anything. One would like to be grand and heroic, if one could; but if not, why try at all? One wants to be *very* something, *very* great, *very* heroic; or if not that, then at least very stylish and very fashionable. It is this everlasting mediocrity that bores me."

"Then, I suppose, you agree with the man we read of, who buried his one talent in the earth, as hardly worth caring for."

"To say the truth, I always had something of a sympathy for that man," said Pheasant. "I can't enjoy goodness and heroism in homoeopathic doses. I want something appreciable. What I can do, being a woman, is a very different thing from what I should try to do if I were a man, and had a man's chances: it is so much less—so poor—that it is scarcely worth trying for."

"You remember," said I, "the apothegm of one of the old divines, that if two angels were sent down from heaven, the one to govern a kingdom, and the other to sweep a street, they would not feel any disposition to change works."

"Well, that just shows that they are angels, and not mortals," said Pheasant; "but we poor human beings see things differently."

"Yet, my child, what could Grant or Sherman have done, if it had not been for the thousands of brave privates who were content to do each their imperceptible little,—if it had not been for the poor, unnoticed, faithful, never failing common soldiers, who did the work and bore the suffering? No *one* man saved our country, or could save it; nor could the men have saved it without the women. Every mother that said to her son, Go; every wife that strengthened the hands of her husband; every girl who sent courageous letters to her betrothed; every woman who worked for a fair; every grandam whose trembling hands knit stockings and scraped lint; every little maiden who hemmed shirts and made comfort-bags for soldiers,—each and all have been the joint doers of a great heroic work, the doing of which has been the regeneration of our era. A whole generation has learned the luxury of thinking heroic thoughts and being conversant with heroic deeds, and I have faith to believe that all this is not to go out in a mere crush of fashionable luxury and folly and frivolous emptiness,—but that our girls are going to merit the high praise given us by De Tocqueville, when he placed first among the causes of our prosperity the *noble character of American women.* Because foolish female persons in New York are striving to outdo the *demi-monde* of Paris in extravagance, it must not follow that every sensible and patriotic matron, and every nice, modest young girl, must forthwith and without inquiry rush as far after them as they possibly can. Because Mrs. Shoddy opens a ball in a two-thousand-dollar lace dress, every girl in the land need not look with shame on her modest white muslin. Somewhere between the fast women of Paris and the daughters of Christian American families there should be established a *cordon sanitaire,* to keep out the contagion of manners, customs, and habits with which a noble-minded, religious democratic people ought to have nothing to do. . . ."

The Cathedral, Harriet Beecher Stowe*

"I am going to build a cathedral one of these days," said I to my wife, as I sat looking at the slant line of light made by the afternoon sun on our picture of the Cathedral of Milan.

"That picture is one of the most poetic things you have among your house ornaments," said Rudolph. "Its original is the world's chief beauty,—a tribute to religion such as Art never gave before and never can again,—as much before the Pantheon as the Alps, with their virgin snows and glittering pinnacles, are above all temples made with hands. Say what you will, those Middle Ages that you call Dark had a glory of faith that never will be seen in our days of cotton-mills and Manchester prints. Where will you marshal such an army of saints as stands in yonder white-marble forest, visibly transfigured and glorified in that celestial Italian air? Saintship belonged to the mediaeval Church; the heroism of religion has died with it."

"That's just like one of your assertions, Rudolph," said I. "You might as well say that Nature has never made any flowers since Linnaeus shut up his herbarium. We have no statues and pictures of modern saints; but saints themselves, thank God, have never been wanting. 'As it was in the beginning, is now, and ever shall be' "—

"But what about your cathedral?" said my wife.

"Oh yes!—my cathedral,—yes. When my stocks in cloudland rise, I'll build a cathedral larger than Milan's; and the

* Originally published in *The Atlantic Monthly* in 1864, "The Cathedral" was later collected in volume VIII of *The Writings of Harriet Beecher Stowe* entitled *Household Papers and Stories* (Cambridge, Massachusetts, 1896).

men, but more particularly the women, thereon, shall be those who have done even more than Saint Paul tells of in the days of old, who 'subdued Kingdoms, wrought righteousness, quenched the violence of fire, escaped the edge of the sword, out of weakness were made strong, waxed valiant in fight, turned to flight the armies of the aliens.' I am not now thinking of Florence Nightingale, nor of the host of women who have been walking worthily in her footsteps, but of nameless saints of more retired and private state,—domestic saints, who have tended children not their own through whooping-cough and measles, and borne the unruly whims of fretful invalids, —stocking-darning, shirt-making saints,—saints who were no visible garment of haircloth, bound themselves with no belts of spikes and nails, yet in their inmost souls were marked and seared with the red cross of a lifelong self-sacrifice,—saints for whom the mystical terms self-annihilation and self-crucifixion had a real and tangible meaning, all the stronger because their daily death was marked by no outward sign. No mystical rites consecrated them; no organ-music burst forth in solemn rapture to welcome them; no habit of their order proclaimed to themselves and the world that they were the elect of Christ, the brides of another life: but small, eating cares, daily prosaic duties, the petty friction of all the littleness and all the inglorious annoyances of every day, were as dust that hid the beauty and grandeur of their calling even from themselves; they walked unknown even to their households, unknown even to their own souls; but when the Lord comes to build his New Jerusalem, we shall find many a white stone with a new name thereon, and the record of deeds and words which only. He that seeth in secret knows. Many a humble soul will be amazed to find that the seed it sowed in such weakness, in the dust of daily life, has blossomed into immortal flowers under the eye of the Lord.

"When I build my cathedral, that woman," I said, pointing to a small painting by the fire, "shall be among the first of my saints. You see her there, in an every-day dress-cap with a mortal thread-lace border, and with a very ordinary worked collar, fastened by a visible and terrestrial breastpin.

There is no nimbus around her head, no sign of the cross upon her breast; her hands are clasped on no crucifix or rosary. Her clear, keen, hazel eye looks as if it could sparkle with mirthfulness, as in fact it could; there are in it both the subtle flash of wit and the subdued light of humor; and though the whole face smiles, it has yet a certain decisive firmness that speaks the soul immutable in good. That woman shall be the first saint in my cathedral, and her name shall be recorded as Saint Esther. What makes saintliness in my view, as distinguished from ordinary goodness, is a certain quality of magnanimity and greatness of soul that brings life within the circle of the heroic. To be really great in little things, to be truly noble and heroic in the insipid details of every-day life, is a virtue so rare as to be worthy of canonization,—and this virtue was hers. New England Puritanism must be credited with the making of many such women. Severe as was her discipline, and harsh as seems now her rule, we have yet to see whether women will be born of modern systems of tolerance and indulgence equal to those grand ones of the olden times whose places now know them no more. The inconceivable austerity and solemnity with which Puritanism invested this mortal life, the awful grandeur of the themes which it made household words, the sublimity of the issues which it hung upon the commonest acts of our earthly existence, created characters of more than Roman strength and greatness; and the good men and women of Puritan training excelled the saints of the Middle Ages, as a soul fully developed intellectually, educated to closest thought, and exercised in reasoning, is superior to a soul great merely through impulse and sentiment.

My earliest recollections of Aunt Esther, for so our saint was known, were of a bright faced, cheerful, witty, quick-moving little middle-aged person, who came into our house like a good fairy whenever there was a call of sickness or of trouble. If an accident happened in the great roystering family of eight or ten children (and when was not something happening to some of us?), and we were shut up in a sick-room, then duly as daylight came the quick step and cheerful face of Aunt Esther,—not solemn and lugubrious like so many sick-room nurses, but with a never failing flow of wit and story that could beguile even the most doleful into laughing at their own afflictions. I remember how a fit of the quinsy—most tedious of all sicknesses to an active child—was gilded and glorified into quite a fete by my having Aunt Esther all to myself for two whole days, with nothing to do but amuse me. She charmed me into smiling at the very pangs which had made me weep before, and of which she described her own experiences in a manner to make me think that, after all, the quinsy was something with an amusing side to it. Her knowledge of all sorts of medicines, gargles, and alleviatives, her perfect familiarity with every canon and law of good nursing and tending, was something that could only have come from long experience in those good old New England days when there were no nurses recognized as a class in the land, but when watching and the care of the sick were among those offices of Christian life which the families of a neighborhood reciprocally rendered each other. Even from early youth she had obeyed a special vocation as sister of charity in many a sick-room, and, with the usual keen intelligence of New England, had widened her powers of doing good by the reading of medical and physiological works. Her legends of nursing in those days of long typhus fever and other formidable and protracted forms of disease were to our ears quite wonderful, and we regarded her as a sort of patron saint of the sick-room. She seemed always so cheerful, so bright, and so devoted, that it never occurred to us youngsters to doubt that she enjoyed, above all things, being with us, waiting on us all day, watching over us by night, telling us stories, and answering, in her lively and always amusing and instructive way, that incessant fire of questions with which a child persecutes a grown person.

"Sometimes, as a reward of goodness, we were allowed to visit her in her own room, a neat little parlor in the neighborhood, whose windows looked down a hillside on one hand, under the boughs of an apple-orchard, where daisies and clover and bobolinks always abounded in summer time; and on the other faced the street, with a green yard flanked by one or two shady elms between them and the street. No nun's cell was ever neater, no bee's cell ever more compactly and carefully arranged; and to us, familiar with the confusion of a great family of little ones, there was always something inviting about its stillness, its perfect order, and the air of thoughtful repose that breathed over it. She lived there in perfect independence, doing, as it was her delight to do, every office of life for herself. She was her own cook, her own parlor and chamber maid, her own laundress; and very faultless the cooking, washing, ironing, and care of her premises were. A slice of Aunt Esther's gingerbread, one of Aunt Esther's cookies, had, we all believed, certain magical properties such as belonged to no other mortal mixture. Even a handful of walnuts that were brought from the depths of her mysterious closet had virtues in our eyes such as no other walnuts could approach. The little shelf of books that hung suspended by cords against her wall was sacred in our regard; the volumes were like no other books; and we supposed that she derived from them those stores of knowledge on all subjects which she unconsciously dispensed among us,—for she was always telling us something of metals, or minerals, or gems, or plants, or animals, which awakened our curiosity, stimulated our inquiries, and, above all, led us to wonder where she had learned it all. Even the slight restrictions which her neat habits imposed on our breezy and turbulent natures seemed all quite graceful and becoming. It was right, in our eyes, to cleanse our shoes on scraper and mat with extra diligence, and then to place a couple of chips under the heels of our boots when we essayed to dry our feet at her spotless hearth. We marveled to see our own faces reflected in a thousand smiles and winks from her bright brass andirons,—such andirons we thought were seen on earth in no other place,—and a pair of radiant brass candlesticks, that illustrated the mantelpiece, were viewed with no less respect.

"Aunt Esther's cat was a model for all cats,—so sleek, so

intelligent, so decorous and well-trained, always occupying exactly her own cushion by the fire, and never transgressing in one iota the proprieties belonging to a cat of good breeding. She shared our affections with her mistress, and we were allowed as a great favor and privilege, now and then, to hold the favorite on our knees, and stroke her satin coat to a smoother gloss.

"But it was not for us alone that she had attractions. She was in sympathy and fellowship with everything that moved and lived; knew every bird and beast with a friendly acquaintanceship. The squirrels that inhabited the trees in the front yard were won in time by her blandishments to come and perch on her window-sills, and thence, by means of nuts adroitly laid, to disport themselves on the shining cherry tea-table that stood between the windows; and we youngsters used to sit entranced with delight as they gamboled and waved their feathery tails in frolicsome security, eating rations of gingerbread and bits of seedcake with as good a relish as any child among us.

"The habits, the rights, the wrongs, the wants, and the sufferings of the animal creation formed the subject of many an interesting conversation with her; and we boys, with the natural male instinct of hunting, trapping, and pursuing, were often made to pause in our career, remembering her pleas for the dumb things which could not speak for themselves.

"Her little hermitage was the favorite resort of numerous friends. Many of the young girls who attended the village academy made her acquaintance, and nothing delighted her more than that they should come there and read to her the books they were studying, when her superior and wide information enabled her to light up and explain much that was not clear to the immature students.

"In her shady retirement, too, she was a sort of Egeria to certain men of genius, who came to read to her their writings, to consult her in their arguments, and to discuss with her the literature and politics of the day,—through all which her mind moved with an equal step, yet with a sprightliness and vivacity peculiarly feminine.

"Her memory was remarkably retentive, not only of the contents of books, but of all that great outlying fund of anecdote and story which the quaint and earnest New England life always supplied. There were pictures of peculiar characters, legends of true events stranger than romance, all stored in the cabinets of her mind; and these came from her lips with the greater force because the precision of her memory enabled her to authenticate them with name, date, and circumstances of vivid reality. From that shadowy line of incidents which marks the twilight boundary between the spiritual world and the present life she drew legends of peculiar clearness, but invested with the mysterious charm which always dwells in that uncertain region; and the shrewd flash of her eye, and the keen, bright smile with which she answered the wondering question, 'What *do* you suppose it was?' or, 'What could it have been?' showed how evenly rationalism in her mind kept pace with romance.

"The retired room in which she thus read, studied, thought, and surveyed from afar the whole world of science and literature, and in which she received friends and entertained children, was perhaps the dearest and freshest spot to her in the world. There came a time, however, when the neat little independent establishment was given up, and she went to associate herself with two of her nieces in keeping house for a boarding-school of young girls. Here her lively manners and her gracious interest in the young made her a universal favorite, though the cares she assumed broke in upon those habits of solitude and study which formed her delight. From the day that she surrendered this independency of hers, she had never, for more than a score of years, a home of her own, but filled the trying position of an accessory in the home of others. Leaving the boarding-school, she became the helper of an invalid wife and mother in the early nursing and rearing of a family of young children,—an office which leaves no privacy and no leisure. Her bed was always shared with some little one; her territories were exposed to the constant inroads of little pattering feet; and all the various sicknesses and ailments of delicate childhood made absorbing drafts upon her time.

"After a while she left New England with the brother to whose family she devoted herself. The failing health of the wife and mother left more and more the charge of all things in her hands; servants were poor, and all the appliances of living had the rawness and inconvenience which in those days attended Western life. It became her fate to supply all other people's defects and deficiencies. Wherever a hand failed, there must her hand be. Whenever a foot faltered, she must step into the ranks. She was the one who thought for and cared for and toiled for all, yet made never a claim that any one should care for her.

"It was not till late in my life that I became acquainted with the deep interior sacrifice, the constant self-abnegation, which all her life involved. She was born with a strong, vehement, impulsive nature,—a nature both proud and sensitive,—a nature whose tastes were passions, whose likings and whose aversions were of the most intense and positive character. Devoted as she always seemed to the mere practical and material, she had naturally a deep romance and enthusiasm of temperament which exceeded all that can be written in novels. It was chiefly owing to this that a home and a central affection of her own were never hers. In her early days of attractiveness, none who would have sought her could meet the high requirements of her ideality; she never saw her hero, and so never married. Family cares, the tending of young children, she often confessed, were peculiarly irksome to her. She had the head of a student, a passionate love for the world of books. A Protestant convent, where she might devote herself without interruption to study, was her ideal of happiness. She had, too, the keenest appreciation of poetry, of music, of painting, and of natural scenery. Her enjoyment in any of these things was intensely vivid whenever, by chance, a stray sunbeam of the kind darted across the dusty path of her life; yet in all these her life was a constant repression. The eagerness with which she would listen to any account from those more fortunate ones who had known these things, showed how ardent a passion was constantly held in check. A short time before her death, talking with a friend who had visited Switzerland, she said, with great feeling: 'All my life my desire to visit the beautiful places of this earth has been so intense, that I cannot but hope that after my death I shall be permitted to go and look at them.'

"The completeness of her self-discipline may be gathered from the fact that no child could ever be brought to believe she had not a natural fondness for children, or that she found the care of them burdensome. It was easy to see that she had naturally all those particular habits, those minute pertinacities in respect to her daily movement and the arrangement of all her belongings, which would make the meddling, intrusive demands of infancy and childhood peculiarly hard for her to meet. Yet never was there a pair of toddling feet that did not make free with Aunt Esther's room, never a curly head that did not look up, in confiding assurance of a welcome smile, to her bright eyes. The inconsiderate and never ceasing requirements of children and invalids never drew from her other than a cheerful response; and to my mind there is more saintship in this than in the private wearing of any number of haircloth shirts or belts lined with spikes.

"In a large family of careless, noisy children there will be constant losing of thimbles and needles and scissors; but Aunt Esther was always ready, without reproach, to help the careless and the luckless. Her things, so well kept and so treasured, she was willing to lend, with many a caution and injunction, it is true, but also with a relish of right good will. And, to do us justice, we generally felt the sacredness of the trust, and were more careful of her things than of our own. If a shade of sewing-silk were wanting, or a choice button, or a bit of braid or tape, Aunt Esther cheerfully volunteered something from her well-kept stores, not regarding the trouble she made herself in seeking the key, unlocking the drawer, and searching out in bag or parcel just the treasure demanded. Never was more perfect precision, or more perfect readiness to accommodate others.

"Her little income, scarcely reaching a hundred dollars yearly, was disposed of with a generosity worthy a fortune. One tenth was sacredly devoted to charity, and a still further sum laid by every year for presents to friends. No Christmas or New Year ever came round that Aunt Esther, out of this very tiny fund, did not find something for children and servants. Her gifts were trifling in value, but well timed,—a ball of thread-wax, a paper of pins, a pin-cushion,—something generally so well chosen as to show that she had been running over our needs, and noting what to give. She was no less gracious as receiver than as giver. The little articles that we made for her, or the small presents that we could buy out of our childish resources, she always declared were exactly what she needed; and she delighted us by the care she took of them and the value she set upon them.

"Her income was a source of the greatest pleasure to her, as maintaining an independence without which she could not have been happy. Though she constantly gave to every family in which she lived services which no money could repay, it would have been the greatest trial to her not to be able to provide for herself. Her dress, always that of a true gentlewoman,—refined, quiet, and neat,—was bought from this restricted sum, and her small traveling expenses were paid out of it. She abhorred anything false or flashy: her caps were trimmed with real thread lace, and her silk dresses were of the best quality, perfectly well made and kept; and, after all, a little sum always remained over in her hands for unforeseen exigencies.

"This love of independence was one of the strongest features of her life, and we often playfully told her that her only form of selfishness was the monopoly of saintship,—that she who gave so much was not willing to allow others to give to her; that she who made herself servant of all was not willing to allow others to serve her.

"Among the trials of her life must be reckoned much ill health, borne, however, with such heroic patience that it was not easy to say when the hand of pain was laid upon her. She inherited, too, a tendency to depression of spirits, which at times increased to a morbid and distressing gloom. Few knew or suspected these sufferings, so completely had she learned to suppress every outward manifestation that might interfere with the happiness of others. In her hours of depression she resolutely forbore to sadden the lives of those around her with her own melancholy, and often her darkest moods were so lighted up and adorned with an outside show of wit and humor, that those who had known her intimately were astonished to hear that she had ever been subject to depression.

"Her truthfulness of nature amounted almost to superstition. From her promise once given she felt no change of purpose could absolve her; and therefore rarely would she give it absolutely, for she *could not* alter the thing that had gone forth from her lips. Our belief in the certainty of her fulfilling her word was like our belief in the immutability of the laws of nature. Whoever asked her got of her the absolute truth on every subject, and, when she had no good thing to say, her silence was often truly awful. When anything mean or ungenerous was brought to her knowledge, she would close her lips resolutely; but the flash in her eyes showed what she would speak were speech permitted. In her last days she spoke to a friend of what she had suffered from the strength of her personal antipathies. 'I thank God,' she said, 'that I believe at last I have overcome all that too, and that there has not been, for some years, any human being toward whom I have felt a movement of dislike.'

"The last year of her life was a constant discipline of unceasing pain, borne with that fortitude which could make her an entertaining and interesting companion even while the sweat of mortal agony was starting from her brow. Her own room she kept as a last asylum, to which she would silently retreat when the torture became too intense for the repression of society, and there alone, with closed doors, she wrestled with her agony. The stubborn independence of her nature took refuge in this final fastness, and she prayed only that she might go down to death with the full ability to steady herself all the way, needing the help of no other hand.

"The ultimate struggle of earthly feeling came when this proud self-reliance was forced to give way, and she was obliged to leave herself helpless in the hands of others. 'God requires that I should give up my last form of self-will,' she said; 'now I have resigned this, perhaps He will let me go home.'

"In a good old age, Death, the friend, came and opened the door of this mortal state, and a great soul, that had served a long apprenticeship to little things, went forth into the joy of its Lord; a life of self-sacrifice and self-abnegation passed into a life of endless rest."

"But," said Rudolph, "I rebel at this life of self-abnegation and self-sacrifice. I do not think it the duty of noble women, who have beautiful natures and enlarged and cultivated tastes, to make themselves the slaves of the sickroom and nursery."

"Such was not the teaching of our New England faith," said I. "Absolute unselfishness,—the death of self,—such were its teachings, and such as Esther's the characters it made. 'Do the duty nearest thee' was the only message it gave to 'women with a mission;' and from duty to duty, from one self-denial to another, they rose to a majesty of moral strength impossible to any form of mere self-indulgence. It is of souls thus sculptured and chiseled by self-denial and self-discipline that the living temple of the perfect hereafter is to be built. The pain of the discipline is short, but the glory of the fruition is eternal."

Sarah Orne Jewett was born in Berwick, Maine, in 1849, and died there sixty years later. The daughter of a physician, she often accompanied her father on his rounds, and after his death she saved, and read, his medical library. Although she often protested that she was wholly uneducated, her personal library and her literary observations, particularly in letters to friends, reveal not only that she was well-read, but that she was consciously aware of which authors had had the most influence on her own writing. She had originally been inspired by Harriet Beecher Stowe's *Pearl of Orr's Island,* a romantic tale set in a decaying village in Maine, and later sustained in her meticulous attention to detail by the literary credo of Flaubert.

Sarah Orne Jewett published her first story in the late 1860s and her first collection of stories, *Deephaven,* in 1877. Other collections followed, as well as three children's books and several novels, including *A Country Doctor, A White Heron, and Other Stories,* and *The Country of the Pointed Firs,* which were published in 1884, 1886, and 1896, respectively. By the time Sarah Orne Jewett began to write, Berwick was no longer a major inland port, but a station on a branch railroad line. Her grandfather had been a sea captain, and she never forgot the extra dimension which the tales of adventure he and his fellow seamen told had added to New England life. Sarah Jewett later described herself as the kind of child for whom grandfathers and granduncles and aunts were the best playmates, and she remained convinced, despite warm friendships with Annie Fields, wife of the publisher James T. Fields, William Dean Howells, Thomas Bailey Aldrich, and, later, Willa Cather, that she would always feel most at home with her parents' generation.

In a letter to John Greenleaf Whittier written towards the end of her life she summarized her permanently elegiac mood: "Nobody has mourned more than I over the forsaken farmhouses which I see everywhere as I drive about the country out of which I grew, and where every bush and tree seem like my cousins." Sarah Orne Jewett believed that a distinction could be made between sentiment strongly felt and a weak-kneed sentimentality, and it is perhaps not too melodramatic to say that she devoted her life to making that distinction clear.

The Courting of Sister Wisby, Sarah Orne Jewett*

All the morning there had been an increasing temptation to take an out-door holiday, and early in the afternoon the temptation outgrew my power of resistance. A far-away pasture on the long southwestern slope of a high hill was persistently present to my mind, yet there seemed to be no particular reason why I should think of it. I was not sure that I wanted anything from the pasture, and there was no sign, except the temptation, that the pasture wanted anything of me. But I was on the farther side of as many as three fences before I stopped to think again where I was going, and why.

There is no use in trying to tell another person about that afternoon unless he distinctly remembers weather exactly like it. No number of details concerning an Arctic ice-blockade will give a single shiver to a child of the tropics. This was one of those perfect New England days in late summer, when the spirit of autumn takes a first stealthy flight, like a spy, through the ripening country-side, and, with feigned sympathy for those who droop with August heat, puts her cool cloak of bracing air about leaf and flower and human shoulders. Every living thing grows suddenly cheerful and strong; it is only when you catch sight of a horror-stricken little maple in swampy soil—a little maple that has second-sight and fore-knowledge of coming disaster to her race—only then does a distrust of autumn's friendliness dim your joyful satisfaction.

In the midwinter there is always a day when one has the

* "The Courting of Sister Wisby" was first published in *The Atlantic Monthly* in 1887, and was reprinted in William Dean Howells, ed., *Great Modern American Stories* (New York, 1920).

first foretaste of spring; in late August there is a morning when the air is for the first time autumn-like. Perhaps it is a hint to the squirrels to get in their first supplies for the winter hoards, or a reminder that summer will soon end, and everybody had better make the most of it. We are always looking forward to the passing and ending of winter, but when summer is here it seems as if summer must always last. As I went across the fields that day, I found myself half lamenting that the world must fade again, even that the best of her budding and bloom was only a preparation for another springtime, for an awakening beyond the coming winter's sleep.

The sun was slightly veiled; there was a chattering group of birds, which had gathered for a conference about their early migration. Yet, oddly enough, I heard the voice of a belated bobolink, and presently saw him rise from the grass and hover leisurely, while he sang a brief tune. He was much behind time if he were still a housekeeper; but as for the other birds who listened, they cared only for their own notes. An old crow went sagging by, and gave a croak at his despised neighbor, just as a black reviewer croaked at Keats— so hard it is to be just to one's contemporaries. The bobolink was indeed singing out of season, and it was impossible to say whether he really belonged most to this summer or to the next. He might have been delayed on his northward journey; at any rate, he had a light heart now, to judge from his song, and I wished that I could ask him a few questions— how he liked being the last man among the bobolinks, and where he had taken singing lessons in the South.

Presently I left the lower fields, and took a path that led higher, where I could look beyond the village to the northern country mountainward. Here the sweet fern grew thick and fragrant, and I also found myself heedlessly treading on pennyroyal. Nearby, in a field corner, I long ago made a most comfortable seat by putting a stray piece of board and bit of rail across the angle of the fences. I have spent many a delightful hour there, in the shade and shelter of a young pitch-pine and a wild-cherry tree, with a lovely outlook toward the village, just far enough away beyond the green slopes and tall elms of the lower meadows. But that day I still had the feeling of being outward bound, and did not turn aside nor linger. The high pasture land grew more and more enticing.

I stopped to pick some blackberries that twinkled at me like beads among their dry vines, and two or three yellow-birds fluttered up from the leaves of a thistle and then came back again, as if they had complacently discovered that I was only an overgrown yellow-bird, in strange disguise but perfectly harmless. They made me feel as if I were an intruder, though they did not offer to peck at me, and we parted company very soon. It was good to stand at last on the great shoulder of the hill. The wind was coming in from the sea, there was a fine fragrance from the pines, and the air grew sweeter every moment. I took new pleasure in the thought that in a piece of wild pasture land like this one may get closest to Nature, and subsist upon what she gives of her own free will. There have been no drudging, heavy-shod plough-man to overturn the soil, and vex it into yielding artificial crops. Here one has to take just what Nature is pleased to give, whether one is a yellow-bird or a human being. It is very good entertainment for a summer wayfarer, and I am asking my reader now to share the winter provision which I harvested that day. Let us hope that the small birds are also faring well after their fashion, but I give them an anxious thought while the snow goes hurrying in long waves across the buried fields, this windy winter night.

I next went farther down the hill, and got a drink of fresh cool water from the brook, and pulled a tender sheaf of sweet flag beside it. The mossy old fence just beyond was the last barrier between me and the pasture which had sent an invisible messenger earlier in the day, but I saw that some-body else had come first to the rendezvous: there was a brown gingham cape-bonnet and a sprigged shoulder-shawl bobbing up and down, a little way off among the junipers. I had taken such uncommon pleasure in being alone that I in-stantly felt a sense of disappointment; then a warm glow of pleasant satisfaction rebuked my selfishness. This could be

no one but dear old Mrs. Goodsoe, the friend of my childhood and fond dependence of my maturer years. I had not
seen her for many weeks, but here she was, out on one of
her famous campaigns for herbs, or perhaps just returning
from a blueberrying expedition. I approached with care, so
as not to startle the gingham bonnet; but she heard the
rustle of the bushes against my dress, and looked up quickly,
as she knelt, bending over the turf. In that position she was
hardly taller than the luxuriant junipers themselves.

"I'm a-gittin' in my mulleins," she said briskly, "an' I've
been thinking o' you these twenty times since I come out o'
the house. I begun to believe you must ha' forgot me at last."

"I have been away from home," I explained. "Why don't
you get in your pennyroyal too? There's a great plantation of
it beyond the next fence but one."

"Pennyr'yal!" repeated the dear little old woman, with an
air of compassion for inferior knowledge; "'tain't the right
time, darlin'. Pennyr'yal's too rank now. But for mulleins this
day is prime. I've got a dreadful graspin' fit for 'em this year;
seems if I must be goin' to need 'em extry. I feel like the
squirrels must when they know a hard winter's comin'." And
Mrs. Goodsoe bent over her work again, while I stood by and
watched her carefully cut the best full-grown leaves with a
clumsy pair of scissors, which might have served through at
least half a century of herb-gathering. They were fastened
to her apron-strings by a long piece of list.

"I'm going to take my jack-knife and help you," I suggested, with some fear of refusal. "I just passed a flourishing
family of six or seven heads that must have been growing on
purpose for you."

"Now be keerful, dear heart," was the anxious response;
"choose 'em well. There's odds in mulleins same's there is in
angels. Take a plant that's all run up to stalk, and there ain't
but little goodness in the leaves. This one I'm at now must
ha' been stepped on by some creatur and blighted of its
bloom, and the leaves is han'some! When I was small I used
to have a notion that Adam an' Eve must ha' took mulleins
fer their winter wear. Ain't they just like flannel, for all the

world? I've had experience, and I know there's plenty of sickness might be saved to folks if they'd quit horse-radish and such fiery, exasperating things, and use mullein drarves in proper season. Now I shall spread these an' dry 'em nice on my spare floor in the garrit, an' come to steam 'em for use along in the winter there'll be the valley of the whole summer's goodness in 'em, sartin." And she snipped away with the dull scissors while I listened respectfully, and took great pains to have my part of the harvest present a good appearance.

"This is most too dry a head," she added presently, a little out of breath. "There! I can tell you there's win'rows o' young doctors, bilin' over with book-larnin', that is truly ignorant of what to do for the sick, or how to p'int out those paths that well people foller toward sickness. Book-fools I call 'em, them young men, an' some on 'em never'll live to know much better, if they git to be Methuselahs. In my time every middle-aged woman who had brought up a family had some proper ideas of dealin' with complaints. I won't say but there was some fools amongst *them*, but I'd rather take my chances, unless they'd forsook herbs and gone to dealin' with patent stuff. Now my mother really did sense the use of herbs and roots. I never see anybody that come up to her. She was a meek-looking woman, but very understandin' mother was."

"Then that's where you learned so much yourself, Mrs. Goodsoe," I ventured to say.

"Bless your heart, I don't hold a candle to her; 'tis but little I can recall of what she used to say. No, her larnin' died with her," said my friend, in a self-deprecating tone. "Why, there was as many as twenty kinds of roots alone that she used to keep by her, that I forgot the use of; an' I'm sure I shouldn't know where to find the most of 'em, any. There was an herb"—*airb* she called it—"an herb called Pennsylvany; and she used to think everything of noble-liverwort, but I never could seem to get the right effects from it as she could. Though I don't know as she ever really did use masterwort where somethin' else wouldn't ha' served. She had a cousin married out in Pennsylvany that used to take pains to get it to her every year or two, and so she felt 't was important to have it. Some set more by such things as come from a distance, but I rec'lect mother always used to maintain that folks was meant to be doctored with the stuff that grew right about 'em; 'twas sufficient, an' so ordered. That was before the whole population took to livin' on wheels, the way they do now. 'Twas never my idee that we was meant to know what's goin' on all over the world to once. There's goin' to be some sort of a set-back one o' these days, with these telegraphs an' things, an' letters comin' every hand's turn, and folks leavin' their proper work to answer 'em. I may not live to see it. 'Twas allowed to be difficult for folks to get about in old times, or to get word across the country, and they stood in their lot an' place, and weren't all just alike, either, same as pine-spills."

We were kneeling side by side now, as if in penitence for the march of progress, but we laughed as we turned to look at each other.

"Do you think it did much good when everybody brewed a cracked quart mug of herb-tea?" I asked, walking away on my knees to a new mullein.

"I've always lifted my voice against the practice, far's I could," declared Mrs. Goodsoe; "an' I won't deal out none o' the herbs I save for no such nonsense. There was three houses along our road—I call no names—where you couldn't go into the livin' room without findin' a mess o' herb-tea drorin' on the stove or side o' the fireplace, winter or summer, sick or well. One was thoroughwut, one would be camomile, and the other, like as not, yellow dock; but they all used to put in a little new rum to git out the goodness, or keep it from spilin'." (Mrs. Goodsoe favored me with a knowing smile.) "Land, how mother used to laugh! But, poor creatures, they had to work hard, and I guess it never done 'em a mite o' harm; they was all good herbs. I wish you could hear the quawkin' there used to be when they was indulged with a real case o' sickness. Everybody would collect from far an' near; you'd see 'em coming along the road and across the pastures then;

everybody clamorin' that nothin' would do no kind o' good but her choice o' teas or drarves to the feet. I wonder there was a babe lived to grow up in the whole lower part o' the town; an' if nothin' else 'peared to ail 'em, word was passed about that 'twas likely Mis' So-and-So's last young one was goin' to be foolish. Land, how they'd gather! I know one day the doctor come to Widder Peck's and the house was crammed so't he could scercely git inside the door; and he says, just as polite, 'Do send for some of the neighbors!' as if there wa'n't a soul to turn to, right or left. You'd ought to seen 'em begin to scatter."

"But don't you think the cars and telegraphs have given people more to interest them, Mrs. Goodsoe? Don't you believe people's lives were narrower then, and more taken up with little things?" I asked, unwisely, being a product of modern times.

"Not one mite, dear," said my companion stoutly. "There was as big thoughts then as there is now; these times was born o' them. The difference is in folks themselves; but now, instead o' doin' their own housekeepin' and watchin' their own neighbors—though that was carried to excess—they git word that a niece's child is ailin' the other side o' Massachusetts, and they drop everything and git on their best clothes, and off they jiggit in the cars. 'Tis a bad sign when folks wear out their best clothes faster 'n they do their everyday ones. The other side o' Massachusetts has got to look after itself by rights. An' besides that, Sunday-keepin's all gone out o' fashion. Some lays it to one thing an' some another, but some o' them old ministers that folks are all a'sighin' for did preach a lot o' stoff that wa'n't nothin' but chaff; 'twa'n't the word o' God out o' either Old Testament or New. But everybody went to meetin' and heard it, and come home, and was set to fightin' with their next door neighbor over it. Now I'm a believer, and I try to live a Christian life, but I'd as soon hear a surveyor's book read out, figgers an' all, as try to get any simple truth out o' most sermons. It's them as is most to blame."

"What was the matter that day at Widow Peck's?" I hastened to ask, for I knew by experience that the good, clear-minded soul beside me was apt to grow unduly vexed and distressed when she contemplated the state of religious teaching.

"Why, there wa'n't nothin' the matter, only a gal o' Miss Peck's had met with a dis'pintment and had gone into screechin' fits. 'Twas a rovin' creatur that had come along hayin' time, and he'd gone off an' forsook her betwixt two days; nobody ever knew what become of him. Them Pecks was 'Good Lord, anybody!' kind o' gals, and took up with whoever they could get. One of 'em married Heron, the Irishman; they lived in that little house that was burnt this summer, over on the edge o' the plains. He was a good-hearted creatur, with a laughin' eye and a clever word for everybody. He was the first Irishman that ever came this way, and we was all for gettin' a look at him, when he first used to go by. Mother's folks was what they call Scotch-Irish, though; there was an old race of 'em settled about here. They could foretell events, some on 'em, and had second sight. I know folks used to say mother's grandmother had them gifts, but mother was never free to speak about it to us. She remembered her well, too."

"I suppose that you mean old Jim Heron, who was such a famous fiddler?" I asked with great interest, for I am always delighted to know more about that rustic hero, parochial Orpheus that he must have been!

"Now, dear heart, I suppose you don't remember him, do you?" replied Mrs. Goodsoe, earnestly. "Fiddle! He'd about break your heart with them tunes of his, or else set your heels flying up the floor in a jig, though you was minister o' the First Parish and all wound up for a funeral prayer. I tell ye there win't no tunes sounds like them used to. It used to seem to me summer nights when I was comin' along the plains road, and he set by the window playin', as if there was a be-twitched human creatur in that old red fiddle o' his. He could make it sound just like a woman's voice tellin' somethin' over and over, as if folks could help her out o' her sorrows if she could only make 'em understand. I've set by the stone-wall and cried as if my heart was broke, and dear knows it wa'n't in them days. How he would twirl off them jogs and dance

tunes! He used to make somethin' han'some out of 'em in fall
an' winter, playin' at huskins and dancin' parties; but he was
unstiddy by spells, as he got along in years, and never knew
what it was to be forehanded. Everybody felt bad when
he died; you couldn't help likin' the creatur. He'd got the gift
—that's all you could say about it.

"There was a Mis' Jerry Foss, that lived over by the brook
bridge, on the plains road, that had lost her husband early,
and was left with three child'n. She set the world by 'em, and
was a real pleasant, ambitious little woman, and was workin'
on as best she could with that little farm, when there come a
rage o' scarlet fever, and her boy and two girls was swept off
and laid dead within the same week. Every one o' the neighbors did what they could, but she'd had no sleep since they
was taken sick, and after the funeral she set there just like a
piece o' marble, and would only shake her head when you
spoke to her. They all thought her reason would go; and
'twould certain, if she couldn't have shed tears. An' one o'
the neighbors—'twas like mother's sense, but it might have
been somebody else—spoke o' Jim Heron. Mother an' one or
two o' the women that knew her best was in the house with
her. 'T was right in the edge o' the woods and some of us
younger ones was over by the wall on the other side of the
road where there was a couple of old willows—I remember
just how the brook damp felt—and we kept quiet's we could,
and some other folks come along down the road, and stood
waitin' on the little bridge, hopin' somebody'd come out, I
suppose, and they'd git news. Everybody was wrought up, and
felt a good deal for yer, you know. By an' by Jim Heron come
stealin' right out o' the shadows an' set down on the door-
step, an' 'twas a good while before we heard a sound; then,
oh, dear me! 'twas what the whole neighborhood felt for that
mother all spoke in the notes, an' they told me afterwards
that Mis' Foss's face changed in a minute, and she come right
over an' got into my mother's lap—she was a little woman—
an' laid her head down, and there she cried herself into a
blessed sleep. After awhile one o' the other women stole out

an' told the folks, and we all went home. He only played that one tune.

"But there!" resumed Mrs. Goodsoe, after a silence, during which my eyes were filled with tears. "His wife always complained that the fiddle made her nervous. She never 'peared to think nothin' o' poor Heron after she'd once got him."

"That's often the way," said I, with harsh cynicism, though I had no guilty person in my mind at the moment; and we went straying off, not very far apart, up through the pasture. Mrs. Goodsoe cautioned me that we must not get so far off that we could not get back the same day. The sunshine began to feel very hot on our backs, and we both turned toward the shade. We had already collected a large bundle of mullein leaves, which were carefully laid into a clean, calico apron, held together by the four corners, and proudly carried by me, though my companion regarded them with anxious eyes. We sat down together at the edge of the pine woods, and Mrs. Goodsoe proceeded to fan herself with her limp cape-bonnet.

"I declare, how hot it is! The east wind's all gone again," she said. "It felt so cool this forenoon that I overburdened myself with as thick a petticoat as any I've got. I'm despri't afeared of having a chill, now that I ain't so young as once. I hate to be housed up."

"It's only August, after all," I assured her unnecessarily, confirming my statement by taking two peaches out of my pocket, and laying them side by side on the brown pine needles between us.

"Dear sakes alive!" exclaimed the old lady, with evident pleasure. "Where did you get them, now? Doesn't anything taste twice better out'o'-doors? I ain't had such a peach for years. Do le's keep the stones, an' I'll plant 'em; it only takes four years for a peach pit to come to bearing, an' I guess I'm good for four years, 'thout I meet with some accident."

I could not help agreeing, or taking a fond look at the thin little figure, and her wrinkled brown face and kind, twinkling eyes. She looked as if she had properly dried herself, by mistake, with some of her mullein leaves, and was likely to keep her goodness, and to last the longer in consequence. There never was a truer, simple-hearted soul made out of the old-fashioned country dust than Mrs. Goodsoe. I thought, as I looked away from her across the wide country, that nobody was left in any of the farmhouses so original, so full of rural wisdom and reminiscence, so really able and dependable, as she. And nobody had made better use of her time in a world foolish enough to sometimes under-value medicinal herbs.

When we had eaten our peaches we still sat under the pines, and I was not without pride when I had poked about in the ground with a little twig, and displayed to my crony a long fine root, bright yellow to the eye, and a wholesome bitter to the taste.

"Yis, dear, goldthread," she assented indulgently. "Seems to me there's more of it than anything except grass an' hard-tack. Good for canker, but no better than two or three other things I can call to mind; but I always lay in a good wisp of it, for old times sake. Now, I want to know why you should ha' bit it, and took away all the taste o' your nice peach? I was just thinkin' what a han'some entertainment we've had. I've got so I 'sociate certain things with certain folks, and gold-thread was somethin' Lizy Wisby couldn't keep house without, no ways whatever. I believe she took so much it kind o' puckered her disposition."

"Lizy Wisby?" I repeated inquiringly.

"You knew her, if ever, by the name of Mis' Deacon Brimblecom," answered my friend, as if this were only a brief preface to further information, so I waited with respectful expectation. Mrs. Goodsoe had grown tired out in the sun, and a good story would be an excuse for sufficient rest. It was a most lovely place where we sat, half-way up the long hillside; for my part, I was perfectly contented and happy. "You've often heard of Deacon Brimblecom?" she asked, as if a great deal depended upon his being properly introduced.

"I remember him," said I. "They called him Deacon Brim-full, you know, and he used to go about with a witch-hazel branch to show people where to dig wells."

"That's the one," said Mrs. Goodsoe, laughing. "I didn't

know's you could go so far back. I'm always divided between whether you can remember everything I can, or are only a babe in arms."

"I have a dim recollection of there being something strange about their marriage," I suggested, after a pause, which began to appear dangerous. I was so much afraid the subject would be changed.

"I can tell you all about it," I was quickly answered. "Deacon Brimblecom was very pious accordin' to his lights in his early years. He lived way back in the country then, and there come a rovin' preacher along, and set everybody up that way all by the ears. I've heard the old folks talk it over, but I forget most of his doctrine, except some of his followers was persuaded they could dwell among the angels while yet on airth, and this Deacon Brimfull, as you call him, felt sure he was called by the voice of a spirit bride. So he left a good, deservin' wife he had, an' four children, and built him a new house over to the other side of the land he'd had from his father. They didn't take much pains with the buildin', because they expected to be translated before long, and then the spirit brides and them folks was goin' to appear and divide up the airth amongst 'em, and the world's folks and on-believers was goin' to serve 'em or be sent to torments. They had meetin's about in the schoolhouses, an' all sorts o' goin' on; some on 'em went crazy, but the deacon held on to what wits he had, an' by an' by the spirit bride didn't turn out to be much of a housekeeper, an' he had always been used to good livin', so he sneaked home ag'in. One o' mother's sisters married up to Ash Hill, where it all took place; that's how I come to have the particulars."

"Then how did he come to find his Eliza Wisby?" I inquired. "Do tell me the whole story; you've got mullein leaves enough."

"There's all yisterday's at home, if I haven't," replied Mrs. Goodsoe. "The way he come a-courtin' o' Sister Wisby was this: she went a-courtin' o' him.

"There was a spell he lived to home, and then his poor wife died, and he had a spirit bride in good earnest, an' the childr'n was placed about with his folks and hers, for they was both out o' good families; and I don't know what come over him, but he had another pious fit that looked for all the world like the real thing. He hadn't no family cares, and he lived with his brother's folks, and turned his land in with theirs. He used to travel to every meetin' an' conference that was within reach of his old sorrel hoss's feeble legs; he j'ined the Christian Baptists that was just in their early prime, and he was a great exhorter, and got to be called deacon, though I guess he wa'n't deacon, 'less it was for a spare hand when deacon times was scercer'n usual. An' one time there was a four-days' protracted meetin' to the church in the lower part of the town. 'Twas a real solemn time; somethin' more'n usual was goin' forward, an' they collected from the whole country round. Women folks liked it, an' the men too; it give 'em a change, an' they was quartered round free, same as conference folks now. Some on 'em, for a joke, sent Silas Brimblecom up to Lizy Wisby's, though she'd give out she couldn't accommodate nobody, because of expectin' her cousin's folks. Everybody knew 'twas a lie; she was amazin' close considerin' she had plenty to do with. There was a streak that wa'n't just right somewheres in Lizy's wits, I always thought. She was very kind in case o' sickness, I'll say that for her.

"You know where the house is, over there on what they call Windy Hill? There the deacon went, all unsuspectin', and 'stead o' Lizy's resentin' of him she put in her own hoss, and they come back together to evenin' meetin'. She was prominent among the sect herself, an' he bawled and talked, and she bawled and talked, an' took up more'n the time allotted in the exercises, just as if they was showin' off to each what they was able to do at expoundin'. Everybody was laughin' at 'em after the meetin' broke up, and that next day an' the next, an' all through, they was constant, and seemed to be havin' a beautiful occasion. Lizy had always give out she scorned the men, but when she got a chance at a particular one 'twas altogether different, and the deacon seemed to please her somehow or 'nother, and—There! you don't want to listen to this old stuff that's past an' gone?"

"Oh, yes, I do," said I.

"I run on like a clock that's onset her striking hand," said Mrs. Goodsoe mildly. "Sometimes my kitchen time-piece goes on half the forenoon, and I says to myself the day before yisterday I would let it be a warnin', and keep it in mind for a check on my own speech. The next news that was heard was that the deacon an' Lizy—well, opinions differed which of 'em had spoke first, but them fools settled it before the protracted meetin' was over, and give away their hearts before he started for home. They considered 'twould be wise, though, considerin' their short acquaintance, to take one another on trial a spell; 'twas Lizy's notion, and she asked him why he wouldn't come over and stop with her till spring, and then, if both continued to like, they could git married any time 'twas convenient. Lizy, she come and talked it over with mother, and mother disliked to offend her, but she spoke pretty plain; and Lizy felt hurt, an' thought they was showin' excellent judgment, so much harm come from hasty unions and folks comin' to a realizin' sense of each other's failin's when 'twas too late.

"So one day our folks saw Deacon Brimful a-ridin' by with a gre't coopful of hens in the back o' his wagon, and bundles o' stuff tied to top and hitched to the exes underneath; and he riz a hymn just as he passed the house, and was speedin' the old sorrel with a willer switch. 'Twas most Thanksgivin' time, an' sooner'n she expected him. New Year's was the time she set; but he thought he'd come while the roads was fit for wheels. They was out to meetin' together Thanksgivin' Day, an' that used to be a gre't season for marryin'; so the young folks nudged each other, and some on 'em ventured to speak to the couple as they come down the aisle. Lizy carried it off real well; she wa'n't afraid o' what nobody said or thought, and so home they went. They'd got out her yaller sleigh and her hoss; she never would ride after the deacon's poor old creatur, and I believe it died long o' the winter from stiffenin' up.

"Yes," said Mrs. Goodsoe, emphatically, after we had silently considered the situation for a short space of time, "yes, there was consider'ble talk, now I tell you! The raskil boys pestered 'em just about to death for a while. They used to collect up there an' rap on the winders, and they'd turn out all the deacon's hens 'long at nine o'clock o' night, and chase 'em all over the dingle; an' one night they even lugged the pig right out o' the sty, and shoved it into the back entry, an' run for their lives. They'd stuffed its mouth full o' somethin', so it couldn't squeal till it got there. There wa'n't a sign o' nobody to be seen when Lizy hasted out with the light, and she an' the deacon had to persuade the creatur back as best they could; 'twas a cold night, and they said it took 'em till towards mornin'. You see the deacon was just the kind of a man that a hog wouldn't budge for; it takes a masterful man to deal with a hog. Well, there was no end to the works nor the talk, but Lizy left 'em pretty much alone. She did 'pear kind of dignified about it, I must say!"

"And then, were they married in the spring?"

"I was tryin' to remember whether it was just before Fast Day or just after," responded my friend, with a careful look at the sun, which was nearer the west than either of us had noticed. "I think likely 'twas along in the last o' April, any way some of us looked out o' the window one Monday mornin' early, and says, 'For goodness' sake! Lizy's sent the deacon home again!' His old sorrel havin' passed away, he was ridin' in Ezry Welsh's hoss-cart, with his hen-coop and more bundles than he had when he come, and looked as meechin' as ever you see. Ezry was drivin', and he let a glance fly swiftly round to see if any of us was lookin' out; an' then I declare if he didn't have the malice to turn right in towards the barn, where he see my oldest brother, Joshuay, an' says he real natural, 'Joshuay, just step out with your wrench. I believe I hear my kingbolt rattlin' kind o' loose.' Brother, he went out an' took in the sitooation, an' the deacon bowed kind of stiff. Joshuay was so full o' laugh, and Ezry Welsh, that they couldn't look one another in the face. There wa'n't nothing ailed the kingbolt, you know, an' when Josh riz up he says, 'Goin' up country for a spell, Mr. Brimblecom?'

"'I be,' says the deacon, lookin' dreadful mortified and cast down.

"'Ain't things turned out well with you an' Sister Wisby?'

says Joshuay: 'You had ought to remember that the woman is the weaker vessel.'

"'Hang her, let her carry less sail, then!' the deacon bu'st out, and he stood right up an' shook his fist there by the hen-coop, he was so mad; an' Ezry's hoss was a young creatur, an' started up and set the deacon right over backwards into the chips. We didn't know but he'd broke his neck; but when he see the women folks runnin' out he jumped up quick as a cat, an' clim into the cart, an' off they went. Ezry said he told him that he couldn't git along with Lizy, she was so fractious in thundery weather; if there was a rumble in the daytime she must go right to bed an' screech, and 'twas night she must git right up an' go an' call him out of a sound sleep. But everybody knew he'd never gone home unless she'd sent him.

"Somehow they made it up ag'in, him an' Lizy, and she had him back. She's been countin' all along on not havin' to hire nobidy to work about the gardin' an' so on, an' she said she wa'n't goin' to let him have a whole winter's board for nothin'. So the old hens was moved back, and they was married right off fair an' square, an' I don't know but they got along well as most folks. He brought his youngest girl down to live with 'em after a while, an' she was a real treasure to Lizy; everybody spoke well o' Phoebe Brimblecom. The deacon got over his pious fit, and there was consider'ble work in him if you kept right after him. He was an amazin' cider-drinker, and he airnt the name you know him by in his latter days. Lizy never trusted him with nothin', but she kep' him well. She left everything she owned to Phoebe, when she died, 'cept somethin' to satisfy the law. There, they're all gone now; seems to me sometimes, when I get thinkin', as if I'd lived a thousand years!"

I laughed, but I found Mrs. Goodsoe's thoughts had taken a serious turn.

"There, I come by some old graves down here in the lower edge of the pasture," she said as we rose to go. "I couldn't help thinking how I should like to be laid right out in the pasture ground, when my time comes; it looked sort o' comfortable, and I have ranged these slopes so many summers.

Seems as if I could see right up through the turf and tell when the weather was pleasant, and get the goodness o' the sweet fern. Now, dear, just hand me my apernful o' mulleins out o' the shade. I hope you won't come to need none this winter, but I'll dry some special for you."

"I'm going by the road," said I, "or else by the path across the meadows, so I will walk as far as the house with you. Aren't you pleased with my company?" for she demurred at my going the least bit out of the way.

So we strolled toward the little gray house, with our plunder of mullein leaves slung on a stick which we carried between us. Of course I went in to make a call, as if I had not seen my hostess before; she is the last maker of muster-gingerbread, and before I came away I was kindly measured for a pair of mittens.

"You'll be sure to come an' see them two peach-trees after I get 'em well growin'?" Mrs. Goodsoe called after me when I had said good-by, and was almost out of hearing down the road.

Elizabeth Cady Stanton was born in 1815, the third of five daughters, in Johnstown, New York. Her father, Judge Cady, was frankly disappointed that his wife had borne him only one male child; however, he managed to satisfy his desire for sons by taking a series of young men into his law office to study for the bar. Several of these students married Cady daughters, and it is clear that at least one of them, Edward Bayard, had a marked influence on Elizabeth Cady, although he in fact chose to marry her older sister. Bayard took it upon himself to introduce his young sister-in-law to liberal theology —she had been raised a Calvinist and as an adolescent had suffered the tortures of the unconverted—and at the same time (although perhaps less consciously) he and his fellow students managed to impress on her just how unequal women were in the eyes of the law.

Educated at the local academy and at Emma Willard's seminary, Elizabeth Cady fell in love with the eloquent abolitionist Henry Stanton and, over her father's protest, married him. The first years of their marriage were spent in Boston where the new Mrs. Stanton threw her energies into scientific housekeeping and lecture going. But in the belief that the raw ocean air was injuring Mr. Stanton's health, they moved back to upstate New York, this time to Seneca Falls. There, far from her reform-minded friends, and responsible for a family of seven children, Elizabeth Cady Stanton decided on a career. The humiliation she and the other American women had experienced in 1840 when they were refused seats on the main floor of the World Anti-Slavery Convention and thus deprived of their votes, her knowledge of the legal injustices done her sex, and her sense of claustrophobia with no one but children to talk to, came together in her growing determination to call a women's rights convention at Seneca Falls in 1848.

Her friendship with Susan B. Anthony did not really begin until the early 1850s, but from then on they were a team, Mrs. Stanton doing the writing and Miss Anthony the organizing. After several years spent assuring her co-worker that their lives would only begin at fifty, Mrs. Stanton at last was able to disentangle herself from her family obligations and to devote full time to the cause of women's rights, often speaking on the lyceum circuit seven or eight months at a stretch. Never able to convince herself that the vote was a panacea, Mrs. Stanton insisted on the broadest possible platform for the woman's movement. She championed liberalized divorce laws, attacked the literal-mindedness of the clergy, and the venal orthodoxy of physicians. She believed in the legal equality of the sexes, but was open to the possibility that women might in fact be superior—not in a narrowly moral way, but insofar as their maternal instincts were the source of all that was known as civilization.

Mrs. Stanton wrote voluminously, largely speeches and articles, but her most significant contribution to feminist literature was probably not her observations about the position of women, the past existence of a matriarchate, or the follies of taking the Bible literally, but her own recollections, published in *Eighty Years and More* and her collected diary and letters. Mrs. Stanton died in 1902, dissatisfied by the "politic" rhetoric of the official suffrage movement in America, but relishing the passionate impatience of younger women, women like her own daughter Harriot Stanton Blatch, who seemed as unwilling as she had always been to limit themselves to well-bred requests for the vote.

Reminiscences, Elizabeth Cady Stanton*

With several generations of vigorous, enterprising ancestors behind me, I commenced the struggle of life under favorable circumstances on the twelfth day of November, 1815, the same year that my father, Daniel Cady, a distinguished lawyer and judge in the state of New York, was elected to Congress. Perhaps the excitement of a political campaign, in which my mother took the deepest interest, may have had an influence on my life and given me the strong desire that I have always felt to participate in the rights and duties of government.

My father was a man of firm character and unimpeachable integrity, and yet sensitive and modest to a painful degree. There were but two places in which he felt at ease—in the courthouse and at his own fireside. Though gentle and tender, he had such a dignified repose and reserve of manner that, as children, we regarded him with fear rather than affection.

My mother, Margaret Livingston, a tall, queenly looking woman, was courageous, self-reliant, and at her ease under all circumstances and in all places. She was the daughter of Colonel James Livingston, who took an active part in the war of the Revolution. . . .

The first event engraved on my memory was the birth of a sister when I was four years old. It was a cold morning in January when the brawny Scotch nurse carried me to see the little stranger, whose advent was a matter of intense interest to me for many weeks after. The large, pleasant room with the

* Mrs. Stanton's reminiscences, which originally appeared in 1898 with the title *Eighty Years and More*, together with her diary and collected letters, were published in a two-volume work, *Elizabeth Cady Stanton*, by her son and daughter in New York in 1922.

white curtains and bright wood fire on the hearth, where panada, catnip, and all kinds of little messes which we were allowed to taste were kept warm, was the center of attraction for the older children. I heard so many friends remark, "What a pity it is she's a girl!" that I felt a kind of compassion for the little baby. . . .

I am told that I was pensively looking out of the nursery window one day when Mary Dunn, the Scotch nurse, who was something of a philosopher, and a stern Presbyterian, said: "Child, what are you thinking about; are you planning some new form of mischief?" "No, Mary," I replied, "I was wondering why it was that everything we like to do is a sin, and that everything we dislike is commanded by God or some one on earth. I am so tired of that everlasting no! no! no! At school, at home, everywhere it is 'no'! Even at church all the commandments begin 'Thou shalt not.' I suppose God will say 'no' to all we like in the next world, just as you do here." Mary was dreadfully shocked at my dissatisfaction with the things of time and prospective eternity, and exhorted me to cultivate the virtues of obedience and humility. . . .

I have a confused memory of being often under punishment for what in those days were called "tantrums." I suppose they were really justifiable acts of rebellion against the tyranny of those in authority. I have often listened since, with real satisfaction, to what some of our friends had to say of the high-handed manner in which sister Margaret and I defied all the transient orders and strict rules laid down for our guidance. If we had observed them we might as well have been embalmed as mummies, for all the pleasure and freedom we should have had in our childhood. As very little was then done for the amusement of children, happy were those who conscientiously took the liberty of amusing themselves. . . .

When I was eleven years old two events occurred which changed the current of my life. My only brother, who had just graduated from Union College, came home to die. A young man of great talent and promise, he was the pride of my father's heart. We early felt that his son filled a larger place in our father's affections and future plans than the five daughters together. Well do I remember how tenderly he watched my brother in his last illness, the sighs and tears he gave vent to as he slowly walked up and down the hall, and, when the last sad moment came, and we were all assembled to say farewell in the silent chamber of death, how broken were his utterances as he knelt and prayed for comfort and support. I still recall, too, going into the large darkened parlor to see my brother, and finding the casket, mirrors, and pictures all draped in white, and my father seated by his side, pale, immovable. As he took no notice of me, after standing a long while, I climbed upon his knee, when he mechanically put his arm about me and, with my head resting against his beating heart, we both sat in silence, he thinking of the wreck of all his hopes in the loss of a dear son, and I wondering what could be said or done to fill the void in his breast. At length he heaved a deep sigh and said: "Oh, my daughter, would that you were a boy!"

Then and there I resolved that I would not give so much time as heretofore to play, but would study and strive to be at the head of all my classes and thus delight my father's heart. All that day and far into the night I pondered the problem of boyhood. I thought that the chief thing to be done in order to equal boys was to be learned and courageous. So I decided to study Greek and learn to manage a horse. Having formed this conclusion I fell asleep. My resolutions, unlike many such made at night, did not vanish with the coming dawn. I arose early and hastened to put them into execution. They were resolutions never to be forgotten—destined to mold my character anew. As soon as I was dressed I hastened to our good pastor, Simon Hosack, who was always early at work in his garden.

"Doctor," said I, "which do you like best, boys or girls?"

"Why, girls, to be sure; I would not give you [one girl] for all the boys in Christendom."

"My father," I replied, "prefers boys; he wishes I was one, and I intend to be as near like one as possible. I am going to ride on horseback and study Greek. Will you give me a Greek lesson now? I want to begin at once."

"Yes, child," said he throwing down his hoe. "Come into my library and we will begin without delay."

He entered fully into the feeling of suffering and sorrow which took possession of me when I discovered that a girl weighed less in the scale of being than a boy, and he praised my determination to prove the contrary. The old grammar which he had studied in the University of Glasgow was soon in my hands, and the Greek article was learned before breakfast.

Then came the sad pageantry of death; the weeping of friends, the dark rooms, the ghostly stillness, the exhortation to the living to prepare for death, the solemn prayer, the mournful chant, the funeral cortege, the solemn, tolling bell, the burial. How I suffered during those sad days! What strange undefined fears of the unknown took possession of me! For months afterward, at the twilight hour, I went with my father to the new-made grave. Near it stood two tall poplar trees, against one of which I leaned, while my father threw himself on the grave with outstretched arms, as if to embrace his child. At last the frosts and storms of November came and threw a chilling barrier between the living and the dead, and we went there no more.

During all this time I kept up my lessons at the parsonage, and made rapid progress. I surprised even my teacher, who thought me capable of doing anything. I learned to drive, and to leap a fence and ditch on horseback. I taxed every power, hoping some day to hear my father say, "Well, a girl is as good as a boy, after all." But he never said it. When the doctor came over to spend the evening with us I would whisper in his ear, "Tell my father how fast I get on," and he would tell him, and was lavish in his praises. But my father only paced the room, sighed, and showed that he wished I were a boy; and I, not knowing why he felt thus, would hide my tears of vexation on the doctor's shoulder.

Soon after this I began to study Latin, Greek, and mathematics with a class of boys in the village academy, many of whom were much older than I. For three years one boy kept his place at the head of the class, and I always stood next. Two prizes were offered in Greek. I strove for one, and took the second. How well I remember my joy in receiving that prize. There was no sentiment of ambition, rivalry, or triumph over my companions, nor feeling of satisfaction in receiving this honor in the presence of those assembled on the day of the exhibition. One thought alone filled my mind. "Now," said I, "my father will be satisfied with me." So, as soon as we were dismissed, I ran down the hill, rushed breathless into his office, laid the Greek Testament, which was my prize, on his table and exclaimed: "There, I got it!" He took up the book, asked me some questions about the class, the teachers, the spectators, and, evidently pleased, handed it back to me. Then, while I stood looking and waiting for him to say something which would show that he recognized the equality of the daughter with the son, he kissed me on the forehead and exclaimed, with a sigh, "Ah, you should have been a boy!" . . .

I can truly say that all the cares and anxieties, the trials and disappointments of my whole life, are light, when balanced with my sufferings in childhood and youth from the theological dogmas which I sincerely believed, and the gloom connected with everything associated with the name of religion, the church, the graveyard, and the solemn, tolling bell. Everything connected with death was then rendered inexpressibly dolorous. The body, covered with a black pall, was borne on the shoulders of men; the mourners were in crape and walked with bowed heads, while the neighbors who had tears to shed did so copiously, and summoned up their saddest facial expressions. At the grave came the sober warnings to the living, and sometimes frightful prophesies as to the state of the dead. All this pageantry of woe and visions of the unknown land beyond the tomb, often haunted my midnight dreams and shadowed the sunshine of my days.

The church, which was bare, with no furnace to warm us, no organ to gladden our hearts, no choir to lead our songs of praise in harmony, was sadly lacking in all attractions for the youthful mind. The preacher, even when my gentle friend Simon Hosack, shut up in an octagonal box high above our heads, gave us sermons over an hour long, and the chorister, in a similar box below him, intoned line after line of David's Psalms, while, like a flock of sheep at the heels of their shepherd, the congregation, without regard to time or tune, straggled after their leader.

Years later, the introduction of stoves, a violoncello, Wesley's hymns, and a choir, split the church in twain. These old Scotch Presbyterians were opposed to all innovations. So, when the thermometer was twenty degrees below zero on the Johnstown Hills, four hundred feet above the Mohawk Valley, we trudged along through the snow, foot-stoves in hand, to the cold hospitalities of the Lord's House, there to be chilled to the very core by listening to sermons on predestination, justification by faith, and eternal damnation. . . .

As my father's office joined the house, I spent there much of my time, when out of school, listening to the clients stating their cases, talking with the students, and reading the laws in regard to woman. In our Scotch neighborhood many men still retained the old feudal ideas of women and property. Fathers, at their death, would will the bulk of their property to the eldest son, with the proviso that the mother was to have a home with him. Hence, it was not unusual for the mother, who had brought all the property into the family, to be made an unhappy dependent on the bounty of an uncongenial daughter-in-law and a dissipated son. The tears and complaints of the women who came to my father for legal advice touched my heart, and early drew my attention to the injustice and cruelty of the laws. As the practice of the law was my father's business, I could not exactly understand why he could not alleviate the sufferings of these women. So, in order to enlighten me, he would take down his books and show me the inexorable statutes. The students, observing my interest, would amuse themselves by reading to us all the worst laws they could find, over which I would laugh and cry by turns. One Christmas morning I ran into the office to show them my present of a coral necklace and bracelet. They all admired the jewelry, and then began to tease me with hypothetical cases of future ownership. "Now," said Henry Bayard, "if in due time you should be my wife, those ornaments would be mine. I could take them and lock them up, and you could never wear them except with my permission. I could even exchange them for a cigar, and you could watch them evaporate in smoke."

With this constant bantering from students, and the sad complaints of women clients, my mind was sorely perplexed. So when, from time to time, my attention was called to these odious laws, I would mark them with a pencil, and becoming more and more convinced of the necessity of taking some active measures against these unjust provisions, I resolved to seize the first opportunity, when alone in the office, to cut every one of them out of the books; supposing my father and his library were the beginning and the end of the law. However, this mutilation of his volumes was never accomplished, for dear old Flora Campbell, to whom I confided my plan for the amelioration of her wrongs, warned my father of what I proposed to do. Without letting me know that he had discovered my secret, he explained to me one evening how laws were made, the large number of lawyers and libraries there were all over the state, and that if his library should burn up it would make no difference in woman's condition. "When you are grown up, and able to prepare a speech," said he, "you must go down to Albany and talk to the legislators; tell them all you have seen in this office—the sufferings of these Scotchwomen, robbed of their inheritance and left dependent on their unworthy sons, and, if you can persuade them to pass new laws, the old ones will be a dead letter." Thus was the future object of my life suggested and my duty plainly outlined by him who was most opposed to my public career when, in due time, it was entered upon. . . .

The next happening in Troy* that seriously influenced my character was the advent of the Rev. Charles G. Finney, a pulpit orator, who, as a terrifier of human souls, proved himself the equal of Savonarola. He held a protracted meeting, which many of my schoolmates attended. We were at all the public services beside the daily prayer and experience meetings held in the seminary. Our studies, for the time, held a subordinate place to the more important duty of saving our souls. The result of six weeks of untiring effort on the part of Mr. Finney and his confreres was one of those intense revival seasons that swept over the city and through the seminary like an epidemic, attacking in its worst form the most susceptible. Owing to my gloomy Calvinistic training in the old Scotch Presbyterian Church, and my vivid imagination, I was one of the first victims.

The revival fairly started, the most excitable were soon on the anxious seat. There we learned the total depravity of human nature, and the sinner's awful danger of everlasting punishment. This was enlarged upon until the most innocent girl believed herself a monster of iniquity, and felt certain of eternal damnation. Then God's hatred of sin was emphasized, and his irreconcilable position toward the sinner so justified that one felt like a miserable, helpless, forsaken worm of the dust in trying to approach him, even in prayer. Having brought you into a condition of profound humility, the only cardinal virtue for one under conviction, in the depths of your despair you were told that it required no herculean effort on your part to be transformed into an angel, to be reconciled to God, to escape endless perdition. The way to salvation was short and simple. We had naught to do but to repent and believe and give our hearts to Jesus, who was ever ready to receive them. How to do all this was the puzzling question.

With the natural reaction from despair to hope, many of us imagined ourselves converted, prayed and gave our experiences in the meetings, and at times rejoiced in the thought

* At this time Elizabeth Cady was a student at Emma Willard, a female academy in Troy, New York.

that we were Christians—chosen children of God—rather than sinners and outcasts.

But Doctor Finney's terrible anathemas on the depravity and deceitfulness of the human heart soon shortened our new-born hopes. His appearance in the pulpit on these memorable occasions is indelibly impressed on my mind. I can see him now, his great eyes rolling around and his arms flying about in the air like a windmill. One evening he described hell and the devil and the long procession of sinners being swept down the rapids, about to make the awful plunge into the burning depths of liquid fire below, and the rejoicing hosts in the inferno coming up to meet them, with the shouts of the devils echoing through the vaulted arches. He suddenly halted, and, pointing his index finger at the supposed procession, he exclaimed:

"There, do you not see them?"

I was wrought up to such a pitch that I actually jumped up and gazed in the direction to which he pointed, while the picture glowed before my eyes and remained with me for months afterwards. I cannot forbear saying that, although high respect is due to the intellectual, moral, and spiritual gifts of the venerable ex-president of Oberlin College, such preaching worked incalculable harm to the very soul he sought to save. Fear of the Judgment seized my soul. Visions of the lost haunted my dreams. Mental anguish prostrated my health. Returning home, I often at night roused my father from his slumbers to pray for me lest I should be cast into the bottomless pit before morning.

To change the current of my thoughts a trip was planned to Niagara, and it was decided that the subject of religion was to be tabooed altogether. Accordingly, our party, consisting of my sister, her husband, Edward Bayard, my father, and myself, started in our private carriage, and for six weeks I heard nothing on the subject. My religious superstitions gave place to rational ideas based on scientific facts, and in proportion, as I looked at everything from a new standpoint, I grew more and more happy, day by day. Thus, with a delightful journey and entire change in the current of my thoughts, my mind was restored to its normal condition. I view it as one of the greatest crimes to shadow the minds of the young with these gloomy superstitions, and with fears of the unknown and the unknowable to poison all their joy in life.

After the restraint of childhood at home and in school, what a period of irrepressible joy and freedom comes to us in girlhood with the first taste of liberty. Then is our individuality in a measure recognized, and our feelings and opinions consulted; then we decide where and when we will come and go, what we will eat, drink, wear, and do. To suit one's own fancy in clothes, to buy what one likes, and wear what one chooses, is a great privilege to most young people. To go out at pleasure, to walk, to ride, to drive, with no one to say us nay or question our right to liberty, this is indeed like a birth into a new world of happiness and freedom.

This is the period too, when the emotions rule us, and we idealize everything in life. Then comes that dream of bliss that throws a halo of glory around the most ordinary characters in everyday life, holding the strongest and most common-sense young men and women in a thraldom from which few mortals escape—the period when love, in soft silver tones, whispers his first words of adoration. What dignity it adds to a young girl's estimate of herself when some man makes her feel that in her hands rest his future peace and happiness! Though these seasons of intoxication may come once to all, they are seldom repeated. How often in after-life we long for one more such rapturous dream of bliss, one more season of supreme love and passion!

After leaving school, until my marriage, I had the most pleasant years of my girlhood. With frequent visits to a large circle of friends and relatives in various towns and cities, the monotony of home life was sufficiently broken to make our simple country pleasures always delightful and enjoyable. An entirely new life now opened to me. The old bondage of fear of the visible and the invisible was broken, and, no longer subject to absolute authority, I rejoiced in the dawn of a new day of freedom in thought and action. . . .

Part of the time Margaret Christie, a young girl of Scotch descent, was a member of our family circle. She taught us French and music. Our days were too short for all we had to do, for our time was not wholly given to pleasure. We were required to keep our rooms in order, mend and make our clothes, and do our own ironing. The latter was one of my mother's politic requirements, to make our laundry lists as short as possible. Ironing on hot days in summer was a sore trial to all of us; but Miss Christie, being of an inventive turn of mind, soon taught us a short way out of it. She folded and smoothed her undergarments with her hands, and then sat on them for a specified time. We all followed her example and thus utilized the hours devoted to reading *Corinne* and *Telemaque* in this primitive style of ironing our clothes. But for dresses, collars and cuffs, and pocket handkerchiefs, we were compelled to wield the hot iron; hence with these articles we used all due economy, and my mother's object was thus accomplished. . . .

The puzzling questions of theology and poverty that had occupied so much of my thoughts now gave place to the practical one, "What to do with a baby?" Though motherhood is the most important of all the professions—requiring more knowledge than any other department in human affairs—there was no attention given to preparation for this office. If we buy a plant of a horticulturist we ask him many questions as to its needs, whether it thrives best in sunshine or in shade, whether it needs much or little water, what degrees of heat or cold; but when we hold in our arms for the first time a being of infinite possibilities, in whose wisdom may rest the destiny of a nation, we take it for granted that the laws governing its life, health, and happiness are intuitively understood, that there is nothing new to be learned in regard to it. Here is a science to which philosophers have as yet given but little attention. An important fact has only been discovered and acted upon within the last ten years; that children come into the world tired, and not hungry, exhausted with the perilous journey. Instead of being kept on the rack while the nurse makes a prolonged toilet and feeds it some nostrum supposed to have much-needed medicinal influence, the child's face, eyes, and mouth should be carefully washed, and the rest of its body thoroughly oiled, and then it should be slipped into a soft pillow case, wrapped in a blanket, and laid to sleep. Ordinarily, in the proper conditions, with its face uncovered in a cool, pure atmosphere, it will sleep twelve hours. Then it should be bathed, fed, and clothed in a high-neck, long-sleeved silk shirt and a blanket. As babies lie still most of the time for the first six weeks, they need no elaborate dressing. I think the nurse was a full hour bathing and dressing my first-born, who protested with a melancholy wail every blessed minute.

Ignorant myself of the initiative steps on the threshold of time, I supposed this proceeding was approved by the best authorities. However, I had been thinking, reading, observing, and had as little faith in the popular theories in regard to babies as on any other subject. I saw them, on all sides, ill half the time, pale and peevish, dying early, having no joy in life. I heard parents complaining of weary days and sleepless nights, while each child in turn ran the gauntlet of red gum, whooping cough, chicken pox, mumps, measles, and fits. Everyone seemed to think these inflictions were a part of the eternal plan—that Providence had a kind of Pandora's box, from which he scattered these venerable diseases most liberally among those whom he especially loved. Having gone through the ordeal of bearing a child, I was determined, if possible, to keep him, so I read everything I could find on babies. But the literature on this subject was as confusing and unsatisfactory as the longer and shorter catechism and the Thirty-nine Articles of our faith. I had recently visited our dear friends, Theodore and Angeline Grimké-Weld, and they warned me against books on this subject. They had been so misled by one author, who assured them that the stomach of a child could only hold one tablespoonful, that they nearly starved their first-born to death. Though the child dwindled day by day, and, at the end of a month looked like a little old man, yet they still stood by the distinguished author.

Fortunately, they both went off one day and left the child with "Sister Sarah," who thought she would make an experiment and see what a child's stomach could hold, as she had grave doubts about the tablespoonful theory. To her surprise the baby took a pint bottle full of milk, and had the sweetest sleep thereon he had known in his earthly career. After that he was permitted to take what he wanted, and "the author" was informed of his libel on the infantile stomach. . . .

Mrs. Oliver Johnson and I spent two days at the Brook Farm Community when in the height of its prosperity. There I met the Ripleys—who were, I believe, the backbone of the experiment—William Henry Channing, Bronson Alcott, Charles A. Dana, Frederick Cabot, William Chase, Mrs. Horace Greeley, who was spending a few days there, and many others, whose names I cannot recall. Here was a charming family of intelligent men and women, doing their own farm and house work, with lectures, readings, music, dancing, and games when desired. The story of the beginning and end of this experiment of community life has been told so often that I will simply say that its failure was a grave disappointment to those most deeply interested in its success. Mr. Channing told me, years after, when he was pastor of the Unitarian church in Rochester that, when the Roxbury community was dissolved, and he was obliged to return to the old life of competition, he would gladly have been laid under the sod, as the isolated home seemed so solitary, silent, and selfish. . . .

My second son was born in Albany, in March, 1844, under more favorable auspices than the first, as I knew then what to do with a baby. Returning to Chelsea we commenced housekeeping, which afforded me another chapter of experience. A new house, newly furnished, with beautiful views of Boston Bay, was all I could desire. Mr. Stanton announced to me, in starting, that his business would occupy all his time, and that I must take entire charge of the housekeeping. So, with two good servants, and two babies under my sole supervision, my time was pleasantly occupied.

When first installed as mistress over an establishment, one has that same feeling of pride and satisfaction that a young minister must have in taking charge of his first congregation. It is a proud moment in a woman's life to reign supreme within four walls, to be the one to whom all questions of domestic pleasure and economy are referred, and to hold in her hand that little family book in which the daily expenses, the outgoings and incomings, are duly registered. I studied up everything pertaining to housekeeping, and enjoyed it all. Even washing day—that day so many people dread—had its charms for me. The clean clothes on the lines and on the grass looked so white, and smelled so sweet, that it was to me a pretty sight to contemplate. I inspired my laundress with an ambition to have her clothes look white and to get them out earlier than our neighbors, and to have them ironed and put away sooner.

As Mr. Stanton did not come home to dinner, we made a picnic of our noon meal on Mondays, and all thoughts and energies were turned to speed the washing. No unnecessary sweeping or dusting, no visiting nor "entertaining angels unawares" on that day—it was held sacred to soap suds, blue-bags, and clotheslines. The children, only, had no deviation in the regularity of their lives. They had their drives and walks, their naps and rations, in quantity and time, as usual. I had all the most approved cookbooks, and spent time preserving, pickling, and experimenting in new dishes. I felt the same ambition to excel in all departments of the culinary art that I did at school in the different branches of learning. My love of order and cleanliness was carried throughout, from parlor to kitchen, from the front door to the back. I gave a man an extra shilling to pile the logs of firewood with their smooth ends outward, though I did not have them scoured white, as did my Dutch grandmother. I tried, too, to give an artistic touch to everything—the dress of my children and servants included. My dining table was round, always covered with a clean cloth of a pretty pattern and a centerpiece of flowers in their season, pretty dishes, clean silver, and set with neatness and care. I put my soul into everything, and hence enjoyed it. I never could understand how housekeepers could rest with rubbish all round their back doors; eggshells, broken dishes, tin cans, and old shoes scattered round their premises; servants ragged and dirty, with their hair in papers, and with the kitchen and dining room full of flies. I have known even artists to be indifferent to their personal appearance and their surroundings. Surely a mother and child, tastefully dressed, and a pretty home for a framework, is, as a picture, even more attractive than a domestic scene hung on the wall. The love of the beautiful can be illustrated as well in life as on canvas. There is such a struggle among women to become artists that I really wish some of their gifts could be illustrated in clean, orderly, beautiful homes. . . .

In 1846 we moved to Seneca Falls. Here we spent sixteen years of our married life, and here our other children—two sons and two daughters—were born.

I was already acquainted with many of the people and the surroundings in Seneca Falls, as my sister, Mrs. Bayard, had lived there several years, and I had frequently made her long visits. We had quite a magnetic circle of reformers, too, in Central New York. At Rochester were William Henry Channing, Frederick Douglas [sic], the Posts, Hallowells, Stebbins, old Quaker families at Farmington; the Mays, Sedgwicks, and Mills at Syracuse; Gerrit Smith at Peterboro, and Beriah Green at Whitesboro.

The house we were to occupy had been closed for some years, and needed many repairs, and the grounds, comprising five acres, were overgrown with weeds. My father gave me a check and said with a smile, "You believe in woman's capacity to do and dare; now go ahead and put your place in order." After a minute survey of the premises, and due consultation with one or two sons of Adam, I set the carpenters, painters, paperhangers, and gardeners at work, built a new kitchen and woodhouse, and in one month took possession. Having left my children with my mother, there were no impediments to a full display of my executive ability. In the purchase of brick, timber, paint, etc., and in making bargains with workmen, I was in frequent consultation with my neighbors, Judge Sackett and Mr. Bascom. The latter was a member of the Constitutional Convention, then in session in Albany, and as he used to walk down whenever he was at home to see how my work progressed, we had long talks, sitting on boxes in the midst of tools and shavings, on the status of women. I urged him to propose an amendment to Article II, Section 3, of the State Constitution, striking out the word "male," which limits the suffrage to men. But, while he fully agreed with all I had to say on the political equality of women, he had not the courage to "make himself the laughingstock" of the convention. Whenever I cornered him on this point, manlike he turned the conversation to the painters and carpenters. However, these conversations had the effect of bringing him into the first woman's convention, where he did us good service.

In Seneca Falls my life was comparatively solitary, and the change from Boston was somewhat depressing. There, all my immediate friends were reformers. I had near neighbors, a new house with all the modern conveniences, and well-trained servants. Here, our residence was on the outskirts of the town, roads were often muddy and no sidewalks most of the way, Mr. Stanton was frequently from home, I had poor servants and an increasing number of children. To keep a house and grounds in good order, purchase every article for daily use, keep the wardrobes of half a dozen human beings in proper trim, take the children to dentists, shoemakers, and different schools, or find teachers at home, altogether made sufficient work to keep one brain busy, as well as all the hands I could impress into the service. Then, too, the novelty of housekeeping had passed away, and much that was once attractive in domestic life was now irksome.

There was an Irish settlement at a short distance, and continual complaints were coming to me that my boys threw stones at their pigs, cows, and the roofs of their houses. This involved constant diplomatic relations in the settlement of various difficulties, in which I was so successful that at length they constituted me a kind of umpire in all their own quarrels. If a drunken husband was pounding his wife the children would run for me. Hastening to the scene of action, I would take Patrick by the collar, and, much to his surprise and shame, make him sit down and promise to behave himself. I never had one of them offer me the least resistance, and in time they all came to regard me as one having authority. I strengthened my influence by cultivating good feeling. I lent the men papers to read, and invited their children into our grounds, giving them fruit, of which we had abundance, and my children's old clothes, books, and toys. I was their physician, also—with my box of homeopathic medicines I took charge of the men, women, and children in sickness. Thus the most amiable relations were established, and, in any emergency, these poor neighbors were good friends and always ready to serve me.

But I found police duty rather irksome, especially when called out dark nights to prevent drunken fathers from disturbing their sleeping children, or to minister to poor mothers in the pangs of maternity. Alas! alas! who can measure the mountains of sorrow and suffering endured in unwelcome motherhood in the abodes of ignorance, poverty, and vice, where terror-stricken women and children are the victims of strong men frenzied with passion and intoxicating drink?

Up to this time life had glided by with comparative ease, but now the real struggle was upon me. My duties were too numerous and varied, and none sufficiently exhilarating or intellectual to bring into play my higher faculties. I suffered with mental hunger, which, like an empty stomach, is very depressing. I had books, but no stimulating companionship. To add to my general dissatisfaction at the change from Boston, I found that Seneca Falls was a malarial region, and in due time all the children were attacked with chills and fever. The servants were afflicted in the same way. The love of order and the beautiful and artistic all seemed fading away in the struggle to accomplish what was absolutely necessary from hour to hour.

I now fully understood the practical difficulties most women had to contend with in the isolated household, and the impossibility of woman's best development if in contact, the chief part of her life, with servants and children. Fourier's phalansterie community life and co-operative household had a new significance for me. Emerson says, "A healthy discontent is the first step to progress." The general discontent I felt with woman's portion as wife, mother, housekeeper, physician, and spiritual guide, the chaotic conditions into which everything fell without her constant supervision, and the wearied, anxious look of the majority of women impressed me with a strong feeling that some active measures should be taken to remedy the wrongs of society in general, and of women in particular. My experience at the World's Antislavery Convention, all I had read of the legal status of women, and the oppression I saw everywhere, together swept across my soul, intensified now by many personal experiences. It seemed as if all the elements had conspired to impel me to some onward step. I could not see what to do or where to begin—my only thought was a public meeting for protest and discussion.

In this tempest-tossed condition of mind I received an invitation to spend the day with Lucretia Mott, at Richard Hunt's, in Waterloo. There I met several members of different families of Friends, earnest, thoughtful women. I poured out the torrent of my long-accumulating discontent with such vehemence and indignation that I stirred myself, as well as the rest of the party, to do and dare anything. My discontent, according to Emerson, must have been healthy, for it moved us all to prompt action, and we decided, then and there, to call a "Woman's Rights Convention." We wrote the call that evening and published it in the Seneca County *Courier* the next day, the 14th of July, 1848, giving only five days' notice, as the convention was to be held on the 19th and 20th.

Elizabeth Cady Stanton, Letters*

Johnstown, *March 16, 1842*

Dear Henry [Stanton],—The baby's shoulder was bandaged both by Dr. Childs and Dr. Clark. But I thought their bandages were too severe and made the child uncomfortable; so, with my usual conceit, I removed both successfully and turned surgeon myself. I first rubbed the arm and shoulder well with arnica, then put a wet compress on the collar bone, some cotton batting rolled in linen under the arm, and over the shoulder two bands of linen, like suspenders, pinned to the belly band. This we removed night and morning, washed the shoulder with cold water and arnica and wet the compress anew. The surgeons pronounced my work all very good, and this morning the child is dressed for the first time in ten days. I did not write you about the bandaging until I felt sure I had done well. You know it is a great thing to impress husbands, as Susan Nipper did the devoted Toots, with the belief that their wives are indeed wonderful women!

Boston, *April 11, 1846*

Dear Mr. Whittier [John Greenleaf],—When I was in Edinburgh I bought one day a little volume because of its title, *Records of Woman.* It was by Mrs. Hemans. I took it up by chance this morning and read it for the first time. It is a charming series of poems all in honor of our sex. Mrs. Hemans—so I was told by some of her friends in her native city, Liverpool, whom I met the day before I sailed, and by

* From Theodore Stanton and Harriot Stanton Blatch, *Elizabeth Cady Stanton* (New York, 1922).

other friends in Dublin, where she lived the last years of her short life—had a great liking for our country. So I am not surprised to find in this volume many references to the United States. "Edith," which is described by its author as "A Tale of the Woods," is founded on incidents related in an American work, *Sketches of Connecticut,** written by I do not know whom. Henry, who, you remember, was born in Griswold in that state, would like to find out something about this book. Can you aid us, you who browse so much among dusty volumes? "Edith," by the way, contains a pretty song that ought to be set to music. "The Indian Woman's Death Song," which is not the one I refer to in the preceding sentence, has also an American setting, being based on facts found in Keating's "Narrative of an Expedition to the Source of St. Peter's River." But I confess I do not know just where this river is, though, judging from the name, it may be somewhere in the celestial regions. Speaking of this volume, Mrs. Hemans says: "I have put my heart and individual feelings into it more than in anything else I have written." However this may be, this little collection is a worthy contribution to high-minded womanhood from the pen of a brilliant poetess. How proud I am when I see one of my sex doing anything well; and I know you are too, which is the reason why I have called your attention to this book. Henry's best wishes with this, and mine too.

To George G. Cooper,
Editor of the *National Reformer,*
Rochester, New York.

Seneca Falls, *September 14, 1848*

Dear Sir,—There is no danger of the Woman Question dying for want of notice. Every paper you take up has something to say about it, and just in proportion to the refinement and intelligence of the editor has this movement

* *Sketch of Connecticut Forty Years Since* (1824), by Lydia Howard Sigourney (1791–1865), educator and author.

been favorably noticed. But one might suppose from the articles that you find in some papers, that there are editors so ignorant as to believe that the chief object of these recent conventions was to seat every lord at the foot of a cradle, and to clothe every woman in her lord's attire. Now neither of these points, however important they be considered by humble minds, was touched upon in the conventions. We did not meet to discuss fashions, customs, or dress, the rights of man or the propriety of the sexes changing positions, but simply our own inalienable rights, our duties, our true sphere. If God has assigned a sphere to man and one to woman, we claim the right ourselves to judge of His design in reference to us, and we accord to man the same privilege. We think that a man has quite enough to do to find out his own individual calling, without being taxed to find out also where every woman belongs. The fact that so many men fail in the business they undertake, calls loudly for their concentrating more thought on their own faculties, capabilities, and sphere of action. We have all seen a man making a failure in the pulpit, at the bar, or in our legislative halls, when he might have shone as a general in our Mexican war, as a captain of a canal boat or as a tailor on the bench. Now, is it to be wondered at that woman has doubts about the present position assigned her being the true one, when everyday experience shows us that man makes such fatal mistakes in regard to himself? There is no such thing as a sphere for sex. Every man has a different sphere, in which he may or may not shine, and it is the same with every woman, and the same woman may have a different sphere at different times. For example, the highly gifted Quakeress, Lucretia Mott, married early in life and brought up a large family of children. All who have seen her at home agree that she was a pattern as a wife, mother, and housekeeper. No one ever fulfilled all the duties of that sphere more perfectly than did she. Her children settled in their own homes, Lucretia Mott has now no domestic cares. She has a talent for public speaking. Her mind is of a high order, her moral perceptions remarkably clear, her religious fervor deep and intense; and who shall tell us that this divinely inspired woman is out of her sphere in her public endeavors to rouse this wicked nation to a sense of its awful guilt, to its great sins of war, slavery, injustice to woman, and to the laboring poor?

Seneca Falls, *April 2, 1852*

My Dear Friend [Susan B. Anthony],—I think you are doing up the temperance business just right. But do not let the conservative element control. For instance, you must take Mrs. Bloomer's suggestions with great caution, for she has not the spirit of the true reformer. At the first woman's rights convention, but four years ago, she stood aloof and laughed at us. It was only with great effort and patience that she has been brought up to her present position. In her paper, she will not speak against the fugitive slave law, nor in her work to put down intemperance will she criticize the equivocal position of the Church. She trusts to numbers to build up a cause rather than to principles, to the truth and the right. Fatal error! The history of the antislavery agitation is, on this point, a lesson to thinking minds. Among the abolitionists, the discussion began by some insisting on compromises in order to draw in numbers and bring over to them a large and respectable body of priests and rabbis. They also decided to turn the cold shoulder on woman's co-operation, as well as let the Church go unrebuked. Where now is that brilliant host in panoply so sacred and so respected? Gone back to learn anew the a, b, c, of the reformer. All this I say to you and to no one else, and you will understand why. I would not speak aught to injure Mrs. Bloomer. Yes, I repeat, beware of her conservative suggestions. We shall test the church people at our next annual meeting by getting up some strong resolutions touching upon this "brotherhood of thieves"—the slave-holding oligarchy of the South. The Church is a terrible engine of oppression, especially as concerns woman. I shall keep my Appeal in this connection as a text for my next speech. Oh, what a dose it will be at the end of the year!

I shall elaborate it and double distill it. Lord have mercy on those who gag in swallowing! By the way, you know many temperance advocates are prepared to carry this question into the churches. Shall our society lead or follow? I say, lead. Have you read Emerson's speech? If not, read it and note what he says of majorities. I will gladly do all in my power to aid you in getting up such a lecture as you desire. In due time I, as an individual, will speak to the women of the state. If my speech as it stands would serve you as a kind of skeleton for a lecture I will send it to you and you can fill out the heads more fully. In reference to "thinking on one's feet," I have no doubt that a little practice will render you an admirable lecturer. But you must dress loosely, take a great deal of exercise, be particular about your diet, and sleep enough. The body has great influence on the mind. If you are attacked in your meetings, be good-natured and keep cool; and if you are simple and truth-loving no sophistry can confound you. I have been re-reading the report of the London convention of 1840. How thoroughly humiliating it was to us! How I could have sat there quietly and listened to all that was said and done, I do not now understand. It is amazing that man can be so utterly unconscious of his brutality to woman. In the good time coming, what a cause of wonder it will be to recall the fact that the champions of freedom, the most progressive men of the nineteenth century, denied women the right of free speech in an antislavery convention, when, at the same time, they would have received with the greatest *eclat* the most degraded man from a rice plantation. If Sambo had been cast out of the convention for any reason, I wonder if Wendell Phillips and George Thompson would have coolly remarked on his discomfiture, "Well, he is as happy outside as in!" Men and angels give me patience! I am at the boiling point! If I do not find some day the use of my tongue on this question, I shall die of an intellectual repression, a woman's rights convulsion! Oh, Susan! Susan! Susan! You must manage to spend a week with me before the Rochester convention, for I am afraid that I cannot attend it; I have so much care with all these boys on my hands. But I will write a letter. How much I do long to be free from housekeeping and children, so as to have some time to read, and think, and write. But it may be well for me to understand all the trials of woman's lot, that I may more eloquently proclaim them when the time comes. Good night.

Seneca Falls, *October 22, 1852*

Dear Lucretia [Mott],—I am at length the happy mother of a daughter. I never felt such sacredness in carrying a child as I have in the case of this one. She is the largest and most vigorous baby I have ever had, weighing twelve pounds. And yet my labor was short and easy. I laid down about fifteen minutes, and alone with my nurse and one female friend brought forth this big girl. I sat up immediately, changed my own clothes, put on a wet bandage, and, after a few hours' repose, sat up again. Am I not almost a savage? For what refined, delicate, genteel, civilized woman would get well in so indecently short a time? Dear me, how much cruel bondage of mind and suffering of body poor woman will escape when she takes the liberty of being her own physician of both body and soul! I have been wishing to write you ever since the convention to say how pleased I was with the whole proceedings. As to the presidency, it is a matter of congratulation, and argues a great advance in our movement that we now have competitors for the office, when at our first convention no woman could be found with the moral hardihood to take that post of honor. I was greatly pleased too that a bloomer was the pet of the meeting. Depend upon it, Lucretia, that woman can never develop in her present drapery. She is a slave to her rags. But I cannot prove that to you now, for I must write about my daughter to a dozen other friends.

A Happy Mother.

Seneca Falls, *June 20, 1853*

Dear Liz [Elizabeth Smith Miller],—Having just finished breakfast, I leave house cares, children and everything to announce to you the melancholy fact that I am still in the flesh in this low, circumscribed and much abused sphere. And what is worse, I am coolly informed by physiologists on earth and by disembodied spirits who are supposed to be in heaven, but who come to us through our tables, that I shall probably remain here to suffer and struggle for about half a century longer—barring accidents and God being willing. That is to say, it appears that my machinery is capable of running a long time. Of course I may burst my boiler screaming to boys to come out of the cherry trees and to stop throwing stones, or explode from accumulated steam of a moral kind that I dare not let off, or be hung for breaking the pate of some stupid Hibernian for burning my meat or pudding on some company occasion. My babies, the boys and these Irish girls, as well as the generally unsettled condition of the moral, religious, and political world, are enough to fret to pieces the best constructed machinery. Some days I feel a general giving away, but I find that a new sun brings me fresh courage and vigor. It is a great comfort to know that the children are now all well. Seated on my front piazza in a big chair, listening to the birds and all the pleasant summer sounds, alternately thinking and reading, I have been enjoying Mrs. Child's sketch of Madame de Staël. What a magnificent creature that mortal was! How I do love that woman! It is seldom we see the intellectual and affectional natures so harmoniously developed as in her. In the midst of all her triumphs, she sighed for love. How we mortals cheat ourselves out of our birthright; how few ever taste the blessedness of loving, nobly, generously, passionately. In a word, how little we cultivate love, that sentiment which is the highest heaven, and can make a paradise on earth. Have you, dear Liz, lived long enough to enjoy solitude, to look upon a few hours of uninterrupted quiet as a precious feast for the soul, to look for it and long for it as an epicure does for his dinner? If not, you are yet to live. With age comes the inner, the higher life. Who would be forever young, to dwell always in externals?

Seneca Falls, *February 15, 1855*

Dear Susan [Anthony],—I have just been engaged to lecture before the Teachers' Association of this country. Two weeks from Wednesday is the appointed time. My fee is to be $10. I am now absorbed in the subject of education, teachers, visiting committees, scholars, school houses, etc., etc. Pray the gods that I may do well. I have my Rochester and Waterloo lectures blocked out. But oh! I ought to read and think so much. But the days are so short, and the nights too; I live by sleep. If with my brain I had a nervous temperament, I could accomplish so much. But then I would die soon. As soon as you all begin to ask too much of me, I shall have a baby! Now, be careful; do not provoke me to that step. An article for the *Tribune* which I sent Henry three weeks ago, he returns to me to-day for revision and correction. I shall send no more to him for criticism; husbands are too critical. Henceforth, they shall go direct to Greeley, fresh from my brain. I am vexed. Good night.

Peterboro, *September 10, 1855*

Dear Susan,—I wish that I were as free as you and I would stump the state in a twinkling. But I am not, and what is more, I passed through a terrible scourging when last at my father's. I cannot tell you how deep the iron entered my soul. I never felt more keenly the degradation of my sex. To think that all in me of which my father would have felt a proper pride had I been a man, is deeply mortifying to him because I am a woman. That thought has stung me to a fierce decision—to speak as soon as I can do myself credit. But the pressure on me just now is too great. Henry sides with my friends, who oppose me in all that is dearest to my heart. They are not willing that I should write even on the woman question. But

I will both write and speak. I wish you to consider this letter strictly confidential. Sometimes, Susan, I struggle in deep waters. I have rewritten my "Indian," and given it into the hands of Oliver Johnson, who has promised to see it safely in the *Tribune*. I have sent him another article on the "Widow's Teaspoons," and I have mailed you one of mine which appeared in the Buffalo *Democracy*. I have sent six articles to the *Tribune*, and three have already appeared. I have promised to write for the *Una*. I read and write a good deal, as you see. But there are grievous interruptions. However, a good time is coming and my future is always bright and beautiful. Good night.

As ever your friend, sincere and steadfast.

Seneca Falls, *May 1, 1859*

Dear Mr. Higginson [Thomas Wentworth Higginson],— I think our friend's tirades on men are just in some respects and unjust in others. Theodore Parker, Garrison, Phillips, Gerrit Smith, and men of that kidney inspire me with love and respect for the sons of Adam. But alas! when we read the view of the average men, their laws, the literature which they father; when we listen to their every-day talk, to their decisions in the courts, to their sermons in the pulpit, and witness their actions at the fireside, then we feel that they richly deserve all that she says. So if that is her mission, let her attack Mrs. Craik and the door-mat theory. We need some one at that point, while our milder spirited supporters can occupy the middle ground, and go on making tender appeals to man's chivalry and sense of justice, while you and I run up and down the scale, always having a royal encounter on "the door-mat," singing with due asperity in the chorus hallelujas to single women, rebukes for spaniel wives, and reasonable denunciations for all flesh in male form. I may add in closing, that I think if women would indulge more freely in vituperation, they would enjoy ten times the health they do. It seems to me they are suffering from repression. Yours as ever, and with renewed admiration for your championship of my sex.

Seneca Falls, *December 23, 1859*

Dear Susan,—Where are you? Since a week ago last Monday, I have looked for you every day. I had the washing put off, we cooked a turkey, I made a pie in the morning, sent my first-born to the depot and put clean aprons on the children, but lo! you did not come. Nor did you soften the rough angles of our disappointment by one solitary line of excuse. And it would do me such great good to see some reformers just now. The death of my father, the worse than death of my dear Cousin Gerrit, the martyrdom of that grand and glorious John Brown—all this conspires to make me regret more than ever my dwarfed womanhood. In times like these, everyone should do the work of a full-grown man. When I pass the gate of the celestial city and good Peter asks me where I would sit, I shall say, "Anywhere, so that I am neither a negro nor a woman. Confer on me, good angel, the glory of white manhood so that henceforth, sitting or standing, rising up or lying down, I may enjoy the most unlimited freedom." Good night.

New Castle, Delaware, *April 1, 1872*

Dear Lucretia [Mott],—Since leaving you, I have thought much of Mrs. Woodhull and of all the gossip about her past, and have come to the conclusion that it is great impertinence in any of us to pry into her private affairs. To me there is a sacredness in individual experience which it seems like profanation to search into or expose. This woman stands before us to-day as an able speaker and writer. Her face, manners, and conversation all indicate the triumph of the moral, intellectual, and spiritual. The processes and localities of her education are little to us, but the result should be everything. Most women, who, like some tender flower, perish in the first rude blast, think there must be some subtle poison in the hardy plant which grows stronger and more beautiful in poor earth and rough exposure, where they would fall faded, withered, and bleeding to the ground. We have already women enough sacrificed to this sentimental, hypocritical prating about purity, without going out of our way to increase the number. Women have crucified the Mary Wollstonecrafts, the Fanny Wrights and the George Sands of all ages. Men mock us with the fact and say we are ever cruel to each other. Let us end this ignoble record and henceforth stand by womanhood. If this present woman must be crucified, let men drive the spikes.

Elizabeth Cady Stanton, Diary*

Tenafly, *February 22* [1881]

William F. Channing has made us a short visit, which I have enjoyed very much. We sat in the parlor and talked hour after hour on the dual humanity; of what men and women are to each other and what we can, would, and should give to each other. Susan attacked Mr. Channing the next morning in her blunt way, calling a spade a spade, permitting no mysticism, pinning him down most mercilessly with some plain questions. I went to his relief and silenced Susan's guns. Doctor Channing brought me a little poem on motherhood, which, however, I do not like as it expresses the old idea of maternity being a curse. I have come to the conclusion that the first great work to be accomplished for woman is to revolutionize the dogma that sex is a crime, marriage a defilement and maternity a bane.

Basingstoke, *September 6* [1883]

We were six ladies at dinner this evening. No men. We had a free and cheery time. Now and then it is a great relief for either sex to have a little occasion to themselves. I have been reading *Leaves of Grass*. Walt Whitman seems to understand everything in nature but woman. In "There is a Woman Waiting for Me," he speaks as if the female must be forced to the creative act, apparently ignorant of the great natural fact that a healthy woman has as much passion as a man, that she needs nothing stronger than the law of attraction to draw her to the male.

* From Theodore Stanton and Harriot Stanton Blatch, *Elizabeth Cady Stanton* (New York, 1922).

Basingstoke, *September 18*

To-day we gave a party to the wives of the old cottagers to try and interest them in a co-operative laundry Hattie wanted to give them. I talked to them on health, air, diet, and babies. I found, as usual, none of them gave their little ones water. They said they never knew that nurslings needed it. I also spoke to them of over-population. I think I made them clearly understand that so long as they filled their homes with infants their own conditions grew worse and worse with every generation. We offered them a nice supper, Hattie presented her plan, and Alice Blatch played some fine classical music, and then, as the twilight deepened, they returned to their isolated cottage homes. When one reflects on what might be accomplished by co-operation, it is pitiful to observe all our unnecessary miseries arising from competition, in the midst of which the finest and most spiritual natures are totally wrecked.

On Board the *Servia*,
At Sea, *November 22*

The sail from Liverpool to Queenstown was smooth and pleasant. We tarried there several hours. The harbor is beautiful. Crowds of gulls hovered over us. After taking on the U.S. mails, and many passengers, we sailed out for the broad ocean and then our sorrows began. Some blunder must have been made in the arrangement of the ballast, for the ship rolled beyond all endurance. Most of the passengers were sick. I was not; but as it was impossible to walk on deck, I was compelled to remain seated in the dining saloon. My reading during the voyage has been confined to Howells's works, a complete set of which was given to me by my children just as I left Basingstoke. It seems to me there is a lamentable want of common sense in all his women. They may be true to nature, but as it is nature under false conditions, I should rather have some pen portray the ideal woman, and paint a type worthy of our imitation.

Basingstoke, *January 12* [1887]

I have been busy getting off my promised letter to our next National Convention. I am devoting a paragraph to the question of "the ballot and the bullet." There is more than one way of fighting, and I am sure that woman's ingenuity will find means of rendering herself useful in case of a conflict. The recent evictions of Irish tenants on the immense estate of Lord Clanricarde, is an illustration in point. It appears that the women rendered active service in holding the enemy at bay by pouring scalding hot lime water on the heads of their assailants. If all the heroic deeds of women recorded in history and our daily journals have not yet convinced our opponents that women are possessed of superior fighting qualities, the sex may feel called upon in the near future—I see many signs of this even here in slow old England—to give some further examples of their prowess. Of one thing men may be assured, and that is, that the next generation will not argue the question of woman's rights with the infinite patience we have displayed during half a century.

New York, *May 18* [1893]

I am much worked up over the infamous Geary bill against the admission of the Chinese into the United States. How my blood boils over these persecutions of the Africans, the Jews, the Indians, and the Chinese. I suppose the Japanese will come next. I wonder if these fanatical Christians think that Christ died for these peoples, or confined his self-sacrifice to Saxons, French, Germans, Italians, etc.?

Thomaston, Long Island, *May 29* [1894]

I have just finished reading Mrs. Humphry Ward's *Marcella,* an interesting character study. I have much enjoyed the socialistic tendency of the book. When novels begin to take up a kindly consideration of the sociological and industrial problems, we may look for the dawn of a new day of human equality.

Thomaston, *July 4*

For the past month we have had strikes on the railroads running through Chicago. Never before have we had so great a one. A Mr. Debs seems to have inaugurated the movement. The strikers make many blunders. But as labor is never half paid, and those who do the hard work of the world are half clothed, half fed, and poorly sheltered, while those who neither toil nor spin enjoy all the good things of life, it is natural for the masses to occasionally ask why we have these extremes of riches and poverty. There must be something rotten in Denmark. My sympathies are with those who build our railroads, bridges, the mighty ships that plough the deep, our cathedrals, colleges, and palace homes, who raise our grains, vegetables, and fruits, and bring all we eat to our doors. Yes, the present conditions are not just and equal.*

New York, *January 20* [1895]

I have been busy for a week past writing a speech and resolutions for the annual woman suffrage convention to be held this year, not in Washington as has been our habit for twenty-seven years, but in a southern city—Atlanta, Georgia. Susan and Mrs. Chapman Catt have been holding meetings extensively throughout the South, and have aroused so much thought and even enthusiasm that it is expected that the Atlanta gathering will also be a great success. My speech is de-

---

* Late in August occurs this entry: "We have been watching with interest the aftermath of last month's lamentable strike. Well, these things must needs be until all the human race enjoy alike the fruits of their labor. We are perhaps in the midst of the industrial revolution. And see those stupid men in Congress talking against the income tax, one of the most just measures passed in a long time. Well, the time has come for labor to assert its rights. It is good that the working masses should now and then show their power and our dependence. I have just had an article in the *Sun* in which I recommend our friends to join the People's Party. If the

voted largely to the question of immigration, and I air my present belief in an educated suffrage open to men and women alike. My view ought to be well received in a southern city.

New York, *February 21*

Taking up the papers to-day, the first word that caught my eye thrilled my very soul. Frederick Douglass is dead! What memories of the long years since he and I first met chased each other, thick and fast, through my mind and held me spellbound. A graduate from the "Southern Institution," he was well fitted to stand before a Boston audience and, with his burning eloquence, portray his sufferings in the land of bondage. He stood there like an African prince, majestic in his wrath, as with wit, satire, and indignation he graphically described the bitterness of slavery and the humiliation of subjection to those who, in all human virtues and powers, were inferior to himself. Thus it was that I first saw Frederick Douglass, and wondered that any mortal man should have ever tried to subjugate a being with such talents, intensified with the love of liberty. Around him sat the great antislavery orators of the day, earnestly watching the effect of his eloquence on that immense audience, that laughed and wept by turns, completely carried away by the wondrous gifts of his pathos and humor. On this occasion, all the other speakers seemed tame after Frederick Douglass. In imitation of the Methodist preachers of the South, he used to deliver a sermon from the text, "Servants, obey your masters," which some of our literary critics pronounced the finest piece of satire in the English language. The last time I visited his home at Anacosta, near Washington, I asked him if he had the written text of that sermon. He answered, "No, not even notes of it." "Could you give it again?" I asked. "No," he replied; "or at least I could not bring back the old feelings even if I tried, the blessing of liberty I have so long enjoyed having almost obliterated the painful memories of my sad early days."

Prohibitionists, the Populists, the labor organizations and the women would all unite, we should be in the majority."

New York, *January 25* [1899]

I have been somewhat seriously indisposed of late. So a faith-curist gave me a treatment two nights ago. She placed her hands on my hands and knees alternately, and prayed aloud, suggesting to the Lord that I was a worthy child, etc. The next morning I did not see nor did I skip about. The faith-curist said: "The patient must have faith or the work cannot be accomplished." Then I sent for Dr. Caroline Cabot who plied me with beef tea, glycerine and whisky. I inhaled pine steam and took two kinds of pills in quick succession during all my waking hours. Finally she ordered a very hot bath. To-day I am as agile as a grasshopper. Who would believe that I am a homeopathist!

New York, *February 4*

As my eyes grow dimmer from day to day, my intellectual vision grows clearer. But I have written Susan not to lay out any more work for me, but to call on our younger coadjutor to write the letters to senators and congressmen. Say to them I write, that "it requires no courage now to talk suffrage; they should demand equality everywhere—*hoc opus, hic labor, est.*" So many of our followers think they do enough if they sing suffrage, which now calls down no ridicule or persecution. But the battle is not wholly fought until we stand equal in the church, the world of work, and have an equal code of moral for both sexes. Suffrage achieved in some places, we have thrown down the outposts to the land of liberty that lies still beyond. Now for new women, new measures, and the birth day of a new Republic. There are many phases of our question which have not yet been sufficiently studied, many strong holds of the enemy yet to be taken. We have battered away at the old ship of state until she is riddled through and through. This has been the work of half a century, one whole generation of earnest men and women. Now the younger apostle should do the same in the church and society.

New York, *September 30*

During the past two days we have had a celebration in honor of Admiral Dewey and his ship, the *Olympia*. The city is bedecked with flags, and the hotels are crowded to bursting. Our landlord covered the top of the house with seats for his lessees and their guests, so that we saw well and at our ease the naval pageant in the Hudson. Naturally the topic to the fore just now is "expansion." I am strongly in favor of this new departure in our foreign policy. What would this continent have been if we had left it to the Indians? I have no sympathy with all the pessimistic twaddle about the Phillippines.

New York, *December 3*

Susan writes asking me to put on paper what I think ought to be done by our national association at its next annual meeting. So I have replied as follows:

1. A resolution should be passed in favor of establishing a new government in Hawaii. It is a disgrace to the civilization of the nineteenth century to make that island a male oligarchy.

2. We should protest in clarion tones against the proposal by railroad kings to turn women out of all the positions which they hold in the North Western Railroad, especially as it is generally admitted that they have given faithful service.

3. We should discuss and pass a resolution against the proposition of the Knights of Labor to remove women from all factories and industries which take them from home. If these gentlemen propose to provide every woman with a strong right arm on which she may lean until she reaches the other side of Jordan; a robust generous man pledged to feed, clothe and shelter the woman and her children to the end of life; a husband or a brother sure not to die or default on the way— why then this proposal might be worthy of woman's consideration. But as long as she is often forced to be the bread-

winner for herself, husband, and children, it would be suicidal for her to retire to the privacy of home and with folded hands wait for the salvation of the Lord. There is an immense amount of sentimental nonsense talked about the isolated home. This is evident when we see what it really means for the mass of the human family. For Deacon Jones, a millionaire surrounded with every luxury, no material change may be desirable. But for a poor farmer with wife and child in the solitude of a prairie home, a co-operative household with society would be inestimable blessing. Woman's work can never be properly organized in the isolated home. One woman cannot fill all the duties required as housekeeper, cook, laundress, nurse, and educator of her children. Therefore we should oppose all sly moves to chain woman in the home.

4. To my mind, our Association cannot be too broad. Suffrage involves every basic principle of republican government, all our social, civil, religious, educational, and political rights. It is therefore germane to our platform to discuss every invidious distinction of sex in the college, home, trades, and professions, in literature, sacred and profane, in the canon as well as in the civil law. At the inauguration of our movement, we numbered in our Declaration of Rights eighteen grievances covering the whole range of human experience. On none of these did we talk with bated breath. Note the radical claims we made, and think how the world responded. Colleges were built for women, and many of the older male colleges opened their doors to our sex. Laws were modified in our favor. The professions were thrown open to us. In short, in response to our radicalism, the bulwarks of the enemy fell as never since. At that time you gave on many occasions a radical lecture on social purity. I was responsible for an equally advanced one on marriage and divorce. Lucretia Mott was not less outspoken on theological questions. But at present our association has so narrowed its platform for reasons of policy and propriety that our conventions have ceased to point the way.

5. Our national convention should always be held in Washington, where we could examine intelligently the bills before

Congress which nearly or remotely affect the women of the nation. We should have a sort of Woman's Congress, if we can afford it, which should sit at the federal capital for a longer or a shorter period every year.

New York, *December 15*

During the past weeks I have enjoyed these works among others: Andrew D. White's *A History of the Warfare of Science with Theology,* read for the second time; Boswell's *Life of Johnson,* which is pleasant and profitable; Cross's *George Eliot's Life,* whose editing does not wholly please me; *Rev. Amos Barton;* Matthew Arnold's *Essays in Criticism,* both series; Bacon's *Essays;* Herbert Spencer's *Education;* Irving's *Oliver Goldsmith;* Higginson's *Cheerful Yesterdays;* Ingersoll's *Great Speeches,* full of telling passages; Sallie Holley's *Reminiscences;* Ralph Waldo Trine's *In Tune with the Infinite;* Hughes's *Tom Brown at Oxford;* several of the novels of Charlotte Brontë, Thackeray, George Eliot, and Cabot Lodge's *Life of Washington.* The heroic struggles of George Washington show at what a great price we secured our liberty as a nation, and after reading such a book as this last one, I feel more than ever the immense debt we owe posterity to maintain what our revolutionary heroes achieved for us.

The Woman's Bible, Elizabeth Cady Stanton*

Introduction

From the inauguration of the movement for woman's emancipation the Bible has been used to hold her in the "divinely ordained sphere," prescribed in the Old and New Testaments.

The canon and civil law; church and state; priests and legislators; all political parties and religious denominations have alike taught that woman was made after man, of man, and for man, an inferior being, subject to man. Creeds, codes, Scriptures and statutes, are all based on this idea. The fashions, forms, ceremonies and customs of society, church ordinances and discipline all grow out of this idea.

Of the old English common law, responsible for woman's civil and political status, Lord Brougham said, "it is a disgrace to the civilization and Christianity of the Nineteenth Century." Of the canon law, which is responsible for woman's status in the church, Charles Kingsley said, "this will never be a good world for women until the last remnant of the canon law is swept from the face of the earth."

The Bible teaches that woman brought sin and death into the world, that she precipitated the fall of the race, that she was arraigned before the judgment seat of Heaven, tried, condemned and sentenced. Marriage for her was to be a condition of bondage, maternity a period of suffering and anguish,

* Mrs. Stanton organized a committee of women to reinterpret those biblical texts which were commonly believed to define woman's sphere, but the introduction and the appendix ("The Woman's Bible Repudiated") she wrote herself. Her introductory remarks appeared in volume one of the *Woman's Bible,* published in New York in 1895. The appendix concluded the second volume which came out in 1898.

and in silence and subjection, she was to play the role of a dependent on man's bounty for all her material wants, and for all the information she might desire on the vital questions of the hour, she was commanded to ask her husband at home. Here is the Bible position of woman briefly summed up.

Those who have the divine insight to translate, transpose and transfigure this mournful object of pity into an exalted, dignified personage, worthy our worship as the mother of the race, are to be congratulated as having a share of the occult mystic power of the eastern Mahatmas.

The plain English to the ordinary mind admits of no such liberal interpretation. The unvarnished texts speak for themselves. The canon law, church ordinances and Scriptures, are homogeneous, and all reflect the same spirit and sentiments.

These familiar texts are quoted by clergymen in their pulpits, by statesmen in the halls of legislation, by lawyers in the courts, and are echoed by the press of all civilized nations, and accepted by woman herself as "The Word of God." So perverted is the religious element in her nature, that with faith and works she is the chief support of the church and clergy; the very powers that make her emancipation impossible. When, in the early part of the Nineteenth Century, women began to protest against their civil and political degradation, they were referred to the Bible for an answer. When they protested against their unequal position in the church, they were referred to the Bible for an answer.

This led to a general and critical study of the Scriptures. Some, having made a fetish of these books and believing them to be the veritable "Word of God," with liberal translations, interpretations, allegories and symbols, glossed over the most objectionable features of the various books and clung to them as divinely inspired. Others, seeing the family resemblance between the Mosaic code, the canon law, and the old English common law, came to the conclusion that all alike emanated from the same source; wholly human in their origin and inspired by the natural love of domination in the historians. Others, bewildered with their doubts and fears, came to no conclusion. While their clergymen told them on the one hand, that they owed all the blessings and freedom they enjoyed to the Bible, on the other, they said it clearly marked out their circumscribed sphere of action: that the demands for political and civil rights were irreligious, dangerous to the stability of the home, the state and the church. Clerical appeals were circulated from time to time conjuring members of their churches to take no part in the anti-slavery or woman suffrage movements, as they were infidel in their tendencies, undermining the very foundations of society. No wonder the majority of women stood still, and with bowed heads, accepted the situation.

Listening to the varied opinions of women, I have long thought it would be interesting and profitable to get them clearly stated in book form. To this end six years ago I proposed to a committee of women to issue a Woman's Bible, that we might have women's commentaries on women's position in the Old and New Testaments. It was agreed on by several leading women in England and America and the work was begun, but from various causes it has been delayed, until now the idea is received with renewed enthusiasm, and a large committee has been formed, and we hope to complete the work within a year.

Those who have undertaken the labor are desirous to have some Hebrew and Greek scholars, versed in Biblical criticism, to gild our pages with their learning. Several distinguished women have been urged to do so, but they are afraid that their high reputation and scholarly attainments might be compromised by taking part in an enterprise that for a time may prove very unpopular. Hence we may not be able to get help from that class.

Others fear that they might compromise their evangelical faith by affiliating with those of more liberal views, who do not regard the Bible as the "Word of God," but like any other book, to be judged by its merits. If the Bible teaches the equality of Woman, why does the church refuse to ordain women to preach the gospel, to fill the offices of deacons and elders, and to administer the Sacraments, or to admit them as delegates to the Synods, General Assemblies and Conferences of the different denominations? They have never yet invited a woman to join one of their Revising Committees, nor tried to mitigate the sentence pronounced on her by changing one count in the indictment served on her in Paradise.

The large number of letters received, highly appreciative of the undertaking, is very encouraging to those who have inaugurated the movement, and indicate a growing self-respect and self-assertion in the women of this generation. But we have the usual array of objectors to meet and answer. One correspondent conjures us to suspend the work, as it is "ridiculous" for "women to attempt the revision of the Scriptures." I wonder if any man wrote to the late revising committee of Divines to stop their work on the ground that it was ridiculous for men to revise the Bible. Why is it more ridiculous for women to protest against her present status in the Old and New Testament, in the ordinances and discipline of the church, than in the statutes and constitution of the state? Why is it more ridiculous to arraign ecclesiastics for their false teaching and acts of injustice to women, than members of Congress and the House of Commons? Why is it more audacious to review Moses than Blackstone, the Jewish code of laws, than the English system of jurisprudence? Women have compelled their legislators in every state in this Union to so modify their statutes for women that the old common law is now almost a dead letter. Why not compel Bishops and Revising Committees to modify their creeds and dogmas? Forty years ago it seemed as ridiculous to timid, time-serving and retrograde folk for women to demand an expurgated edition of the laws, as it now does to demand an expurgated edition of the Liturgies and the Scriptures. Come, come, my conservative friend, wipe the dew off your spectacles, and see that the world is moving. Whatever your views may be as to the importance of the proposed work, your political and social degradation are but an outgrowth of your status in the Bible. When you express your aversion, based on a blind feeling of reverence in which reason has no control, to the revision of the Scriptures, you do but echo Cowper, who, when asked to read Paine's "Rights of Man," exclaimed, "No man shall convince me that I am improperly governed while I *feel* the contrary."

Others say it is not *politic* to rouse religious opposition. This much-lauded policy is but another word for *cowardice*. How can woman's position be changed from that of a subordinate to an equal, without opposition, without the broadest discussion of all the questions involved in her present degradation? For so far-reaching and momentous a reform as her complete independence, an entire revolution in all existing institutions is inevitable.

Let us remember that all reforms are interdependent, and that whatever is done to establish one principle on a solid basis, strengthens all. Reformers who are always compromising, have not yet grasped the idea that truth is the only safe ground to stand upon. The object of an individual life is not to carry one fragmentary measure in human progress, but to utter the highest truth clearly seen in all directions, and thus to round out and perfect a well balanced character. Was not the sum of influence exerted by John Stuart Mill on political, religious and social questions far greater than that of any statesman or reformer who has sedulously limited his sympathies and activities to carrying one specific measure? We have many women abundantly endowed with capabilities to understand and revise what men have thus far written. But they are all suffering from inherited ideas of their inferiority; they do not perceive it, yet such is the true explanation of their solicitude, lest they should seem to be too self-asserting.

Again there are some who write us that our work is a useless expenditure of force over a book that has lost its hold on the human mind. Most intelligent women, they say, regard it simply as the history of a rude people in a barbarous age, and have no more reverence for the Scriptures than any other work. So long as tens of thousands of Bibles are printed every year, and circulated over the whole habitable globe, and the masses in all English-speaking nations revere it as the word of God; it is vain to belittle its influence. The sentimental feelings we all have for those things we were educated to believe sacred, do not readily yield to pure reason. I distinctly remember the shudder that passed over me on seeing a mother take our family Bible to make a high seat for her child at table. It seemed such a desecration. I was tempted to protest against its use for such a purpose, and this, too, long after my reason had repudiated its divine authority.

To women still believing in the plenary inspiration of the Scriptures, we say give us by all means your exegesis in the light of the higher criticism learned men are now making, and illumine the Woman's Bible, with your inspiration.

Bible historians claim special inspiration for the Old and New Testaments containing most contradictory records of the same events, of miracles opposed to all known laws, of customs that degrade the female sex of all human and animal life, stated in most questionable language that could not be read in a promiscuous assembly, and call all this "The Word of God."

The only points in which I differ from all ecclesiastical teaching is that I do not believe that any man ever saw or talked with God, I do not believe that God inspired the Mosaic code, or told the historians what they say he did about woman, for all the religions on the face of the earth degrade her, and so long as woman accepts the position that they assign her, her emancipation is impossible. Whatever the Bible may be made to do in Hebrew or Greek, in plain English it does not exalt and dignify woman. My standpoint for criticism is the revised edition of 1888. I will so far honor the revising committee of nine men who have given us the best exegesis they can according to their ability, although Disraeli said the last one before he died, contained 150,000 blunders in the Hebrew, and 7,000 in the Greek.

But the verbal criticism in regard to woman's position amounts to little. The spirit is the same in all periods and languages, hostile to her as an equal.

There are some general principles in the holy books of all religions that teach love, charity, liberty, justice and equality for all the human family, there are many grand and beautiful passages, the golden rule has been echoed and re-echoed around the world. There are lofty examples of good and true men and women, all worthy [of] our acceptance and example whose lustre cannot be dimmed by the false sentiments and vicious characters bound up in the same volume. The Bible cannot be accepted or rejected as a whole, its teachings are varied and its lessons differ widely from each other. In criticising the peccadilloes of Sarah, Rebecca and Rachel, we would not shadow the virtues of Deborah, Huldah and Vashti. In criticising the Mosaic code we would not question the wisdom of the golden rule and the fifth Commandment. Again the church claims special consecration for its cathedrals and priesthood, parts of these aristocratic churches are too holy for women to enter, boys were early introduced into the choirs for this reason, woman singing in an obscure corner closely veiled. A few of the more democratic denominations accord women some privileges, but invidious discriminations of sex are found in all religious organizations, and the most bitter outspoken enemies of woman are found among clergymen and bishops of the Protestant religion.

The canon law, the Scriptures, the creeds and codes and church discipline of the leading religions bear the impress of fallible man, and not of our ideal great first cause, "the Spirit of all Good," that set the universe of matter and mind in motion, and by immutable law holds the land, the sea, the planets, revolving round the great centre of light and heat, each in its own elliptic, with millions of stars in harmony all singing together, the glory of creation forever and ever.

Elizabeth Cady Stanton.

"The Woman's Bible" Repudiated

At the twenty-eighth annual convention of the National-American Woman Suffrage Association, held in Washington, D.C., in January, 1896, the following, was reported by the Committee on Resolutions:

"That this Association is non-sectarian, being composed of persons of all shades of religious opinion, and that it has no official connection with the so-called 'Woman's Bible,' or any theological publication."

Charlotte Perkins Stetson [later Charlotte Perkins Gilman] moved to amend by striking out everything after the word "opinion."

Anna R. Simmons moved, as an amendment to the amendment, to omit the words "the so-called Woman's Bible, or."

This was followed by a long and animated discussion, in which the following persons participated:

Frances A. Williamson, Helen Morris Lewis, Annie L. Diggs, Carrie Chapman Catt, Rachel Foster Avery, Henry B. Blackwell, Laura M. Johns, Elizabeth U. Yates, Katie R. Addison, Alice Stone Blackwell and Rev. Anna Howard Shaw, speaking for the resolution; and Charlotte Perkins Stetson, Mary Bentley Thomas, J. B. Merwin, Clara B. Colby, Harriette A. Keyser, Lavina A. Hatch, Lillie Devereux Blake, Caroline Hallowell Miller, Victoria Conkling Whitney, Althea B. Stryker, and Cornelia H. Cary speaking against it.

The President, Susan B. Anthony, left the chair and spoke with much earnestness against the adoption of the resolution as follows:

"The one distinct feature of our Association has been the right of individual opinion for every member. We have been beset at every step with the cry that somebody was injuring the cause by the expression of some sentiments that differed with those held by the majority of mankind. The religious persecution of the ages has been done under what was claimed to be the command of God. I distrust those people who know so well what God wants them to do to their fellows, because it always coincides with their own desires. All the way along the history of our movement there has been this same contest on account of religious theories. Forty years ago one of our noblest men said to me: 'You would better never hold another convention than let Ernestine L. Rose stand on your platform,' because that talented and eloquent Polish woman, who ever stood for justice and freedom, did not believe in the plenary inspiration of the Bible. Did we banish Mrs. Rose? No, indeed! Every new generation of converts threshes over the same old straw. Twenty-five years ago a prominent woman, who stood on our platform for the first time, wanted us to pass a resolution that we were not free lovers; and I was not more shocked than I am to-day at this attempt. The question is whether you will sit in judgment on one who has questioned the Divine inspiration of certain passages in the Bible derogatory to women. If she had written approvingly of these passages, you would not have brought in this resolution because you thought the cause might be injured among the liberals in religion. In other words, if she had written your views, you would not have considered a resolution necessary. To pass this one is to set back the hands on the dial of reform. It is the reviving of old time censorship, which I hoped we had outgrown.

"What you should do is to say to outsiders that a Christian has neither more nor less rights in our Association than an atheist. When our platform becomes too narrow for people of all creeds and of no creeds, I myself shall not stand upon it. Many things have been said and done by our orthodox friends that I have felt to be extremely harmful to our cause; but I should no more consent to a resolution denouncing them than I shall consent to this. Who is to draw the line? Who can tell now whether Mrs. Stanton's commentaries may not prove a great help to woman's emancipation from old superstitions that have barred her way? Lucretia Mott at first thought Mrs. Stanton had injured the cause of all woman's other rights by insisting upon the demand for suffrage, but she had sense enough not to bring in a resolution against it. In 1860, when Mrs. Stanton made a speech before the New York Legislature in favor of a bill making drunkenness a cause for divorce, there was a general cry among the friends that she had killed the woman's cause. I shall be pained beyond expression if the delegates here are so narrow and illiberal as to adopt this resolution. You would better not begin resolving against individual action or you will find no limit. This year it is Mrs. Stanton; next year it may be me or one of yourselves who will be the victim.

"Are you going to cater to the whims and prejudices of people who have no intelligent knowledge of what they condemn? If we do not inspire in woman a broad and catholic spirit, they will fail, when enfranchised, to constitute that power for better government which we have always claimed for them. You would better educate ten women into the practice of liberal principles than to organize ten thousand on a platform of intolerance and bigotry. I pray you, vote for religious liberty, without censorship or inquisition. This resolution, adopted, will be a vote of censure upon a woman who is without a peer in intellectual and statesmanlike ability; one who has stood for half a century the acknowledged leader of progressive thought and demand in regard to all matters pertaining to the absolute freedom of women."

The Resolution was then adopted by a vote of 53 to 41.

"The Truth shall make you free."—*John viii.*, *32*.

Jane Addams was born in 1860 in Cedarville, Illinois, daughter of the richest and most respected man in the region. She was the eighth child of John and Sarah Addams, small and frail with a curved spine which she later insisted had made her notably ugly. Her sense of unworthiness, of somehow not being up to Addams' standards, was manifested in her attempts at an early age to avoid being seen in public with her father lest her own unprepossessing appearance somehow detract from his handsomeness and reputation.

Jane Addams had hoped to go to Smith, but at her father's suggestion she attended the local female seminary at Rockford where he was a trustee. Largely through her efforts, the seminary became a full-fledged college in 1882, and Jane Addams, who had graduated a year before, received a retroactive A.B. After one year at Women's Medical College in Philadelphia, which ended with Jane Addams herself a patient in S. Weir Mitchell's hospital, she spent the next seven years alternately invalided in Cedarville and Baltimore and convalescent in Europe. Only in 1889 at the age of twenty-nine did she manage to escape the "snare of preparation" by purchasing a once handsome house which had been surrounded by Chicago tenements, and beginning her career as a settlement worker.

At Hull-House she and her associates managed to establish an art gallery, a wide variety of social and dramatic clubs, a well-baby clinic, a coffee shop and kitchen where carry-out meals could be purchased, and a co-operative house for working girls. Jane Addams' willingness to let any neighborhood political group meet at Hull-House, and her outrage over the treatment of suspected anarchists in Chicago in the 1890s and again in the early years of the twentieth century, earned her considerable reputation as a radical sympathizer. However, only after the Red Scare which followed World War I was she officially blacklisted by the Daughters of the American Revolution, less perhaps for her support of the Socialist presidential candidate, Eugene Debs, than for her stubborn allegiance to pacifistic principles during the war years themselves. In addition to her faith in international arbitration, Jane Addams was a champion of trade unionism, of protective industrial legislation, of the juvenile court system, and woman's suffrage.

At a dinner in her honor given by the business and professional women of Chicago in the early thirties, she had the temerity to suggest that "A woman should fill a woman's place in the world, not a man's place. There are women's talents and women's energies, as there are men's talents and men's energies. To statesmanship she can contribute sympathy and understanding, to business the feminine instinct for cooperation rather than competition." In her conception of woman's place, Jane Addams was a radical even in the 1930s, but in her analysis of why society should cherish its liberated women, she was profoundly conservative. Her most significant writings, *Democracy and Social Ethics* (1907), *Twenty Years at Hull-House* (1910), and *The Second Twenty Years at Hull-House* (1930), were informed by her sense that the detachment cultivated by businessmen-philanthropists and lady bountifuls alike, represented a perversion of true charity in which the benefactor received as much as he gave. Jane Addams died in 1935.

Twenty Years at Hull-House, Jane Addams*

Perhaps I may record here my protest against the efforts, so often made, to shield children and young people from all that has to do with death and sorrow, to give them a good time at all hazards on the assumption that the ills of life will come soon enough. Young people themselves often resent this attitude on the part of their elders; they feel set aside and belittled as if they were denied the common human experiences. They too wish to climb steep stairs and to eat their bread with tears, and they imagine that the problems of existence which so press upon them in pensive moments would be less insoluble in the light of these great happenings.

An incident which stands out clearly in my mind as an exciting suggestion of the great world of moral enterprise and serious undertakings must have occurred earlier than this, for in 1872, when I was not yet twelve years old, I came into my father's room one morning to find him sitting beside the fire with a newspaper in his hand, looking very solemn; and upon my eager inquiry what had happened, he told me that Joseph Mazzini was dead. I had never even heard Mazzini's name, and after being told about him I was inclined to grow argumentative, asserting that my father did not know him, that he was not an American, and that I could not understand why we should be expected to feel badly about him. It is impossible to recall the conversation with the complete breakdown of my cheap arguments, but in the end I obtained that which I have ever regarded as a valuable possession, a sense of the genuine relationship which

* These excerpts are taken from the first edition of *Twenty Years at Hull-House* (New York, 1911).

may exist between men who share large hopes and like desires, even though they differ in nationality, language, and creed; that those things count for absolutely nothing between groups of men who are trying to abolish slavery in America or to throw off Hapsburg oppression in Italy. At any rate, I was heartily ashamed of my meager notion of patriotism, and I came out of the room exhilarated with the consciousness that impersonal and international relations are actual facts and not mere phrases. I was filled with pride that I knew a man who held converse with great minds and who really sorrowed and rejoiced over happenings across the sea. I never recall those early conversations with my father, nor a score of others like them, but there comes into my mind a line from Mrs. Browning in which a daughter describes her relations with her father:—

"He wrapt me in his large
Man's doublet, careless did it fit or no." . . .

Thousands of children in the sixties and seventies, in the simplicity which is given to the understanding of a child, caught a notion of imperishable heroism when they were told that brave men had lost their lives that the slaves might be free. At any moment the conversation of our elders might turn upon these heroic events; there were red-letter days, when a certain general came to see my father, and again when Governor Oglesby, whom all Illinois children called "Uncle Dick," spent a Sunday under the pine trees in our front yard. We felt on those days a connection with the great world so much more heroic than the village world which surrounded us through all the other days. My father was a member of the state senate for the sixteen years between 1854 and 1870, and even as a little child I was dimly conscious of the grave march of public affairs in his comings and goings at the state capital.

He was much too occupied to allow time for reminiscence, but I remember overhearing a conversation between a visitor and himself concerning the stirring days before the war, when it was by no means certain that the Union men in the legislature would always have enough votes to keep Illinois from seceding. I heard with breathless interest my father's account of the trip a majority of the legislators had made one dark day to St. Louis, that there might not be enough men for a quorum, and so no vote could be taken on the momentous question until the Union men could rally their forces.

My father always spoke of the martyred President as Mr. Lincoln, and I never heard the great name without a thrill. I remember the day—it must have been one of comparative leisure, perhaps a Sunday—when at my request my father took out of his desk a thin packet marked "Mr. Lincoln's Letters," the shortest one of which bore unmistakable traces of that remarkable personality. These letters began, "My dear Double-D'ed Addams," and to the inquiry as to how the person thus addressed was about to vote on a certain measure then before the legislature, was added the assurance that he knew that this Addams "would vote according to his conscience," but he begged to know in which direction the same conscience "was pointing." As my father folded up the bits of paper I fairly held my breath in my desire that he should go on with the reminiscence of this wonderful man, whom he had known in his comparative obscurity, or better still, that he should be moved to tell some of the exciting incidents of the Lincoln-Douglas debates. There were at least two pictures of Lincoln that always hung in my father's room, and one in our old-fashioned upstairs parlor, of Lincoln with little Tad. For one or all of these reasons I always tend to associate Lincoln with the tenderest thoughts of my father. . . .

I remember an incident occurring when I was about fifteen years old, in which the conviction was driven into my mind that the people themselves were the great resource of the country. My father had made a little address of reminiscence at a meeting of "the old settlers of Stephenson County," which was held every summer in the grove beside the mill, relating his experiences in inducing the farmers of the county

to subscribe for stock in the Northwestern Railroad, which
was the first to penetrate the county and to make a connection with the Great Lakes at Chicago. Many of the Pennsyl-
vania German farmers doubted the value of "the whole new-
fangled business," and had no use for any railroad, much less
for one in which they were asked to risk their hard-earned
savings. My father told of his despair in one farmers' community dominated by such prejudice which did not in the
least give way under his argument, but finally melted under the enthusiasm of a high-spirited German matron who
took a share to be paid for "out of butter and egg money."
As he related his admiration of her, an old woman's piping
voice in the audience called out: "I'm here to-day, Mr. Addams, and I'd do it again if you asked me." The old woman,
bent and broken by her seventy years of toilsome life, was
brought to the platform and I was much impressed by my
father's grave presentation of her as "one of the public-
spirited pioneers to whose heroic fortitude we are indebted
for the development of this country." I remember that I
was at that time reading with great enthusiasm Carlyle's
"Heroes and Hero Worship," but on the evening of "Old Settlers' Day," to my surprise, I found it difficult to go on. Its
sonorous sentences and exaltation of the man who "can" suddenly ceased to be convincing. I had already written down
in my commonplace book a resolution to give at least twenty-
five copies of this book each year to noble young people of
my acquaintance. It is perhaps fitting to record in this chapter that the very first Christmas we spent at Hull-House, in
spite of exigent demands upon my slender purse for candy
and shoes, I gave to a club of boys twenty-five copies of the
then new Carl Schurz's "Appreciation of Abraham Lincoln."

In our early effort at Hull-House to hand on to our neighbors whatever of help we had found for ourselves, we made
much of Lincoln. We were often distressed by the children
of immigrant parents who were ashamed of the pit whence
they were digged, who repudiated the language and customs
of their elders, and counted themselves successful as they
were able to ignore the past. Whenever I held up Lincoln

for their admiration as the greatest American, I invariably pointed out his marvelous power to retain and utilize past experiences; that he never forgot how the plain people in Sangamon County thought and felt when he himself had moved to town; that this habit was the foundation for his marvelous capacity for growth; that during those distracting years in Washington it enabled him to make clear beyond denial to the American people themselves, the goal towards which they were moving. I was sometimes bold enough to add that proficiency in the art of recognition and comprehension did not come without effort, and that certainly its attainment was necessary for any successful career in our conglomerate America. . . .

The winter after I left school was spent in the Woman's Medical College of Philadelphia, but the development of the spinal difficulty which had shadowed me from childhood forced me into Dr. Weir Mitchell's hospital for the late spring, and the next winter I was literally bound to a bed in my sister's house for six months. In spite of its tedium, the long winter had its mitigations, for after the first few weeks I was able to read with a luxurious consciousness of leisure, and I remember opening the first volume of Carlyle's "Frederick the Great" with a lively sense of gratitude that it was not Gray's "Anatomy," having found, like many another, that general culture is a much easier undertaking than professional study. The long illness inevitably put aside the immediate prosecution of a medical course, and although I had passed my examinations creditably enough in the required subjects for the first year, I was very glad to have a physician's sanction for giving up clinics and dissecting rooms and to follow his prescription of spending the next two years in Europe.

Before I returned to America I had discovered that there were other genuine reasons for living among the poor than that of practicing medicine upon them, and my brief foray into the profession was never resumed.

The long illness left me in a state of nervous exhaustion

with which I struggled for years, traces of it remaining long after Hull-House was opened in 1889. At the best it allowed me but a limited amount of energy, so that doubtless there was much nervous depression at the foundation of the spiritual struggles which this chapter is forced to record. However, it could not have been all due to my health, for as my wise little notebook sententiously remarked, "In his own way each man must struggle, lest the moral law become a far-off abstraction utterly separated from his active life."

It would, of course, be impossible to remember that some of these struggles ever took place at all, were it not for these selfsame notebooks, in which, however, I no longer wrote in moments of high resolve, but judging from the internal evidence afforded by the books themselves, only in moments of deep depression when overwhelmed by a sense of failure.

One of the most poignant of these experiences, which occurred during the first few months after our landing upon the other side of the Atlantic, was on a Saturday night, when I received an ineradicable impression of the wretchedness of East London, and also saw for the first time the overcrowded quarters of a great city at midnight. A small party of tourists were taken to the East End by a city missionary to witness the Saturday night sale of decaying vegetables and fruit, which, owing to the Sunday laws in London, could not be sold until Monday, and, as they were beyond safe keeping, were disposed of at auction as late as possible on Saturday night. On Mile End Road, from the top of an omnibus which paused at the end of a dingy street lighted by only occasional flares of gas, we saw two huge masses of ill-clad people clamoring around two hucksters' carts. They were bidding their farthings and ha'pennies for a vegetable held up by the auctioneer, which he at last scornfully flung, with a gibe for its cheapness, to the successful bidder. In the momentary pause only one man detached himself from the groups. He had bidden in a cabbage, and when it struck his hand, he instantly sat down on the curb, tore it with his teeth, and hastily devoured it, unwashed and uncooked as it was. He and his fellows were types of the "submerged tenth," as our missionary guide told us, with some little satisfaction in the then new phrase, and he further added that so many of them could scarcely be seen in one spot save at this Saturday night auction, the desire for cheap food being apparently the one thing which could move them simultaneously. They were huddled into ill-fitting, cast-off clothing, the ragged finery which one sees only in East London. Their pale faces were dominated by that most unlovely of human expressions, the cunning and shrewdness of the bargain-hunter who starves if he cannot make a successful trade, and yet the final impression was not of ragged, tawdry clothing nor of pinched and sallow faces, but of myriads of hands, empty, pathetic, nerveless and workworn, showing white in the uncertain light of the street, and clutching forward for food which was already unfit to eat. . . .

I should have been shown either less or more, for I went away with no notion of the hundreds of men and women who had gallantly identified their fortunes with these empty-handed people, and who, in church and chapel, "relief works," and charities, were at least making an effort towards its mitigation.

Our visit was made in November, 1883, the very year when the *Pall Mall Gazette* exposure started "The Bitter Cry of Outcast London," and the conscience of England was stirred as never before over this joyless city in the East End of its capital. Even then, vigorous and drastic plans were being discussed, and a splendid program of municipal reforms was already dimly outlined. Of all these, however, I had heard nothing but the vaguest rumor.

No comfort came to me then from any source, and the painful impression was increased because at the very moment of looking down the East London street from the top of the omnibus, I had been sharply and painfully reminded of "The Vision of Sudden Death" which had confronted De Quincey one summer's night as he was being driven through rural England on a high mail coach. Two absorbed lovers suddenly appear between the narrow, blossoming hedge-

rows in the direct path of the huge vehicle which is sure to
crush them to their death. De Quincey tries to send them a
warning shout, but finds himself unable to make a sound
because his mind is hopelessly entangled in an endeavor to
recall the exact lines from the "Iliad" which describe the
great cry with which Achilles alarmed all Asia militant. Only
after his memory responds is his will released from its momentary paralysis, and he rides on through the fragrant night
with the horror of the escaped calamity thick upon him, but
he also bears with him the consciousness that he had given
himself over so many years to classic learning—that when
suddenly called upon for a quick decision in the world of
life and death, he had been able to act only through a
literary suggestion.

This is what we were all doing, lumbering our minds with
literature that only served to cloud the really vital situation
spread before our eyes. It seemed to me too preposterous
that in my first view of the horror of East London I should
have recalled De Quincey's literary description of the literary suggestion which had once paralyzed him. In my disgust
it all appeared a hateful, vicious circle which even the
apostles of culture themselves admitted, for had not one of
the greatest among the moderns plainly said that "conduct,
and not culture is three fourths of human life."

For two years in the midst of my distress over the poverty
which, thus suddenly driven into my consciousness, had become to me the "Weltschmerz," there was mingled a sense
of futility, of misdirected energy, the belief that the pursuit
of cultivation would not in the end bring either solace
or relief. I gradually reached a conviction that the first
generation of college women had taken their learning too
quickly, had departed too suddenly from the active, emotional life led by their grandmothers and great-grandmothers;
that the contemporary education of young women had developed too exclusively the power of acquiring knowledge
and of merely receiving impressions; that somewhere in the
process of "being educated" they had lost that simple and
almost automatic response to the human appeal, that old

healthful reaction resulting in activity from the mere presence of suffering or of helplessness; that they are so sheltered and pampered they have no chance even to make "the great refusal."

In the German and French *pensions,* which twenty-five years ago were crowded with American mothers and their daughters who had crossed the seas in search of culture, one often found the mother making real connection with the life about her, using her inadequate German with great fluency, gayly measuring the enormous sheets or exchanging recipes with the German Hausfrau, visiting impartially the nearest kindergarten and market, making an atmosphere of her own, hearty and genuine as far as it went, in the house and on the street. On the other hand, her daughter was critical and uncertain of her linguistic acquirements, and only at ease when in the familiar receptive attitude afforded by the art gallery and the opera house. In the latter she was swayed and moved, appreciative of the power and charm of the music, intelligent as to the legend and poetry of the plot, finding use for her trained and developed powers as she sat "being cultivated" in the familiar atmosphere of the classroom which had, as it were, become sublimated and romanticized.

I remember a happy busy mother who, complacent with the knowledge that her daughter daily devoted four hours to her music, looked up from her knitting to say, "If I had had your opportunities when I was young, my dear, I should have been a very happy girl. I always had musical talent, but such training as I had, foolish little songs and waltzes and not time for half an hour's practice a day."

The mother did not dream of the sting her words left and that the sensitive girl appreciated only too well that her opportunities were fine and unusual, but she also knew that in spite of some facility and much good teaching she had no genuine talent and never would fulfill the expectations of her friends. She looked back upon her mother's girlhood with positive envy because it was so full of happy industry and extenuating obstacles, with undisturbed opportunity to believe that her talents were unusual. The girl looked wistfully

at her mother, but had not the courage to cry out what was
in her heart: "I might believe I had unusual talent if I did
not know what good music was; I might enjoy half an hour's
practice a day if I were busy and happy the rest of the time.
You do not know what life means when all the difficulties
are removed! I am simply smothered and sickened with advantages. It is like eating a sweet dessert the first thing in
the morning."

This, then, was the difficulty, this sweet dessert in the
morning and the assumption that the sheltered, educated girl
has nothing to do with the bitter poverty and the social maladjustment which is all about her, and which, after all, cannot be concealed, for it breaks through poetry and literature
in a burning tide which overwhelms her; it peers at her in
the form of heavy-laden market women and underpaid street
laborers, gibing her with a sense of her uselessness. . . .

The two years which elapsed before I again found myself
in Europe brought their inevitable changes. Family arrangements had so come about that I had spent three or four
months of each of the intervening winters in Baltimore, where
I seemed to have reached the nadir of my nervous depression and sense of maladjustment, in spite of my interest in
the fascinating lectures given there by Lanciani of Rome,
and a definite course of reading under the guidance of a
Johns Hopkins lecturer upon the United Italy movement. In
the latter I naturally encountered the influence of Mazzini,
which was a source of great comfort to me, although perhaps
I went too suddenly from a contemplation of his wonderful ethical and philosophical appeal to the workingmen of
Italy, directly to the lecture rooms at Johns Hopkins University, for I was certainly much disillusioned at this time
as to the effect of intellectual pursuits upon moral development.

The summers were spent in the old home in northern
Illinois, and one Sunday morning I received the rite of baptism and became a member of the Presbyterian church in

the village. At this time there was certainly no outside pressure pushing me towards such a decision, and at twenty-five one does not ordinarily take such a step from a mere desire to conform. While I was not conscious of any emotional "conversion," I took upon myself the outward expressions of the religious life with all humility and sincerity. It was doubtless true that I was

"Weary of myself and sick of asking
  What I am and what I ought to be,"

and that various cherished safeguards and claims to self-dependence had been broken into by many piteous failures. But certainly I had been brought to the conclusion that "sincerely to give up one's conceit or hope of being good in one's own right is the only door to the Universe's deeper reaches." Perhaps the young clergyman recognized this as the test of the Christian temper, at any rate he required little assent to dogma or miracle, and assured me that while both the ministry and the officers of his church were obliged to subscribe to doctrines of well-known severity, the faith required of the laity was almost early Christian in its simplicity. I was conscious of no change from my childish acceptance of the teachings of the Gospels, but at this moment something persuasive within made me long for an outward symbol of fellowship, some bond of peace, some blessed spot where unity of spirit might claim right of way over all differences. There was also growing within me an almost passionate devotion to the ideals of democracy, and when in all history had these ideals been so thrillingly expressed as when the faith of the fisherman and the slave had been boldly opposed to the accepted moral belief that the well-being of a privileged few might justly be built upon the ignorance and sacrifice of the many? Who was I, with my dreams of universal fellowship, that I did not identify myself with the institutional statement of this belief, as it stood in the little village in which I was born, and without which testimony in each remote hamlet of Christendom it would be so easy for the world to slip back into the doctrines of selection and aristocracy? . . .

Another Sunday afternoon in the early spring, on the way to a Bohemian mission in the carriage of one of its founders, we passed a fine old house standing well back from the street, surrounded on three sides by a broad piazza which was supported by wooden pillars of exceptionally pure Corinthian design and proportion. I was so attracted by the house that I set forth to visit it the very next day, but though I searched for it then and for several days after, I could not find it, and at length I most reluctantly gave up the search.

Three weeks later, with the advice of several of the oldest residents of Chicago, including the ex-mayor of the city, Colonel Mason, who had from the first been a warm friend to our plans, we decided upon a location somewhere near the junction of Blue Island Avenue, Halsted Street, and Harrison Street. I was surprised and overjoyed on the very first day of our search for quarters to come upon the hospitable old house, the quest for which I had so recently abandoned. The house was of course rented, the lower part of it used for offices and storerooms in connection with a factory that stood back of it. However, after some difficulties were overcome, it proved to be possible to sublet the second floor and what had been the large drawing-room on the first floor.

The house had passed through many changes since it had been built in 1856 for the homestead of one of Chicago's pioneer citizens, Mr. Charles J. Hull, and although battered by its vicissitudes, was essentially sound. Before it had been occupied by the factory, it had sheltered a second-hand furniture store, and at one time the Little Sisters of the Poor had used it for a home for the aged. It had a half-skeptical reputation for a haunted attic, so far respected by the tenants living on the second floor that they always kept a large pitcher full of water on the attic stairs. Their explanation of this custom was so incoherent that I was sure it was a survival of the belief that a ghost could not cross running water, but perhaps that interpretation was only my eagerness for finding folklore.

The fine old house responded kindly to repairs, its wide hall and open fireplaces always insuring it a gracious aspect. Its generous owner, Miss Helen Culver, in the following spring gave us a free leasehold of the entire house. Her kindness has continued through the years until the group of thirteen buildings, which at present comprises our equipment, is built largely upon land which Miss Culver has put at the service of the Settlement which bears Mr. Hull's name. In those days the house stood between an undertaking establishment and a saloon. "Knight, Death, and the Devil," the three were called by a Chicago wit, and yet any mock heroics which might be implied by comparing the Settlement to a knight quickly dropped away under the genuine kindness and hearty welcome extended to us by the families living up and down the street.

We furnished the house as we would have furnished it were it in another part of the city, with the photographs and other impedimenta we had collected in Europe, and with a few bits of family mahogany. While all the new furniture which was bought was enduring in quality, we were careful to keep it in character with the fine old residence. Probably no young matron ever placed her own things in her own house with more pleasure than that with which we first furnished Hull-House. We believed that the Settlement may logically bring to its aid all those adjuncts which the cultivated man regards as good and suggestive of the best life of the past. . . .

In every neighborhood where poorer people live, because rents are supposed to be cheaper there, is an element which, although uncertain in the individual, in the aggregate can be counted upon. It is composed of people of former education and opportunity who have cherished ambitions and prospects, but who are caricatures of what they meant to be—"hollow ghosts which blame the living men." There are

times in many lives when there is a cessation of energy and
loss of power. Men and women of education and refinement
come to live in a cheaper neighborhood because they lack
the ability to make money, because of ill health, because of
an unfortunate marriage, or for other reasons which do not
imply criminality or stupidity. Among them are those who,
in spite of untoward circumstances, keep up some sort of an
intellectual life; those who are "great for books," as their
neighbors say. To such the Settlement may be a genuine
refuge. . . .

On our first New Year's Day at Hull-House we invited
the older people in the vicinity, sending a carriage for the
most feeble and announcing to all of them that we were going to organize an Old Settlers' Party.

Every New Year's Day since, older people in varying numbers have come together at Hull-House to relate early hardships, and to take for the moment the place in the community to which their pioneer life entitles them. Many people
who were formerly residents of the vicinity, but whom prosperity has carried into more desirable neighborhoods, come
back to these meetings and often confess to each other that
they have never since found such kindness as in early Chicago when all its citizens came together in mutual enterprises. Many of these pioneers, so like the men and women
of my earliest childhood that I always felt comforted by their
presence in the house, were very much opposed to "for-
eigners," whom they held responsible for a depreciation of
property and a general lowering of the tone of the neighborhood. Sometimes we had a chance for championship; I recall
one old man, fiercely American, who had reproached me because we had so many "foreign views" on our walls, to whom
I endeavored to set forth our hope that the pictures might
afford a familiar island to the immigrants in a sea of new and
strange impressions. The old settler guest, taken off his guard,
replied, "I see; they feel as we did when we saw a Yankee
notion from down East,"—thereby formulating the dim kinship between the pioneer and the immigrant, both "buffeting

the waves of a new development." The older settlers as well as their children throughout the years have given genuine help to our various enterprises for neighborhood improvement, and from their own memories of earlier hardships have made many shrewd suggestions for alleviating the difficulties of that first sharp struggle with untoward conditions. . . .

From our very first months at Hull-House we found it much easier to deal with the first generation of crowded city life than with the second or third, because it is more natural and cast in a simpler mold. The Italian and Bohemian peasants who live in Chicago, still put on their bright holiday clothes on a Sunday and go to visit their cousins. They tramp along with at least a suggestion of having once walked over plowed fields and breathed country air. The second generation of city poor too often have no holiday clothes and consider their relations a "bad lot." I have heard a drunken man in a maudlin stage, babble of his good country mother and imagine he was driving the cows home, and I knew that his little son who laughed loud at him, would be drunk earlier in life and would have no such pastoral interlude to his ravings.

Filial Relations, Jane Addams*

In considering the changes which our increasing democracy is constantly making upon various relationships, it is impossible to ignore the filial relation. This chapter deals with the relation between parents and their grown-up daughters, as affording an explicit illustration of the perplexity and maladjustment brought about by the various attempts of young women to secure a more active share in the community life. We constantly see parents very much disconcerted and perplexed in regard to their daughters when these daughters undertake work lying quite outside of traditional and family interests. These parents insist that the girl is carried away by a foolish enthusiasm, that she is in search of a career, that she is restless and does not know what she wants. They will give any reason, almost, rather than the recognition of a genuine and dignified claim. Possibly all this is due to the fact that for so many hundreds of years women have had no larger interests, no participation in the affairs lying quite outside personal and family claims. Any attempt that the individual woman formerly made to subordinate or renounce the family claim was inevitably construed to mean that she was setting up her own will against that of her family's for selfish ends. It was concluded that she could have no motive larger than a desire to serve her family, and her attempt to break away must therefore be wilful and self-indulgent.

The family logically consented to give her up at her marriage, when she was enlarging the family tie by founding another family. It was easy to understand that they per-

* The passages here are taken from a chapter entitled "Filial Relations" in Jane Addams' *Democracy and Social Ethics* (New York, 1907).

mitted and even promoted her going to college, travelling in Europe, or any other means of self-improvement, because these merely meant the development and cultivation of one of its own members. When, however, she responded to her impulse to fulfil the social or democratic claim, she violated every tradition.

The mind of each one of us reaches back to our first struggles as we emerged from self-willed childhood into a recognition of family obligations. We have all gradually learned to respond to them, and yet most of us have had at least fleeting glimpses of what it might be to disregard them and the elemental claim they make upon us. We have yielded at times to the temptation of ignoring them for selfish aims, of considering the individual and not the family convenience, and we remember with shame the self-pity which inevitably followed. But just as we have learned to adjust the personal and family claims, and to find an orderly development impossible without recognition of both, so perhaps we are called upon now to make a second adjustment between the family and the social claim, in which neither shall lose and both be ennobled.

The attempt to bring about a healing compromise in which the two shall be adjusted in proper relation is not an easy one. It is difficult to distinguish between the outward act of him who in following one legitimate claim has been led into the temporary violation of another, and the outward act of him who deliberately renounces a just claim and throws aside all obligation for the sake of his own selfish and individual development. The man, for instance, who deserts his family that he may cultivate an artistic sensibility, or acquire what he considers more fulness of life for himself, must always arouse our contempt. Breaking the marriage tie as Ibsen's "Nora" did, to obtain a larger self-development, or holding to it as George Eliot's "Romola" did, because of the larger claim of the state and society, must always remain two distinct paths. The collision of interests, each of which has a real moral basis and a right to its own place in life, is bound to be more or less tragic. It is the struggle between two claims, the destruction of either of which would bring ruin to the ethical life. Curiously enough, it is almost exactly this contradiction which is the tragedy set forth by the Greek dramatist, who asserted that the gods who watch over the sanctity of the family bond must yield to the higher claims of the gods of the state. The failure to recognize the social claim as legitimate causes the trouble; the suspicion constantly remains that woman's public efforts are merely selfish and captious, and are not directed to the general good. This suspicion will never be dissipated until parents, as well as daughters, feel the democratic impulse and recognize the social claim. . . .

It is impossible to bring about the higher development by any self-assertion or breaking away of the individual will. The new growth in the plant swelling against the sheath, which at the same time imprisons and protects it, must still be the truest type of progress. The family in its entirety must be carried out into the larger life. Its various members together must recognize and acknowledge the validity of the social obligation. When this does not occur we have a most flagrant example of the ill-adjustment and misery arising when an ethical code is applied too rigorously and too conscientiously to conditions which are no longer the same as when the code was instituted, and for which it was never designed. . . .

Such glimpses remind us of that tragedy enacted centuries ago in Assisi, when the eager young noble cast his very clothing at his father's feet, dramatically renouncing his filial allegiance, and formally subjecting the narrow family claim to the wider and more universal duty. All the conflict of tragedy ensued which might have been averted, had the father recognized the higher claim, and had he been willing to subordinate and adjust his own claim to it. The father considered his son disrespectful and hard-hearted, yet we know St. Francis to have been the most tender and loving of men, responsive to all possible ties, even to those of inanimate na-

ture. We know that by his affections he freed the frozen life
of his time. The elements of tragedy lay in the narrowness
of the father's mind; in his lack of comprehension and his
lack of sympathy with the power which was moving his son,
and which was but part of the religious revival which swept
Europe from end to end in the early part of the thirteenth
century; the same power which built the cathedrals of the
North, and produced the saints and sages of the South. But
the father's situation was nevertheless genuine; he felt his
heart sore and angry, and his dignity covered with disrespect. He could not, indeed, have felt otherwise, unless he
had been touched by the fire of the same revival, and lifted
out of and away from the contemplation of himself and his
narrower claim. It is another proof that the notion of a larger
obligation can only come through the response to an enlarged interest in life and in the social movements around
us. . . .

It is always difficult for the family to regard the daughter otherwise than as a family possession. From her baby-
hood she has been the charm and grace of the household,
and it is hard to think of her as an integral part of the social
order, hard to believe that she has duties outside of the family, to the state and to society in the larger sense. This assumption that the daughter is solely an inspiration and refinement to the family itself and its own immediate circle, that
her delicacy and polish are but outward symbols of her father's protection and prosperity, worked very smoothly for
the most part so long as her education was in line with it.
When there was absolutely no recognition of the entity of
woman's life beyond the family, when the outside claims
upon her were still wholly unrecognized, the situation was
simple, and the finishing school harmoniously and elegantly
answered all requirements. She was fitted to grace the fireside and to add lustre to that social circle which her parents
selected for her. But this family assumption has been notably
broken into, and educational ideas no longer fit it. Modern
education recognizes woman quite apart from family or so-

ciety claims, and gives her the training which for many years has been deemed successful for highly developing a man's individuality and freeing his powers for independent action. Perplexities often occur when the daughter returns from college and finds that this recognition has been but partially accomplished. When she attempts to act upon the assumption of its accomplishment, she finds herself jarring upon ideals which are so entwined with filial piety, so rooted in the tenderest affections of which the human heart is capable, that both daughter and parents are shocked and startled when they discover what is happening, and they scarcely venture to analyze the situation. The ideal for the education of woman has changed under the pressure of a new claim. The family has responded to the extent of granting the education, but they are jealous of the new claim and assert the family claim as over against it. . . .

In such instances the girl quietly submits, but she feels wronged whenever she allows her mind to dwell upon the situation. She either hides her hurt, and splendid reserves of enthusiasm and capacity go to waste, or her zeal and emotions are turned inward, and the result is an unhappy woman, whose heart is consumed by vain regrets and desires.

If the college woman is not thus quietly reabsorbed, she is even reproached for her discontent. She is told to be devoted to her family, inspiring and responsive to her social circle, and to give the rest of her time to further self-improvement and enjoyment. She expects to do this, and responds to these claims to the best of her ability, even heroically sometimes. But where is the larger life of which she has dreamed so long? That life which surrounds and completes the individual and family life? She has been taught that it is her duty to share this life, and her highest privilege to extend it. This divergence between her self-centred existence and her best convictions becomes constantly more apparent. But the situation is not even so simple as a conflict between her affections and her intellectual convictions, although even that is tumultuous enough, also the emotional nature is di-

vided against itself. The social claim is a demand upon the
emotions as well as upon the intellect, and in ignoring it she
represses not only her convictions but lowers her springs of
vitality. Her life is full of contradictions. She looks out into
the world, longing that some demand be made upon her
powers, for they are too untrained to furnish an initiative.
When her health gives way under this strain, as it often does,
her physician invariably advises a rest. But to be put to bed
and fed on milk is not what she requires. What she needs is
simple, health-giving activity, which, involving the use of all
her faculties, shall be a response to all the claims which she
so keenly feels.

It is quite true that the family often resents her first attempts to be part of a life quite outside their own, because
the college woman frequently makes these first attempts most
awkwardly; her faculties have not been trained in the line of
action. She lacks the ability to apply her knowledge and
theories to life itself and to its complicated situations. This is
largely the fault of her training and of the one-sidedness of
educational methods. The colleges have long been full of
the best ethical teaching, insisting that the good of the whole
must ultimately be the measure of effort, and that the individual can only secure his own rights as he labors to secure
those of others. But while the teaching has included an ever-
broadening range of obligation and has insisted upon the
recognition of the claims of human brotherhood, the training
has been singularly individualistic; it has fostered ambitions
for personal distinction, and has trained the faculties almost
exclusively in the direction of intellectual accumulation.
Doubtless, woman's education is at fault, in that it has failed
to recognize certain needs, and has failed to cultivate and
guide the larger desires of which all generous young hearts
are full.

During the most formative years of life, it gives the young
girl no contact with the feebleness of childhood, the pathos
of suffering, or the needs of old age. It gathers together crude
youth in contact only with each other and with mature men
and women who are there for the purpose of their mental

direction. The tenderest promptings are bidden to bide their time. This could only be justifiable if a definite outlet were provided when they leave college. Doubtless the need does not differ widely in men and women, but women not absorbed in professional or business life, in the years immediately following college, are baldly brought face to face with the deficiencies of their training. Apparently every obstacle is removed, and the college woman is at last free to begin the active life, for which, during so many years, she has been preparing. But during this so-called preparation, her faculties have been trained solely for accumulation, and she has learned to utterly distrust the finer impulses of her nature, which would naturally have connected her with human interests outside of her family and her own immediate social circle. All through school and college the young soul dreamed of self-sacrifice, of succor to the helpless and of tenderness to the unfortunate. . . .

Fortunately a beginning has been made in another direction, and a few parents have already begun to consider even their little children in relation to society as well as to the family. The young mothers who attend "Child Study" classes have a larger notion of parenthood and expect given characteristics from their children, at certain ages and under certain conditions. They quite calmly watch the various attempts of a child to assert his individuality, which so often takes the form of opposition to the wishes of the family and to the rule of the household. They recognize as acting under the same law of development the little child of three who persistently runs away and pretends not to hear his mother's voice, the boy of ten who violently, although temporarily, resents control of any sort, and the grown-up son who, by an individualized and trained personality, is drawn into pursuits and interests quite alien to those of his family.

This attempt to take the parental relation somewhat away from mere personal experience, as well as the increasing tendency of parents to share their children's pursuits and interests, will doubtless finally result in a better understanding

of the social obligation. The understanding, which results
from identity of interests, would seem to confirm the conviction that in the complicated life of to-day there is no education so admirable as that education which comes from
participation in the constant trend of events. There is no
doubt that most of the misunderstandings of life are due to
partial intelligence, because our experiences have been so
unlike that we cannot comprehend each other. The old difficulties incident to the clash of two codes of morals must
drop away, as the experiences of various members of the
family become larger and more identical.

At the present moment, however, many of those difficulties still exist and may be seen all about us. In order to
illustrate the situation baldly, and at the same time to put
it dramatically, it may be well to take an instance concerning
which we have no personal feeling. The tragedy of King
Lear has been selected, although we have been accustomed
so long to give him our sympathy as the victim of the in-
gratitude of his two older daughters, and of the apparent
coldness of Cordelia, that we have not sufficiently considered
the weakness of his fatherhood, revealed by the fact that
he should get himself into so entangled and unhappy a relation to all of his children. In our pity for Lear, we fail to
analyze his character. The King on his throne exhibits utter
lack of self-control. The King in the storm gives way to the
same emotion, in repining over the wickedness of his children, which he formerly exhibited in his indulgent treatment of them.

It might be illuminating to discover wherein he had failed
and why his old age found him roofless in spite of the fact
that he strenuously urged the family claim with his whole
conscience. At the opening of the drama he sat upon his
throne, ready for the enjoyment which an indulgent parent
expects when he has given gifts to his children. From the two
elder, the responses for the division of his lands were graceful and fitting but he longed to hear what Cordelia, his
youngest and best beloved child, would say. He looked to

ward her expectantly, but instead of delight and gratitude there was the first dawn of character. Cordelia made the awkward attempt of an untrained soul to be honest and scrupulously to express her inmost feeling. The king was baffled and distressed by this attempt at self-expression. It was new to him that his daughter should be moved by a principle obtained outside himself, which even his imagination could not follow; that she had caught the notion of an existence in which her relation as a daughter played but a part. She was transformed by a dignity which recast her speech and made it self-contained. She found herself in the sweep of a feeling so large that the immediate loss of a kingdom seemed of little consequence to her. Even an act which might be construed as disrespect to her father was justified in her eyes, because she was vainly striving to fill out this larger conception of duty. . . .

Historically considered, the relation of Lear to his children was archaic and barbaric, indicating merely the beginning of a family life since developed. His paternal expression was one of domination and indulgence, without the perception of the needs of his children, without any anticipation of their entrance into a wider life, or any belief that they could have a worthy life apart from him. If that rudimentary conception of family life ended in such violent disaster, the fact that we have learned to be more decorous in our conduct does not demonstrate that by following the same line of theory we may not reach a like misery.

Wounded affection there is sure to be, but this could be reduced to a modicum if we could preserve a sense of the relation of the individual to the family, and of the latter to society, and if we had been given a code of ethics dealing with these larger relationships, instead of a code designed to apply so exclusively to relationships obtaining only between individuals.

Doubtless the clashes and jars which we all feel most keenly are those which occur when two standards of morals, both honestly held and believed in, are brought sharply together. The awkwardness and constraint we experience when two standards of conventions and manners clash but feebly prefigure this deeper difference.

Charlotte Perkins Gilman was born in 1860 in Hartford, Connecticut. Her father, the son of Mary Beecher Perkins and nephew of Catharine Beecher and Harriet Beecher Stowe, was a librarian, first in Boston and later in San Francisco when he and his wife separated. After a painful childhood devoted to learning to restrain her feelings and relentlessly form her "character," Charlotte Perkins supported herself by teaching art and painting advertising cards. In 1884 she married the artist Charles Stetson. After the birth of their child, Katherine Beecher Stetson, the then Mrs. Stetson had a mental breakdown which she described in her short story "The Yellow Wall-Paper" (1892) and later in her autobiography, *The Living of Charlotte Perkins Gilman* (1935). In 1890 she and her husband separated; four years later they were divorced. In 1900 she married her cousin, G. Houghton Gilman.

Although Mrs. Gilman never felt that she had fully recovered from her breakdown, she was active on the lecture circuit for many years speaking on women's rights and the necessity for social reorganization, and at the same time managed to produce a slim volume of poems, *In This Our World* (1893), to publish, edit, and be the sole contributor to a magazine, *The Forerunner* (1909–16), to write a novel, *What Diantha Did* (1910), and to produce a considerable amount of original and pungent sociology, including *Women and Economics* (1898), *The Home, Its Work and Influence* (1903), and *His Religion and Hers* (1923).

Mrs. Gilman had been strongly influenced by Lester Ward in her thinking. She was charmed by Ward's suggestion that the female was the primary sex and the male a kind of afterthought, and, more importantly, she was convinced by Ward's confidence that human beings could control their social environment through intelligent planning. But her writings were in no sense derivative, and were marked by her mordant wit as well as by a passion for privacy which gave her vision of the good society a somewhat antiseptic quality. Mrs. Gilman committed suicide in 1935 when she began to be bothered by the inoperable cancer she had lived with for more than a year, thereby transforming her death into a final act of self-control.

The Yellow Wall-Paper, Charlotte Perkins Gilman*

It is very seldom that mere ordinary people like John and myself secure ancestral halls for the summer.

A colonial mansion, a hereditary estate, I would say a haunted house, and reach the height of romantic felicity—but that would be asking too much of fate!

Still I will proudly declare that there is something queer about it.

Else, why should it be let so cheaply? And why have stood so long untenanted?

John laughs at me, of course, but one expects that in [him]. John is practical in the extreme. He has no patience with faith, an intense horror of superstition, and he scoffs openly at any talk of things not to be felt and seen and put down in figures.

John is a physician, and *perhaps*—(I would not say it to a living soul, of course, but this is dead paper and a great relief to my mind)—*perhaps* that is one reason I do not get well faster.

You see he does not believe I am sick! And what can one do?

If a physician of high standing, and one's own husband, assures friends and relatives that there is really nothing the matter with one but temporary nervous depression—a slight hysterical tendency—what is one to do?

My brother is also a physician, and also of high standing, and he says the same thing.

So I take phosphates or phosphites—whichever it is—and

---

* "The Yellow Wall-Paper" was first published in *New England Magazine* in 1891 and was reprinted by William Dean Howells in *Great Modern American Stories* (New York, 1920).

tonics, and journeys, and air, and exercise, and am absolutely forbidden to "work" until I am well again.

Personally, I disagree with their ideas.

Personally, I believe that congenial work, with excitement and change, would do me good.

But what is one to do?

I did write for a while in spite of them; but it *does* exhaust me a good deal—having to be so sly about it, or else meet with heavy opposition.

I sometimes fancy that in my condition if I had less opposition and more society and stimulus—but John says the very worst thing I can do is to think about my condition, and I confess it always makes me feel bad.

So I will let it alone and talk about the house.

The most beautiful place! It is quite alone, standing well back from the road, quite three miles from the village. It makes me think of English places that you read about, for there are hedges and walls and gates that lock, and lots of separate little houses for the gardeners and people.

There is a *delicious* garden! I never saw such a garden—large and shady, full of box-bordered paths, and lined with long grape-covered arbors with seats under them.

There were greenhouses, too, but they are all broken now.

There was some legal trouble, I believe, something about the heirs and co-heirs; anyhow, the place has been empty for years.

That spoils my ghostliness, I am afraid, but I don't care—there is something strange about the house—I can feel it.

I even said so to John one moonlight evening, but he said what I felt was a draught, and shut the window.

I get unreasonably angry with John sometimes. I'm sure I never used to be so sensitive. I think it is due to this nervous condition.

But John says if I feel so I shall neglect proper self-control; so I take pains to control myself—before him, at least, and that makes me very tired.

I don't like our room a bit. I wanted one downstairs that

opened on the piazza and had roses all over the window, and such pretty old-fashioned chintz hangings! But John would not hear of it.

He said there was only one window and not room for two beds, and no near room for him if he took another.

He is very careful and loving, and hardly lets me stir without special direction.

I have a schedule prescription for each hour in the day; he takes all care from me, and so I feel basely ungrateful not to value it more.

He said we came here solely on my account, that I was to have perfect rest and all the air I could get. "Your exercise depends on your strength, my dear," said he, "and your food somewhat on your appetite; but air you can absorb all the time." So we took the nursery at the top of the house.

It is a big, airy room, the whole floor nearly, with windows that look all ways, and air and sunshine galore. It was nursery first and then playroom and gymnasium, I should judge; for the windows are barred for little children, and there are rings and things in the walls.

The paint and paper look as if a boys' school had used it. It is stripped off—the paper—in great patches all around the head of my bed, about as far as I can reach, and in a great place on the other side of the room low down. I never saw a worse paper in my life.

One of those sprawling flamboyant patterns committing every artistic sin.

It is dull enough to confuse the eye in following, pronounced enough constantly to irritate and provoke study, and when you follow the lame uncertain curves for a little distance they suddenly commit suicide—plunge off at outrageous angles, destroy themselves in unheard of contradictions.

The color is repellant, almost revolting; a smouldering unclean yellow, strangely faded by the slow-turning sunlight.

It is a dull yet lurid orange in some places, a sickly sulphur tint in others.

No wonder the children hated it! I should hate it myself if I had to live in this room long.

There comes John, and I must put this away—he hates to have me write a word.

* * * * * * * * * * *

We have been here two weeks, and I haven't felt like writing before, since that first day.

I am sitting by the window now, up in this atrocious nursery, and there is nothing to hinder my writing as much as I please, save lack of strength.

John is away all day, and even some nights when his cases are serious.

I am glad my case is not serious!

But these nervous troubles are dreadfully depressing.

John does not know how much I really suffer. He knows there is no *reason* to suffer, and that satisfies him.

Of course it is only nervousness. It does weigh on me so not to do my duty in any way!

I meant to be such a help to John, such a real rest and comfort, and here I am a comparative burden already!

Nobody would believe what an effort it is to do what little I am able—to dress and entertain, and order things.

It is fortunate Mary is so good with the baby. Such a dear baby!

And yet I *cannot* be with him, it makes me so nervous.

I suppose John never was nervous in his life. He laughs at me so about this wall-paper!

At first he meant to repaper the room, but afterwards he said that I was letting it get the better of me, and that nothing was worse for a nervous patient than to give way to such fancies.

He said that after the wall-paper was changed it would be the heavy bedstead, and then the barred windows, and then that gate at the head of the stairs, and so on.

"You know the place is doing you good," he said, "and really, dear, I don't care to renovate the house just for a three months' rental."

"Then do let us go downstairs," I said, "there are such pretty rooms there."

Then he took me in his arms and called me a blessed little goose, and said he would go down cellar, if I wished, and have it whitewashed into the bargain.

But he is right enough about the beds and windows and things.

It is an airy and comfortable room as any one need wish, and, of course, I would not be so silly as to make him uncomfortable just for a whim.

I'm really getting quite fond of the big room, all but that horrid paper.

Out of one window I can see the garden, those mysterious deep-shaded arbors, the riotous old-fashioned flowers, and bushes and gnarly trees.

Out of another I get a lovely view of the bay and a little private wharf belonging to the estate. There is a beautiful shaded lane that runs down there from the house. I always fancy I see people walking in these numerous paths and arbors, but John has cautioned me not to give way to fancy in the least. He says that with my imaginative power and habit of story-making, a nervous weakness like mine is sure to lead to all manner of excited fancies, and that I ought to use my will and good sense to check the tendency. So I try.

I think sometimes that if I were only well enough to write a little it would relieve the press of ideas and rest me.

But I find I get pretty tired when I try.

It is so discouraging not to have any advice and companionship about my work. When I get really well, John says we will ask Cousin Henry and Julia down for a long visit; but he says he would as soon put fireworks in my pillowcase as to let me have those stimulating people about now.

I wish I could get well faster.

But I must not think about that. This paper looks to me as if it _knew_ what a vicious influence it had!

There is a recurrent spot where the pattern lolls like a broken neck and two bulbous eyes stare at you upside down.

I get positively angry with the impertinence of it and the

everlastingness. Up and down and sideways they crawl, and
those absurd, unblinking eyes are everywhere. There is one
place where two breadths didn't match, and the eyes go all
up and down the line, one a little higher than the other.

I never saw so much expression in an inanimate thing before, and we all know how much expression they have! I
used to lie awake as a child and get more entertainment and
terror out of blank walls and plain furniture than most children could find in a toy-store.

I remember what a kindly wink the knobs of our big, old
bureau used to have, and there was one chair that always
seemed like a strong friend.

I used to feel that if any of the other things looked too
fierce I could always hop into that chair and be safe.

The furniture in this room is no worse than inharmonious,
however, for we had to bring it all from downstairs. I suppose when this was used as a playroom they had to take the
nursery things out, and no wonder! I never saw such ravages
as the children have made here.

The wall-paper, as I said before, is torn off in spots, and
it sticketh closer than a brother—they must have had per-
severance as well as hatred.

Then the floor is scratched and gouged and splintered, the
plaster itself is dug out here and there, and this great heavy
bed which is all we found in the room, looks as if it had been
through the wars.

But I don't mind it a bit—only the paper.

There comes John's sister. Such a dear girl as she is, and
so careful of me! I must not let her find me writing.

She is a perfect and enthusiastic housekeeper, and hopes
for no better profession. I verily believe she thinks it is the
writing which made me sick!

But I can write when she is out, and see her a long way off
from these windows.

There is one that commands the road, a lovely shaded winding road, and one that just looks off over the country. A lovely
country, too, full of great elms and velvet meadows.

This wall-paper has a kind of sub-pattern in a different

shade, a particularly irritating one, for you can only see it in certain lights, and not clearly then.

But in the places where it isn't faded and where the sun is just so—I can see a strange, provoking, formless sort of figure, that seems to skulk about behind that silly and conspicuous front design.

There's sister on the stairs!

* * * * * * * * * * *

Well, the Fourth of July is over! The people are all gone and I am tired out. John thought it might do me good to see a little company, so we just had mother and Nellie and the children down for a week.

Of course I didn't do a thing. Jennie sees to everything now.

But it tired me all the same.

John says if I don't pick up faster he shall send me to Weir Mitchell in the fall.

But I don't want to go there at all. I had a friend who was in his hands once, and she says he is just like John and my brother, only more so!

Besides, it is such an undertaking to go so far.

I don't feel as if it was worth while to turn my hand over for anything, and I'm getting dreadfully fretful and querulous.

I cry at nothing, and cry most of the time.

Of course I don't when John is here, or anybody else, but when I am alone.

And I am alone a good deal just now. John is kept in town very often by serious cases, and Jennie is good and lets me alone when I want her to.

So I walk a little in the garden or down that lovely land, sit on the porch under the roses, and lie down up here a good deal.

I'm getting really fond of the room in spite of the wall-paper. Perhaps *because* of the wall-paper.

It dwells in my mind so!

I lie here on this great immovable bed—it is nailed down, I believe—and follow that pattern about by the hour. It is as good as gymnastics, I assure you. I start, we'll say, at the bottom, down in the corner over there where it has not been touched, and I determine for the thousandth time that I *will* follow that pointless pattern to some sort of a conclusion.

I know a little of the principle of design, and I know this thing was not arranged on any laws of radiation, or alternation, or repetition, or symmetry, or anything else that I ever heard of.

It is repeated, of course, by the breadths, but not otherwise.

Looked at in one way each breadth stands alone, the bloated curves and flourishes—a kind of "debased Romanesque" with delirium tremens—go waddling up and down in isolated columns of fatuity.

But, on the other hand, they connect diagonally, and the sprawling outlines run off in great slanting waves of optic horror, like a lot of wallowing sea-weeds in full chase.

The whole thing goes horizontally, too, at least it seems so, and I exhaust myself trying to distinguish the order of its going in that direction.

They have used a horizontal breadth for a frieze, and that adds wonderfully to the confusion.

There is one end of the room where it is almost intact, and there, when the crosslights fade and the low sun shines directly upon it, I can almost fancy radiation after all,—the interminable grotesques seem to form around a common centre and rush off in headlong plunges of equal distraction.

It makes me tired to follow it. I will take a nap I guess.

* * * * * * * * * * * *

I don't know why I should write this.

I don't want to.

I don't feel able.

And I know John would think it absurd. But I *must* say what I feel and think in some way—it is such a relief!

But the effort is getting to be greater than the relief.

Half the time now I am awfully lazy, and lie down ever so much.

John says I mustn't lose my strength, and has me take cod

liver oil and lots of tonics and things, to say nothing of ale and wine and rare meat.

Dear John! He loves me very dearly, and hates to have me sick. I tried to have a real earnest reasonable talk with him the other day, and tell him how I wish he would let me go and make a visit to Cousin Henry and Julia.

But he said I wasn't able to go, nor able to stand it after I got there; and I did not make out a very good case for myself, for I was crying before I had finished.

It is getting to be a great effort for me to think straight. Just this nervous weakness I suppose.

And dear John gathered me up in his arms, and just carried me upstairs and laid me on the bed, and sat by me and read to me till it tired my head.

He said I was his darling and his comfort and all he had, and that I must take care of myself for his sake, and keep well.

He says no one but myself can help me out of it, that I must use my will and self-control and not let any silly fancies run away with me.

There's one comfort, the baby is well and happy, and does not have to occupy this nursery with the horrid wall-paper.

If we had not used it, that blessed child would have! What a fortunate escape! Why, I wouldn't have a child of mine, an impressionable little thing, live in such a room for worlds.

I never thought of it before, but it is lucky that John kept me here after all, I can stand it so much easier than a baby, you see.

Of course I never mention it to them any more—I am too wise—but I keep watch for it all the same.

There are things in that paper that nobody knows but me, or ever will.

Behind that outside pattern the dim shapes get clearer every day.

It is always the same shape, only very numerous.

And it is like a woman stooping down and creeping about behind that pattern. I don't like it a bit. I wonder—I begin to think—I wish John would take me away from here!

* * * * * * * * * * *

It is so hard to talk with John about my case, because he is so wise, and because he loves me so.

But I tried it last night.

It was moonlight. The moon shines in all around just as the sun does.

I hate to see it sometimes, it creeps so slowly, and always comes in by one window or another.

John was asleep and I hated to waken him, so I kept still and watched the moonlight on that undulating wall-paper till I felt creepy.

The faint figure behind seemed to shake the pattern, just as if she wanted to get out.

I got up softly and went to feel and see if the paper *did* move, and when I came back John was awake.

"What is it, little girl?" he said. "Don't go walking about like that—you'll get cold."

I thought it was a good time to talk so I told him that I really was not gaining here, and that I wished he would take me away.

"Why darling!" said he, "our lease will be up in three weeks, and I can't see how to leave before.

"The repairs are not done at home, and I cannot possibly leave town just now. Of course if you were in any danger, I could and would, but you really are better, dear, whether you can see it or not. I am a doctor, dear, and I know. You are gaining flesh and color, your appetite is better, I feel really much easier about you."

"I don't weigh a bit more," said I, "nor as much; and my appetite may be better in the evening when you are here, but it is worse in the morning when you are away!"

"Bless her little heart!" said he with a big hug, "she shall be as sick as she pleases! But now let's improve the shining hours by going to sleep, and talk about it in the morning!"

"And you won't go away?" I asked gloomily.

"Why, how can I, dear? It is only three weeks more and then we will take a nice little trip of a few days while Jennie is getting the house ready. Really, dear, you are better!"

"Better in body perhaps—" I began, and stopped short, for he sat up straight and looked at me with such a stern, reproachful look that I could not say another word.

"My darling," said he, "I beg of you, for my sake and for our child's sake, as well as for your own, that you will never for one instant let that idea enter your mind! There is nothing so dangerous, so fascinating, to a temperament like yours. It is a false and foolish fancy. Can you not trust me as a physician when I tell you so?"

So of course I said no more on that score, and we went to sleep before long. He thought I was asleep first, but I wasn't, and lay there for hours trying to decide whether that front pattern and the back pattern really did move together or separately.

* * * * * * * * * * * *

On a pattern like this, by daylight, there is a lack of sequence, a defiance of law, that is a constant irritant to a normal mind.

The color is hideous enough, and unreliable enough, and infuriating enough, but the pattern is torturing.

You think you have mastered it, but just as you get well underway in following, it turns a back-somersault and there you are. It slaps you in the face, knocks you down, and tramples upon you. It is like a bad dream.

The outside pattern is a florid arabesque, reminding one of a fungus. If you can imagine a toadstool in joints, an interminable string of toadstools, budding and sprouting in endless convolutions—why, that is something like it.

That is, sometimes!

There is one marked peculiarity about this paper, a thing nobody seems to notice but myself, and that is that it changes as the light changes.

When the sun shoots in through the east window—I always watch for that first, long, straight ray—it changes so quickly that I never can quite believe it.

That is why I watch it always.

By moonlight—the moon shines in all night when there is a moon—I wouldn't know it was the same paper.

At night in any kind of light, in twilight, candlelight, lamplight, and worst of all by moonlight, it becomes bars! The outside pattern I mean, and the woman behind it is as plain as can be.

I didn't realize for a long time what the thing was that showed behind, that dim sub-pattern, but now I am quite sure it is a woman.

By daylight she is subdued, quiet. I fancy it is the pattern that keeps her so still. It is so puzzling. It keeps me quiet by the hour.

I lie down ever so much now. John says it is good for me, and to sleep all I can.

Indeed he started the habit by making me lie down for an hour after each meal.

It is a very bad habit I am convinced, for you see I don't sleep.

And that cultivates deceit, for I don't tell them I'm awake —O, no!

The fact is I am getting a little afraid of John.

He seems very queer sometimes, and even Jennie has an inexplicable look.

It strikes me occasionally, just as a scientific hypothesis, that perhaps it is the paper!

I have watched John when he did not know I was looking, and come into the room suddenly on the most innocent excuses, and I've caught him several times *looking at the paper!* And Jennie too. I caught Jennie with her hand on it once.

She didn't know I was in the room, and when I asked her in a quiet, a very quiet voice, with the most restrained manner possible, what she was doing with the paper—she turned around as if she had been caught stealing, and looked quite angry—asked me why I should frighten her so!

Then she said that the paper stained everything it touched, that she had found yellow smooches on all my clothes and John's, and she wished we would be more careful!

Did not that sound innocent? But I know she was studying that pattern, and I am determined that nobody shall find it out but myself!

* * * * * * * * * * *

Life is very much more exciting now than it used to be. You see I have something more to expect, to look forward to, to watch. I really do eat better, and am more quiet than I was.

John is so pleased to see me improve! He laughed a little the other day, and said I seemed to be flourishing in spite of my wall-paper.

I turned it off with a laugh. I had no intention of telling him it was *because* of the wall-paper—he would make fun of me. He might even want to take me away.

I don't want to leave now until I have found it out. There is a week more, and I think that will be enough.

* * * * * * * * * * *

I'm feeling ever so much better! I don't sleep much at night, for it is so interesting to watch developments; but I sleep a good deal in the daytime.

In the daytime it is tiresome and perplexing.

There are always new shoots on the fungus, and new shades of yellow all over it. I cannot keep count of them, though I have tried conscientiously.

It is the strangest yellow, that wall-paper! It makes me think of all the yellow things I ever saw—not beautiful ones like buttercups, but old foul, bad yellow things.

But there is something else about that paper—the smell! I noticed it the moment we came into the room, but with so much air and sun it was not bad. Now we have had a week of fog and rain, and whether the windows are open or not, the smell is here.

It creeps all over the house.

I find it hovering in the dining-room, skulking in the parlor, hiding in the hall, lying in wait for me on the stairs.

It gets into my hair.

Even when I go to ride, if I turn my head suddenly and surprise it—there is that smell!

Such a peculiar odor, too! I have spent hours in trying to analyze it, to find what it smelled like.

It is not bad—at first, and very gentle, but quite the subtlest, most enduring odor I ever met.

In this damp weather it is awful, I wake up in the night and find it hanging over me.

It used to disturb me at first. I thought seriously of burning the house—to reach the smell.

But now I am used to it. The only thing I can think of that it is like is the *color* of the paper! A yellow smell.

There is a very funny mark on this wall, low down, near the mopboard. A streak that runs round the room. It goes behind every piece of furniture, except the bed, a long, straight, even *smooch*, as if it had been rubbed over and over.

I wonder how it was done and who did it, and what they did it for. Round and round and round—round and round and round—it makes me dizzy!

* * * * * * * * * * * *

I really have discovered something at last.

Through watching so much at night, when it changes so, I have finally found out.

The front pattern *does* move—and no wonder! The woman behind shakes it!

Sometimes I think there are a great many women behind, and sometimes only one, and she crawls around fast, and her crawling shakes it all over.

Then in the very bright spots she keeps still, and in the very shady spots she just takes hold of the bars and shakes them hard.

And she is all the time trying to climb through. But nobody could climb through that pattern—it strangles so; I think that is why it has so many heads.

They get through, and then the pattern strangles them off and turns them upside down, and makes their eyes white!

If those heads were covered or taken off it would not be half so bad.

* * * * * * * * * * * *

I think that woman gets out in the daytime!

And I'll tell you why—privately—I've seen her!

I can see her out of every one of my windows!

It is the same woman, I know, for she is always creeping, and most women do not creep by daylight.

I see her in that long shaded lane, creeping up and down. I see her in those dark grape arbors, creeping all around the garden.

I see her on that long road under the trees, creeping along, and when a carriage comes she hides under the blackberry vines.

I don't blame her a bit. It must be very humiliating to be caught creeping by daylight!

I always lock the door when I creep by daylight. I can't do it at night, for I know John would suspect something at once.

And John is so queer now, that I don't want to irritate him. I wish he would take another room! Besides, I don't want anybody to get that woman out at night but myself.

I often wonder if I could see her out of all the windows at once.

But, turn as fast as I can, I can only see out of one at one time.

And though I always see her, she *may* be able to creep faster than I can turn!

I have watched her sometimes away off in the open country, creeping as fast as a cloud shadow in a high wind.

* * * * * * * * * * * *

If only that top pattern could be gotten off from the under one! I mean to try it, little by little.

I have found out another funny thing, but I shan't tell it this time! It does not do to trust people too much.

There are only two more days to get this paper off, and I believe John is beginning to notice. I don't like the look in his eyes.

And I heard him ask Jennie a lot of professional questions about me. She had a very good report to give.

She said I slept a good deal in the daytime.

John knows I don't sleep very well at night, for all I'm so quiet!

He asked me all sorts of questions, too, and pretended to be very loving and kind.

As if I couldn't see through him!

Still, I don't wonder he acts so, sleeping under this paper for three months.

It only interests me, but I feel sure John and Jennie are secretly affected by it.

* * * * * * * * * * * *

Hurrah! This is the last day, but it is enough. John to stay in town over night, and won't be out until this evening.

Jennie wanted to sleep with me—the sly thing! but I told her I should undoubtedly rest better for a night all alone.

That was clever, for really I wasn't alone a bit! As soon as it was moonlight and that poor thing began to crawl and shake the pattern, I got up and ran to help her.

I pulled and she shook, I shook and she pulled, and before morning we had peeled off yards of that paper.

A strip about as high as my head and half around the room.

And then when the sun came and that awful pattern began to laugh at me, I declared I would finish it to-day!

We go away to-morrow, and they are moving all my furniture down again to leave things as they were before.

Jennie looked at the wall in amazement, but I told her merrily that I did it out of pure spite at the vicious thing.

She laughed and said she wouldn't mind doing it herself, but I must not get tired.

How she betrayed herself that time!

But I am here, and no person touches this paper but Me— not *alive*!

She tried to get me out of the room—it was too patent! But I said it was so quiet and empty and clean now that I believed I would lie down again and sleep all I could; and not to wake me even for dinner—I would call when I woke.

So now she is gone, and the servants are gone, and the things are gone, and there is nothing left but that great bedstead nailed down, with the canvas mattress we found on it.

We shall sleep downstairs to-night, and take the boat home to-morrow.

I quite enjoy the room, now it is bare again.

How those children did tear about here!

This bedstead is fairly gnawed!

But I must get to work.

I have locked the door and thrown the key down into the front path.

I don't want to go out, and I don't want to have anybody come in, till John comes.

I want to astonish him.

I've got a rope up here that even Jennie did not find. If that woman does get out, and tries to get away, I can tie her!

But I forgot I could not reach far without anything to stand on!

This bed will *not* move!

I tried to lift and push it until I was lame, and then I got so angry I bit off a little piece at one corner—but it hurt my teeth.

Then I peeled off all the paper I could reach standing on the floor. It sticks horribly and the pattern just enjoys it! All those strangled heads and bulbous eyes and waddling fungus growths just shriek with derision!

I am getting angry enough to do something desperate. To jump out of the window would be admirable exercise, but the bars are too strong even to try.

Besides I wouldn't do it. Of course not. I know well enough that a step like that is improper and might be misconstrued.

I don't like to *look* out of the windows even—there are so many of those creeping women, and they creep so fast.

I wonder if they all come out of that wall-paper as I did?

But I am securely fastened now by my well-hidden rope—you don't get *me* out in the road there!

I suppose I shall have to get back behind the pattern when it comes night, and that is hard!

It is so pleasant to be out in this great room and creep around as I please!

I don't want to go outside. I won't, even if Jennie asks me to.

For outside you have to creep on the ground, and everything is green instead of yellow.

But here I can creep smoothly on the floor, and my shoulder just fits in that long smooch around the wall, so I cannot lose my way.

Why there's John at the door!

It is no use, young man, you can't open it!

How he does call and pound!

Now he's crying for an axe.

It would be a shame to break down that beautiful door!

"John dear!" said I in the gentlest voice, "the key is down by the front steps, under a plantain leaf!"

That silenced him for a few moments.

Then he said, very quietly indeed, "Open the door, my darling!"

"I can't," said I. "The key is down by the front door under a plantain leaf!"

And then I said it again, several times, very gently and slowly, and said it so often that he had to go and see, and he got it of course, and came in. He stopped short by the door.

"What is the matter?" he cried. "For God's sake, what are you doing!"

I kept on creeping just the same, but I looked at him over my shoulder.

"I've got out at last," said I, "in spite of you and Jane. And I've pulled off most of the paper, so you can't put me back!"

Now why should that man have fainted? But he did, and right across my path by the wall, so that I had to creep over him every time!

Two Callings, Charlotte Perkins Gilman*

I

I hear a deep voice through uneasy dreaming,
    A deep, soft, tender, soul-beguiling voice;
A lulling voice that bids the dreams remain,
That calms my restlessness and dulls my pain,
That thrills and fills and holds me till in seeming
    There is no other sound on earth—no choice.

"Home!" says the deep voice, "Home!" and softly singing
    Brings me a sense of safety unsurpassed;
So old! so old! The piles above the wave—
The shelter of the stone-blocked, shadowy cave—
Security of sun-kissed treetops swinging—
    Safety and Home at last!

"Home" says the sweet voice, and warm Comfort rises,
    Holding my soul with velvet-fingered hands;
Comfort of leafy lair and lapping fur,
Soft couches, cushions, curtains, and the stir
Of easy pleasures that the body prizes,
    Of soft, swift feet to serve the least commands.

I shrink—half rise—and then it murmurs "Duty!"
    Again the past rolls out—a scroll unfurled;
Allegiance and long labor due my lord—
Allegiance in an idleness abhorred—
I am the squaw—the slave—the harem beauty—
    I serve and serve, the handmaid of the world.

* "Two Callings" served as an introduction to Mrs. Gilman's book *The Home* (New York, 1910).

My soul rebels—but hark! a new note thrilling,
   Deep, deep, past finding—I protest no more;
The voice says "love!" and all those ages dim
Stand glorified and justified in him;
I bow—I kneel—the woman soul is willing—
   "Love is the law. Be still! Obey! Adore!"

And then—ah, then! The deep voice murmurs
    "Mother!"
   And all life answers from the primal sea;
A mingling of all lullabies; a peace
That asks no understanding; the release
Of nature's holiest power—who seeks another?
   Home? Home is Mother—Mother, Home—to me.

"Home!" says the deep voice; "Home and Easy
    Pleasure!
   Safety and Comfort, Laws of Life well kept!
Love!" and my heart rose thrilling at the word;
"Mother!" it nestled down and never stirred;
"Duty and Peace and Love beyond all measure!
   Home! Safety! Comfort! Mother!"—and I slept.

II

A bugle call! A clear, keen, ringing cry,
   Relentless—eloquent—that found the ear
Through fold on fold of slumber, sweet, profound—
A widening wave of universal sound,
Piercing the heart—filling the utmost sky—
   I wake—I must wake! Hear—for I must hear!

"The World! The World is crying! Hear its needs!
   Home is a part of life—I am the whole!
Home is the cradle—shall a whole life stay
Cradled in comfort through the working day?
I too am Home—the Home of all high deeds—
   The only Home to hold the human soul!

"Courage!—the front of conscious life!" it cried;
   "Courage that dares to die and dares to live!
Why should you prate of safety? Is life meant
In ignominious safety to be spent?
Is Home best valued as a place to hide?
   Come out, and give what you are here to give!

"Strength and Endurance! of high action born!"
   And all that dream of Comfort shrank away,
Turning its fond, beguiling face aside:
So Selfishness and Luxury and Pride
Stood forth revealed, till I grew fierce with scorn,
   And burned to meet the dangers of the day.

"Duty? Aye, Duty! Duty! Mark the word!"
   I turned to my old standard. It was rent
From hem to hem, and through the gaping place
I saw my undone duties to the race
Of man—neglected—spurned—how had I heard
   That word and never dreamed of what it meant!

"Duty! Unlimited—eternal—new!"
   And I? My idol on a petty shrine
Fell as I turned, and Cowardice and Sloth
Fell too, unmasked, false Duty covering both—
While the true Duty, all-embracing, high,
   Showed the clear line of noble deeds to do.

And then the great voice rang out to the sun,
   And all my terror left me, all my shame,
While every dream of joy from earliest youth
Came back and lived!—that joy unhoped was truth,
All joy, all hope, all truth, all peace grew one,
   Life opened clear, and Love? Love was its name!

So when the great word "Mother!" rang once more,
   I saw at last its meaning and its place;
Not the blind passion of the brooding past,
But Mother—the World's Mother—come at last,
To love as she had never loved before—
   To feed and guard and teach the human race.

The world was full of music clear and high!
 The world was full of light! The world was free!
And I? Awake at last, in joy untold,
Saw Love and Duty broad as life unrolled—
Wide as the earth—unbounded as the sky—
 Home was the World—the World was Home to me!

Domestic Mythology, Charlotte Perkins Gilman*

There is a school of myths connected with the home, more tenacious in their hold on the popular mind than even religious beliefs. Of all current superstitions none are deeper rooted, none so sensitive to the touch, so acutely painful in removal. We have lived to see nations outgrow some early beliefs, but others are still left us to study, in their long slow processes of decay. Belief in "the divine right of kings," for instance, is practically outgrown in America; and yet, given a king,—or even a king's brother,—and we show how much of the feeling remains in our minds, disclaim as we may the idea. Habits of thought persist through the centuries; and while a healthy brain may reject the doctrine it no longer believes, it will continue to feel the same sentiments formerly associated with that doctrine.

Wherever the pouring stream of social progress has had little influence,—in remote rural regions, hidden valleys, and neglected coasts,—we find still in active force some of the earliest myths. They may change their names as new religions take the place of old, Santa Claus and St. Valentine holding sway in place of forgotten deities of dim antiquity, but the festival or custom embodied is the same that was enjoyed by those most primitive ancestors. Of all hidden valleys none has so successfully avoided discovery as the Home. Church and State might change as they would—as they must; science changed, art changed, business changed, all human functions changed and grew save those of the home. Every man's home was his castle, and there he maintained as far as pos-

* "Domestic Mythology," excerpted here, was the third chapter of Mrs. Gilman's book *The Home* (New York, 1910).

sible the facts and fancies of the place, unaltered from century to century.

The facts have been too many for him. The domestic hearth, with its undying flame, has given way to the gilded pipes of the steam heater and the flickering evanescence of the gas range. But the sentiment about the domestic hearth is still in play. The original necessity for the ceaseless presence of the woman to maintain that altar fire—and it was an altar fire in very truth at one period—has passed with the means of prompt ignition; the matchbox has freed the housewife from that incessant service, but the *feeling* that women should stay at home is with us yet.

The time when all men were enemies, when out-of-doors was one promiscuous battlefield, when home, well fortified, was the only place on earth where a man could rest in peace, is past, long past. But the *feeling* that home is more secure and protective than anywhere else is not outgrown.

So we have quite a list of traditional sentiments connected with home life well worth our study; not only for their interest as archaeological relics, but because of their positive injury to the life of to-day, and in the hope that a fuller knowledge will lead to sturdy action. So far we have but received and transmitted this group of myths, handed down from the dim past; we continue to hand them down in the original package, never looking to see if they are so; if we, with our twentieth-century brains really believe them.

A resentful shiver runs through the reader at the suggestion of such an examination. "What! Scrutinise the home, that sacred institution, and even question it? Sacrilegious!" This very feeling proves the frail and threadbare condition of this group of ideas. Good healthy young ideas can meet daylight and be handled, but very old and feeble ones, that have not been touched for centuries, naturally dread inspection, and no wonder—they seldom survive it.

Let us begin with one especially dominant domestic myth, that fondly cherished popular idea—"the privacy of the home." In the home who has any privacy? Privacy means the decent seclusion of the individual, the right to do what one likes unwatched, uncriticised, unhindered. Neither father, mother, nor child has this right at home. The young man setting up in "chambers," the young woman in college room or studio, at last they realise what privacy is, at last they have the right to be alone. The home does provide some privacy for the family as a lump—but it remains a lump—there is no privacy for the individual. When homes and families began this was enough, people were simple, unspecialised, their tastes and wishes were similar; it is not enough today.

The progressive socialisation of humanity develops individuals; and this ever-increasing individuality suffers cruelly in the crude familiarity of home life. There sits the family, all ages, both sexes, as many characters as persons; and every budding expression, thought, feeling, or action has to run the gauntlet of the crowd. Suppose any member is sufficiently strong to insist on a place apart, on doing things alone and without giving information thereof to the others—is this easy in the home? Is this relished by the family?

The father, being the economic base of the whole structure, has most power in this direction; but in ninety-nine cases in a hundred he has taken his place and his work outside. In the one hundredth case, where some artist, author, or clergyman has to do his work at home—what is his opinion then of the privacy of that sacred place?

The artist flees to a studio apart, if possible; the author builds him a "den" in his garden, if he can afford it; the clergyman strives mightily to keep "the study" to himself, but even so the family, used to herding, finds it hard to respect anybody's privacy, and resents it.

The mother—poor invaded soul—finds even the bathroom door no bar to hammering little hands. From parlour to kitchen, from cellar to garret, she is at the mercy of children, servants, tradesmen, and callers. So chased and trodden is she that the very idea of privacy is lost to her mind; she never had any, she doesn't know what it is, and she cannot understand why her husband should wish to have any "reserves," any place or time, any thought or feeling, with which she may not make free.

The children, if possible, have less even than the mother. Under the close, hot focus of loving eyes, every act magnified out of all natural proportion by the close range, the child soul begins to grow. Noticed, studied, commented on, and incessantly interfered with; forced into miserable self-consciousness by this unremitting glare; our little ones grow up permanently injured in character by this lack of one of humanity's most precious rights—privacy. . . .

Private?—a place private where we admit to the most intimate personal association an absolute stranger; or more than one? Strangers by birth, by class, by race, by education—as utterly alien as it is possible to conceive—these we introduce in our homes—in our very bedchambers; in knowledge of all the daily habits of our lives—and then we talk of privacy! Moreover, these persons can talk. As they are not encouraged to talk to us, they talk the more among themselves; talk fluently, freely, in reaction from the enforced repression of "their place," and, with perhaps a tinge of natural bitterness, revenging small slights by large comment. With servants living in our homes by day and night, confronted with our strange customs and new ideas, having our family affairs always before them, and having nothing else in their occupation to offset this interest, we find in this arrangement of life a condition as far removed from privacy as could be imagined. . . .

We have seen that the privacy of the mother is at the mercy of four sets of invaders: children, servants, tradesmen, and callers. The tradesmen, in a city flat, are kept at a pleasing distance by the dumb-waiter and speaking tube; and, among rich households everywhere, the telephone is a defence. But, even at such long range, the stillness and peace of the home, the chance to do quiet continued work of any sort, are at the mercy of jarring electric bell or piercing whistle. One of the joys of the country vacation is the escape from just these things; the constant calls on time and attention, the interruption of whatever one seeks to do, by these mercantile demands against which the home offers no protection.

In less favoured situations, in the great majority of comfortable homes, the invader gets far closer. "The lady of the house" is demanded, and must come forth. The front door opens, the back door yawns, the maid pursues her with the calls of tradesmen, regular and irregular; from the daily butcher to the unescapable agent with a visiting card. Of course we resist this as best we may with a bulwark of trained servants. That is one of the main uses of servants—to offer some protection to the inmates of this so private place, the home!

Then comes the fourth class—callers. A whole series of revelations as to privacy comes here; a list so long and deep as to tempt a whole new chapter on that one theme. Here it can be but touched on, just a mention of the most salient points.

First there is the bulwark aforesaid, the servant, trained to protect a place called private from the entrance of a class of persons privileged to come in. To hold up the hands of the servant comes the lie; the common social lie, so palpable that it has no moral value to most of us—"Not at home!"

The home is private. Therefore, to be in private, you must claim to be out of it!

Back of this comes a whole series of intrenchments—the reception room, to delay the attack while the occupant hastily assumes defensive armour; the parlour or drawing room, wherein we may hold the enemy in play, cover the retreat of non-combatants, and keep some inner chambers still reserved; the armour above mentioned—costume and manner, not for the home and its inmates, but meant to keep the observer from forming an opinion as to the real home life; and then all the weapons crudely described in rural regions as "company manners," our whole system of defence and attack; by which we strive, and strive ever in vain, to maintain our filmy fiction of the privacy of the home.

The sanctity of the home is another dominant domestic myth. That we should revere the processes of nature as being the laws of God is good; a healthy attitude of mine. But why revere some more than others, and the lower more than the higher?

The home, as our oldest institution, is necessarily our lowest, it came first, before we were equal to any higher manifestation. The home processes are those which maintain the individual in health and comfort, or are intended to; and those which reproduce the individual. These are vital processes, healthy, natural, indispensable, but why sacred? To eat, to sleep, to breathe, to dress, to rest and amuse one's self—these are good and useful deeds; but are they more hallowed than others?

Then the shocked home-worshipper protests that it is not these physical and personal functions which he holds in reverence, but "the sacred duties of maternity," and "all those precious emotions which centre in the home."

Let us examine this view; but, first let us examine the sense of sanctity itself—see what part it holds in our psychology. In the first dawn of these emotions of reverence and sanctity, while man was yet a savage, the priest-craft of the day forced upon the growing racial mind a sense of darkness and mystery, a system of "tabu"—of "that which is forbidden." In China still, as term of high respect, the imperial seat of government is called "the Forbidden City." To the dim thick early mind, reverence was confounded with mystery and restriction.

To-day, in ever-growing light, with microscope and telescope and Röntgen ray, we are learning the true reverence that follows knowledge, and outgrowing that which rests on ignorance.

The savage reveres a thing because he cannot understand it—we revere because we can understand.

The ancient sacred must be covered up; to honour king or god you must shut your eyes, hide your face, fall prostrate.

The modern sacred must be shown and known of all, and honoured by understanding and observance.

Let not our sense of sanctity shrink so sensitively from the searcher; if the home is really sacred, it can bear the light. So now for these "sacred processes of reproduction." (Protest.

"We did not say 'reproduction,' we said 'maternity!'") And what is maternity but one of nature's processes of reproduction? Maternity and paternity and the sweet conscious duties and pleasures of human child-rearing are only more sacred than reproduction by fission, by parthenogenesis, by any other primitive device, because they are later in the course of evolution, so higher in the true measure of growth; and for that very reason education, the social function of child-rearing, is higher than maternity; later, more developed, more valuable, and so more sacred. Maternity is common to all animals —but we do not hold it sacred, in them. We have stultified motherhood most brutally in two of our main food products —milk and eggs—exploiting this function remorselessly to our own appetites.

In humanity, in some places and classes we do hold it sacred, however. Why? "Because it is the highest, sweetest, best thing we know!" will be eagerly answered. Is it—really? Is it better than Liberty, better than Justice, better than Art, Government, Science, Industry, Religion? How can that function which is common to savage, barbarian, peasant, to all kinds and classes, low and high, be nobler, sweeter, better, than those late-come, hard-won, slowly developed processes which make men greater, wiser, kinder, stronger from age to age? . . .

A good, clean, healthy, modern home, with free people living and loving in it, is no more sacred than a schoolhouse. The schoolhouse represents a larger love, a higher function, a farther development for humanity. Let us revere, let us worship, but erect and open-eyed, the highest, not the lowest; the future, not the past! . . .

It will be a great thing for the human soul when it finally stops worshipping backwards. We are pushed forward by the social forces, reluctant and stumbling, our faces over our shoulders, clutching at every relic of the past as we are forced along; still adoring whatever is behind us. We insist upon worshipping "the God of our fathers." Why not the God of our children? Does eternity only stretch one way?

Another devoutly believed domestic myth is that of the "economy" of the home.

The man is to earn, and the woman to save, to expend judiciously, to administer the products of labour to the best advantage. We honestly suppose that our method of providing for human wants by our system of domestic economy is the cheapest possible; that it would cost more to live in any other way. The economic dependence of women upon men, with all its deadly consequences, is defended because of our conviction that her labour in the home is as productive as his out of it; that the marriage is a partnership in which, if she does not contribute in cash, she does in labour, care, and saving.

It is with a real sense of pain that one remorselessly punctures this beautiful bubble. When plain financial facts appear, when economic laws are explained, then it is shown that our "domestic economy" is the most wasteful department of life. The subject is taken up in detail in the chapter on home industries; here the mere statement is made, that the domestic system of feeding, clothing, and cleaning humanity costs more time, more strength, and more money than it could cost in any other way except absolute individual isolation. The most effort and the least result are found where each individual does all things for himself. The least effort and the most result are found in the largest specialisation and exchange.

The little industrial group of the home—from two to five or ten—is very near the bottom of the line of economic progress. It costs men more money, women more work, both more time and strength than need be by more than half. A method of living that wastes half the time and strength of the world is not economical.

Somewhat along this line of popular belief comes that pretty fiction about "the traces of a woman's hand." It is a minor myth, but very dear to us. We imagine that a woman —any woman—just because she is a woman, has an artistic touch, an aesthetic sense, by means of which she can cure ugliness as kings were supposed to cure scrofula, by the laying on of hands. We find this feelingly alluded to in fiction where some lonely miner, coming to his uncared-for cabin, discovers a flower pot, a birdcage and a tidy, and delightedly proclaims—"A woman has been here." He thinks it is beautiful because it is feminine—a sexuo-aesthetic confusion common to all animals.

The beauty-sense, as appealed to by sex-distinctions, is a strange field of study. The varied forms of crests, combs, wattles, callosities of blue and crimson, and the like, with which one sex attracts the other, are interesting to follow; but they do not appeal to the cultivated sense of beauty. Beauty—beauty of sky and sea, of flower and shell, of all true works of art—has nothing to do with sex.

When you turn admiring eyes on the work of those who *have* beautified the world for us; on the immortal marbles and mosaics, vessels of gold and glass, on building and carving and modelling and painting; the enduring beauty of the rugs and shawls of India, the rich embroideries of Japan, you do not find in the great record of world-beauty such conspicuous traces of a woman's hand.

Then study real beauty in the home—any home—all homes. There are women in our farm-houses—women who painfully strive to produce beauty in many forms; crocheted, knitted, crazy-quilted, sewed together, stuck together, made of wax; made—of all awful things—of the hair of the dead! . . .

In her house or on her person "the traces of a woman's hand" may speak loud of sex, and so please her opposite; but there is no assurance of beauty in the result. This sweet tradition is but another of our domestic myths.

Among them all, most prominent of all, is one so general and so devoutly accepted as to call for most thorough exposure. This is our beloved dogma of "the maternal instinct." The mother, by virtue of being a mother, is supposed to know just what is right for her children. We honestly believe, men and women both, that in motherhood inheres the power rightly to care for childhood.

This is a nature-myth, far older than humanity. We base the theory on observation of the lower animals. We watch the birds and beasts and insects, and see that the mother does all for the young; and as she has no instruction and no assistance, yet achieves her ends, we attribute her success to the maternal instinct.

What is an instinct? It is an inherited habit. It is an automatic action of the nervous system, developed in surviving species of many generations of repetition; and performing most intricate feats.

There is an insect which prepares for its young to eat a carefully paralysed caterpillar. This ingenious mother lays her eggs in a neatly arranged hole, then stings a caterpillar, so accurately as to deprive him of motion but not of life, and seals up the hole over eggs and fresh meat in full swing of the maternal instinct. A cruelly inquiring observer took out the helpless caterpillar as soon as he was put in; but the instinct-guided mother sealed up the hole just as happily. She had done the trick, as her instinct prompted, and there was no allowance for scientific observers in that prompting. She had no intelligence, only instinct. You may observe mother instinct at its height in a fond hen sitting on china eggs—instinct, but no brains.

We, being animals, do retain some rudiments of the animal instincts; but only rudiments. The whole course of civilisation has tended to develop in us a conscious intelligence, the value of which to the human race is far greater than instinct. Instinct can only be efficient in directing actions which are unvaryingly repeated by each individual for each occasion. It is that repetition which creates the instinct. When the environment of an animal changes he has to use something more than instinct, or he becomes ex-tinct!

The human environment is in continual flux, and changes more and more quickly as social evolution progresses. No personal conditions are so general and unvarying with us as to have time to develop an instinct; the only true ones for our race are the social instincts—and maternity is not a social process.

Education is a social process, the very highest. To collect the essentials of human progress and supply them to the young, so that each generation may improve more rapidly, that is education. The animals have no parallel to this. The education of the animal young by the animal mother tends only to maintain life, not to improve it. The education of a child, and by education is meant every influence which reaches it, from birth to maturity, is a far more subtle and elaborate process.

The health and growth of the body, the right processes of mental development, the ethical influences which shape character—these are large and serious cares, for which our surviving driblets of instinct make no provision. If there were an instinct inherent in human mothers sufficient to care rightly for their children, then all human mothers would care rightly for their children.

Do they?

What percentage of our human young live to grow up? About fifty per cent. What percentage are healthy? We do not even expect them to be healthy. So used are we to "infantile diseases" that our idea of a mother's duty is to nurse sick children, not to raise well ones! What percentage of our children grow up properly proportioned, athletic and vigorous? Ask the army surgeon who turns down the majority of applicants for military service. What percentage of our children grow up with strong, harmonious characters, wise and good? Ask the great army of teachers and preachers who are trying for ever and ever to somewhat improve the adult humanity which is turned out upon the world from the care of its innumerable mothers and their instincts.

Our eyes grow moist with emotion as we speak of our mothers—our own mothers—and what they have done for us. Our voices thrill and tremble with pathos and veneration as we speak of "the mothers of great men—" mother of Abraham Lincoln! Mother of George Washington! and so on. Had Wilkes Booth no mother? Was Benedict Arnold an orphan?

Who, in the name of all common sense, raises our huge

and growing crop of idiots, imbeciles, cripples, defectives, and degenerates, the vicious and the criminal; as well as all the vast mass of slow-minded, prejudiced, ordinary people who clog the wheels of progress? Are the mothers to be credited with all that is good and the fathers with all that is bad?

That we are what we are is due to these two factors, mothers and fathers.

Our physical environment we share with all animals. Our social environment is what modifies heredity and develops human character. The kind of country we live in, the system of government, of religion, of education, of business, of ordinary social customs and convention, this is what develops mankind, this is given by our fathers.

What does maternal instinct contribute to this sum of influences? Has maternal instinct even evolved any method of feeding, dressing, teaching, disciplining, educating children which commands attention, not to say respect? It has not.

The mothers of each nation, governed only by this rudimentary instinct, repeat from generation to generation the mistakes of their more ignorant ancestors; like a dog turning around three times before he lies down on the carpet, because his thousand-remove progenitors turned round in the grass!

That the care and education of children have developed at all is due to the intelligent efforts of doctors, nurses, teachers, and such few parents as chose to exercise their human brains instead of their brute instincts.

That the care and education of children are still at the disgraceful level generally existent is due to our leaving these noble functions to the unquestioned dominance of a force which, even among animals, is not infallible, and which, in our stage of socialisation, is practically worthless.

Of all the myths which befog the popular mind, of all false worship which prevents us from recognising the truth, this matriolatry is one most dangerous. Blindly we bow to the word "mother"—worshipping the recreative processes of nature as did forgotten nations of old time in their great phallic religions.

The processes of nature are to be studied, not worshipped; the laws of nature find best reverence in our intelligent understanding and observance, not in obsequious adoration. When the human mother shows that she understands her splendid function by developing a free, strong, healthy body; by selecting a vigorous and noble mate; by studying the needs of childhood, and meeting them with proficient services, her own or that of others better fitted; by presenting to the world a race of children who do not die in infancy, who are not preyed upon by "preventable diseases," who grow up straight, strong, intelligent, free-minded, and right-intentioned; then we shall have some reason to honour motherhood, and it will be brain-work and soul-work that we honour. Intelligence, study, experience, science, love that has more than a physical basis—human motherhood—not the uncertain rudiments of a brute instinct!

The Living of Charlotte Perkins Gilman, Charlotte Perkins Gilman*

When about fifteen years old I was told of our extremely remote connection with English royalty, and wrote eagerly to my learned father to inquire as to the facts—*was* I related to Queen Victoria? To which he solemnly replied, "It is quite true that you are related to Queen Victoria, but there are a great many persons between you and the throne and I should not advise you to look forward to it." . . .

The immediate line I am really proud of is the Beecher family. Dr. Lyman Beecher was my father's grandfather, his twelve children were world-servers. It is the fashion of late among juveniles of quite different origins to contemptuously dismiss the settlers and builders of New England as "Puritanic." One needs more historical perspective than is possessed by these persons to appreciate the physical and moral courage of those Great Adventurers; their energy and endurance; their inventive progressiveness. The "Blue Laws" of Connecticut, so widely sneered at, were a great advance in liberality from the English laws behind them.

As characters broadened with the spread of the growing nation new thinkers appeared, the urge toward heaven was humanized in a widening current of social improvement, making New England a seed-bed of progressive movements, scientific, mechanical, educational, humanitarian as well as religious. Into this moving world the Beechers swung forward, the sons all ministers, the daughters as able. Harriet Beecher

* Mrs. Gilman's autobiography was published in New York in 1935.

Stowe is best known, but Catherine Beecher, who so scandalized the German theologian by her answer to "Edwards on the Will," is still honored in the middle west for her wide influence in promoting the higher education of women; and Isabella Beecher Hooker was one of the able leaders in the demand for equal suffrage.

Mary Beecher, my grandmother, the only daughter not doing public work, married Thomas C. Perkins, a lawyer of Hartford, Connecticut, and had four children, Frederick, Emily, Charles and Katherine. Emily married Edward Everett Hale, the distinguished Unitarian divine, author and lecturer; Katherine married William C. Gilman; Charles followed his father's footsteps in the Hartford law office; and Frederick, the oldest, my father, took to books as a duck to water. He read them, he wrote them, he edited them, he criticized them, he became a librarian and classified them. Before he married he knew nine languages, and continued to learn others afterward.

As an editor he helped to found, or worked on, the *Independent,* the *Christian Union* (now the *Outlook*), the *Galaxy,* Old and New, and various other papers and magazines. As a librarian he introduced the decimal system of classification, and his reference book, *The Best Reading,* was for long the standard. When I first visited the British Museum, Dr. Garnett was most polite to me for my father's sake. In those days, when scholarship could still cover a large proportion of the world's good books, he covered them well. Uncle E. E. Hale told me that he never asked my father a question that he could not immediately answer, or tell him where to find the answer.

But—with all these abilities went certain marked characteristics which prevented assured success. While a student in Yale he thrashed a professor, who had, he said, insulted him; which exhibition of temper cut short his college attendance. He was keen to feel injustice and quick to resent it; impatient of any dictation, careless of consequences when aroused. In an Irish riot in New York, during the Civil War, a Negro was being chased through the streets by a mob. Down rushed Mr. Perkins from his office, dragged the Negro into the hallway and faced the mob, but was himself pulled into safety by friends. A courageous man and a good boxer, but unwise. He did not, be it noted, enlist. When about thirty-one he married Mary Fitch Westcott of Providence, Rhode Island, and they had three children in three years, of whom I was the third.

The doctor said that if my mother had another baby she would die. Presently my father left home. Whether the doctor's dictum was the reason or merely a reason I do not know. What I do know is that my childhood had no father. He was an occasional visitor, a writer of infrequent but always amusing letters with deliciously funny drawings, a sender of books, catalogues of books, lists of books to read, and also a purchaser of books with money sadly needed by his family.

Once I remember his holding me by the heels when I had casually swallowed a pin. "It *cannot* be a pin!" protested my mother, but I managed to explain that I had put it in the bread and milk myself—why, I cannot imagine.

Once he brought some black Hamburg grapes to mother, and would not let her give them to us as her heart desired. There was a game of chess at which I beat him, or thought I did—being but nine I now doubt the genuineness of that victory; one punishment, half-hearted, and never repeated, at the same age; and a visit some two years later, when we lived in the country and he brought my twelve-year-old brother a gun; these are the sum of my memories of my father in childish years.

There must have been other visits. I think he used to come at Christmas when possible, but nothing else has stayed in my mind. He made no official separation, said his work kept him elsewhere. No word of criticism did I ever hear, mother held him up to us as a great and admirable character. But he was a stranger, distant and little known. The word Father, in the sense of love, care, one to go to in trouble, means nothing to me, save indeed in advice about books and the care of them—which seems more the librarian than the father.

By heredity I owe him much; the Beecher urge to social service, the Beecher wit and gift of words and such small sense of art as I have; but his learning he could not bequeath, and far more than financial care I have missed the education it would have been to have grown up in his society. . . .

Mary Westcott [Charlotte Gilman's mother], darling of an elderly father and a juvenile mother, petted, cossetted and indulged, grew up in frail health. She was "given up" by one physician, who said she had consumption and could not survive a date he set. She did, but he signified his displeasure by not recognizing her afterward. Delicate and beautiful, well educated, musical, and what was then termed "spiritual minded," she was femininely attractive in the highest degree.

Her adventures and sorrows in this field began when she was a schoolgirl of fifteen in pantalettes, and an admiring gentleman, named Wilder, asked permission of the thirty-three-year-old mother to "pay his addresses" to her daughter. From that time there were always lovers, various and successive. The still childlike Mary, even at seventeen, used to excuse herself from callers and go upstairs to put her dolls to bed.

Engagements were made, broken and renewed, and re-broken. One sudden adorer proposed to her at first sight. The penultimate engagement—with a Mr. Glazier, a theological student in the strongly Baptist city of Providence—was broken on account of his faith; but he saw another light and became a Unitarian. They were again betrothed, and he was visiting at the house immediately before their approaching marriage, when he contracted typhoid fever and died. Poor mother!

In course of time she met her mother's second cousin, Frederick Beecher Perkins of Hartford. They were engaged, that engagement also was broken, but finally, at the extreme old maidenhood of twenty-nine, she married him.

Of those three swiftly appearing babies the first died from some malpractice at birth; the second, Thomas A. Perkins, is still living, and in fourteen months I followed, on the afternoon of July third, 1860. If only I'd been a little slower and made it the glorious Fourth! This may be called the first misplay in a long game that is full of them.

There now follows a long-drawn, triple tragedy, quadruple perhaps, for my father may have suffered too; but mother's life was one of the most painfully thwarted I have ever known. After her idolized youth, she was left neglected. After her flood of lovers, she became a deserted wife. The most passionately domestic of home-worshiping housewives, she was forced to move nineteen times in eighteen years, fourteen of them from one city to another. After a long and thorough musical education, developing unusual talent, she sold her piano when I was two, to pay the butcher's bill, and never owned another. She hated debt, and debts accumulated about her, driving her to these everlasting moves. Absolutely loyal, as loving as a spaniel which no ill treatment can alienate, she made no complaint, but picked up her children and her dwindling furniture and traveled to the next place. She lived with her husband's parents, with her own parents, with his aunts, in various houses here and there when he so installed her, fleeing again on account of debt. . . .

After some thirteen years of this life, mother, urged by friends, and thinking to set my father free to have another wife if he would not live with her, divorced him. This he bitterly resented, as did others of the family. So long as "Mary Fred" was a blameless victim they pitied her and did what they could to help, but a divorce was a disgrace. Divorced or not she loved him till her death, at sixty-three. She was with me in Oakland, California, at the time, and father was then a librarian in San Francisco, just across the bay. She longed, she asked, to see him before she died. As long as she was able to be up, she sat always at the window watching for that beloved face. He never came. That's where I get my implacable temper.

This tragic life carried another grief, almost equal to loss of home and husband—the perplexed distress of the hen who hatched ducks. My mother was a baby-worshiper, even in her own childhood, always devoted to them, and in her starved life her two little ones were literally all; all of duty, hope, ambition, love and joy. She reared them with unusual intelligence and effectiveness, using much of the then new

Kindergarten method, and so training herself with medical books that the doctor said he could do no better by us.

But as these children grew they grew away from her, both of them. The special gift for baby-care did not apply so well to large youngsters; the excellent teaching in first steps could not cope with the needs of changing years; and the sublime devotion to duty, the unflinching severity of discipline made no allowance for the changing psychology of children whose characters were radically different from her own. She increasingly lost touch with them, wider and wider grew the gulf between; it reminds one of that merciless old text: "From him who hath not shall be taken away even that which he hath."

There is a complicated pathos in it, totally unnecessary. Having suffered so deeply in her own list of early love affairs, and still suffering for lack of a husband's love, she heroically determined that her baby daughter should not so suffer if she could help it. Her method was to deny the child all expression of affection as far as possible, so that she should not be used to it or long for it. "I used to put away your little hand from my cheek when you were a nursing baby," she told me in later years; "I did not want you to suffer as I had suffered." She would not let me caress her, and would not caress me, unless I was asleep. This I discovered at last, and then did my best to keep awake till she came to bed, even using pins to prevent dropping off, and sometimes succeeding. Then how carefully I pretended to be sound asleep, and how rapturously I enjoyed being gathered into her arms, held close and kissed.

If love, devotion to duty, sublime self-sacrifice, were enough in child-culture, mothers would achieve better results; but there is another requisite too often lacking—knowledge. Yet all the best she had, the best she knew, my mother gave, at any cost to herself. . . .

My brother, with his garden, hens and hunting had a somewhat fuller life, outside, but no one had a richer, more glorious life than I had, inside. It grew into fairy-tales, one I have yet; it spread to limitless ambitions. With "my wishes" I modestly chose to be the most beautiful, the wisest, the best person in the world; the most talented in music, painting, literature, sculpture—why not, when one was wishing?

But no personal wealth or glory satisfied me. Soon there developed a Prince and Princess of magic powers, who went about the world collecting unhappy children and taking them to a guarded Paradise in the South Seas. I had a boundless sympathy for children, feeling them to be suppressed, misunderstood.

It speaks volumes for the lack of happiness in my own actual life that I should so industriously construct it in imagination. I wanted affection, expressed affection. My brother was really very fond of me, but his teasing hid it from me entirely. Mother loved us desperately, but her tireless devotion was not the same thing as petting, her caresses were not given unless we were asleep, or she thought us so.

My dream world was no secret. I was but too ready to share it, but there were no sympathetic listeners. It was my life, but lived entirely alone. Then, influenced by a friend with a pre-Freudian mind, alarmed at what she was led to suppose this inner life might become, mother called on me to give it up. This was a command. According to all the ethics I knew I must obey, and I did. . . .

Just thirteen. This had been my chief happiness for five years. It was by far the largest, most active part of my mind. I was called upon to close off the main building as it were and live in the "L." No one could tell if I did it or not, it was an inner fortress, open only to me. . . .

But obedience was Right, the thing had to be done, and I did it. Night after night to shut the door on happiness, and hold it shut. Never, when dear, bright, glittering dreams pushed hard, to let them in. Just thirteen. . . .

In June [1874] mother joined a "cooperative housekeeping" group, with Dr. and Mrs. Stevens whom she had previously visited in Rehoboth, Mrs. Isham and her two boys, with whom we had lived in Hartford, and a Mr. Wellman of Cambridge, Massachusetts. All of these people were Swedenborgians, mother presently joined their church, and had us children enter it also—an impermanent experience. There was a strong flavor of Spiritualism on the part of Mrs. Stevens, the dominant figure of the group.

Cooperative housekeeping is inherently doomed to failure. From early experience and later knowledge I thoroughly learned this fact, and have always proclaimed it. Yet such is the perversity of the average mind that my advocacy of the professionalizing of housework—having it done by the hour by specially trained persons, with the service of cooked meals to the home—has always been objected to as "cooperative housekeeping." Upton Sinclair's ill-fated Helicon Hall experiment he attributed to my teachings, without the least justification. . . .

It was a strange group, immersed in the mystic doctrine of "Correspondence," according to which everything in the Bible means something else; floating and wallowing about in endless discussion of proofless themes and theories of their own, with a sort of revelation occasionally added by Mrs. Stevens, the real leader. They would sit around the table long after meals were over, interminably talking on matters of religion and ethics.

My brother and I got from this atmosphere a settled distaste for anything smacking of the esoteric or occult; but it had one advantage, to me at least, that of hearing ideas discussed as the important things of life, instead of gossip and personalities. . . .

One may have a brain specialized in its grasp of ethics, as well as of mechanics, mathematics or music. Even as a child I had noted that the whole trouble and difficulty in a story was almost always due to lying or deceit. "He must never know," she cries, or "She must never know," he insists, and the mischief begins. Also, I observed a strange disproportion in the order of virtues, the peculiar way in which they vary in the order of their importance, by race, class, age, sex.

So I set about the imperative task of building my own religion, based on knowledge. This, to the "believer," is no satisfactory foundation. All religions of the past have rested on some one's say so, have been at one in demanding faith as the foremost virtue. Understanding was never required, nor expected, in fact it was forbidden and declared impossible, quite beyond "the poor human intellect."

"It may be poor," said young Charlotte to herself, "but it is all the intellect there is. I know of none better. At any rate it is all I have, and I'll use it." As this religion of mine underlies all my Living, is the most essential part of my life, and began in these years, it will have to go in.

"Here I am," said I, "in the world, conscious, able to do this or that. What is it all about? How does it work? What is my part in it, my job—what ought I to do?" Then I set to work calmly and cheerfully, sure that the greatest truths were the simplest, to review the story of creation and see what I could see. The first evident fact is action, something doing, this universe is a going concern.

"Power," said I. "Force. Call it God. Now then, is it one, or more?" There are various forces at work before us, as centripetal and centrifugal, inertia and others, but I was trying to get a view of the whole show, to see if there was any dominant underlying power.

Looking rapidly along the story of the world's making and growing, with the development of life upon it, I could soon see that in spite of all local variations and back-sets, the process worked all one way—up. This of course involves deciding on terms, as to what is better or worse, higher or lower, but it seemed to me mere sophistry to deny that vegetable forms and activities are higher than mineral; animal higher than vegetable: and of animal life man the highest form and still going on. This long, irresistible ascent showed a single dominant force. "Good!" said I. "Here's God—One God and it Works!"

The next question was of the character of this Force and its effect on the growing world, was it Good? Or Bad?

Here loomed before me the problem of evil, long baffling so many. But I knew that mighty thinkers had thought for

ages without discovering some of the most patent facts; their
failure did not prove the facts difficult to discover, it merely
showed that they had not thought of them. Also, I was
strengthened by an innate incredulity which refused to accept
anybody's say-so, even if it had been said for a thousand
years. If a problem was said to be insoluble, I forthwith set
out to solve it. So I sat me down before the problem of evil,
thus:

"I will go back to the period of a molten world, where we
can call nothing right or wrong, and follow carefully up the
ages—see where it comes in." So I followed the process until
the earth was cool enough to allow the formation of crystals,
each square or pentagonal or whatever was its nature, and
then if one was broken or twisted, I pounced upon the fact
—"here it is! It is right for this to be a hexagon, wrong for it
to be squeezed flat." Following this thought in vegetable and
animal growth, I was soon able to make my first ethical generalization: "That is right for a given organism which leads
to its best development."

It is told that Buddha, going out to look on life, was greatly
daunted by death. "They all eat one another!" he cried, and
called it evil. This process I examined, changed the verb,
said, "They all feed one another," and called it good. Death?
Why this fuss about death? Use your imagination, try to vis-
ualize a world *without* death! The first form of life would be
here yet, miles deep by this time, and nothing else; a static
world. If birth is allowed, without death, the resulting mass
would leave death as a blessed alternative. Death is the essential condition of life, not an evil.

As to pain—? I observed that the most important continuous
functions of living are unconsciously carried on within us;
that the most external ones, involving a changing activity on
our part, as in obtaining food, and mating, are made desirable
by pleasure; that just being alive is a pleasure; that pain does
not come in unless something goes wrong. "Fine!" said I. "An
admirable world. God is good."

As to the enormous suffering of our humankind, that we

make, ourselves, by erroneous action—and can stop it when we choose.

Having got thus far, there remained to study the two main processes of religion, the Intake and the Output. (The phrasing of all this is of more recent years, but the working out of it was done in those years of early girlhood from sixteen to twenty.)

The Intake; the relation of the soul to God. All manner of religions have wandered around this point, and in spite of wide difference in terminology, the fact is established that the individual can derive renewed strength, peace and power from inner contact with this Central Force. They *do it,* Christian, Hebrew, Moslem, Buddhist. It is evident that this Force does not care what you call it, but flows in, as if we had tapped the reservoir of the universe.

However, one cannot put a quart in a pint cup. Sucking away on this vast power and not doing anything with it, results in nothing, unless it may be a distention of the mind, unfitting it for any practical contacts. So we sometimes see the most profoundly religious persons accomplishing the least good, while more is done by some who spend less time in prayer.

Seeking to clarify my mind on this point I deliberately put myself in God's place, so to speak, tried to imagine how I should feel toward my creatures, what I should expect of them. If that Power is conscious we may assume it to be rational, surely, and in no way *less* than we! If not conscious, we must simply find out how it works. What does God want of the earth? To whirl and spin and keep its times and seasons. What of the vegetable world? To blossom and bear fruit. Of the animals? The same fulfilment of function. Of us? The same and more. We, with all life, are under the great law, Evolution.

I figured it out that the business of mankind was to carry out the evolution of the human race, according to the laws of nature, adding the conscious direction, the telic force, proper to our kind—we are the only creatures that can assist evolution; that we could replenish our individual powers by application to the reservoir; and the best way to get more power was to use what one had.

Social evolution I easily saw to be in human work, in the crafts, trades, arts and sciences through which we are related, maintained and developed. Therefore the first law of human life was clear, and I made my second ethical generalization: "The first duty of a human being is to assume right functional relation to society"—more briefly, to find your real job, and do it. This is the first duty, others accompany and follow it, but not all of them together are enough without this.

This I found perfectly expressed in a story read in later years, of a noted English engineer, whose personal life was open to much criticism, and who was about to die of heart disease. His nurse, a redoubtable Nova Scotian, annoyed him by concern about his soul, his approaching Judgment and probable damnation.

"My good woman," said he, "when I die, if I come to judgment, I believe that I shall be judged by the bridges I have built."

Life, duty, purpose, these were dear to me. God was Real, under and in and around everything, lifting, lifting. We, conscious of that limitless power, were to find our places, our special work in the world, and when found, do it, do it at all costs.

There was one text on which I built strongly: "Whoso doeth the will shall know of the doctrine." "Good," said I. "That's *provable;* I'll try it." And I set to work, with my reliable system of development, to "do the will" as far as I could see it. . . .

Aside from such safe and limited companionship, mother was rigorous in refusing all manner of invitations for me. I was denied so often that I found it saved emotion to "fight fire with fire," to deny myself beforehand, and, strengthened by Emerson, Socrates, Epictetus and Marcus Aurelius, I became a genuine stoic.

This process was promoted by one experience so drastic as to render later deprivations of small account. During my seventeenth year one of mother's cousins, ten years older than I, invited me to a students' concert at Brown. Mother declined for me. She, in her lovely girlhood, had known many college boys—she had some obscure objection to my "getting in with the students." I made no complaint, being already inured to denial. But that same day another of those cousins, twenty years older than I, asked me to go with him and his sisters to sit in a box, and see Edwin Booth in *Hamlet*.

Booth! *Hamlet!* A box! Nothing in all the world could have meant so much to me at the time. And mother refused. Why? She afterwards explained that having refused Robert, she feared that if she accepted Edward's invitation it would hurt Robert's feelings. How about mine? . . . The unparalleled glory offered and the pitiful inadequacy of the reason for its denial made a ghastly impression on my mind. Something broke. Perhaps it was like what is called "a broken heart." At any rate I have never since that day felt the sharp sting of disappointment, only a numb feeling. So deep was the effect of continuous denials and my own drastic training in endurance, that it was many years later before I learned to accept an offered pleasure naturally. . . .

Up to sixteen or seventeen there was no character to be specially proud of; impressionable, vacillating, sensitive, uncontrolled, often loafing and lazy—only a few years earlier good Mrs. Smith had said to mother that I seemed "all froth and foam." Mother told me this, for my good, knowing how much I respected that lady, and I laid up the saying most solemnly. Five or six years from the time of her dictum I asked her if she still thought so, and she reversed her opinion completely, said I was the most determined and firmly based young woman she knew, to my immense satisfaction. Perhaps that relentless memory and determination to make her "eat her words" shows some inner force of character, if only contradictoriness.

The flaccidity of will which had impressed that kind critic I saw to be a weakness to be outgrown, and set about it. The first step was to establish prompt and easy execution of decisions, to connect cerebral action with the motor nerves. Short of idiocy we all have this power, but most of us neglect it. "You couldn't do it if you hadn't inherited the capacity!" says the fatalist. Of course we inherit it. If you inherit a fortune does it prove that you haven't any? We do have the capacity, and can develop it, like any other power, by use.

My advantage was the Yankee inventiveness which devised means for doing easily what is usually found difficult. I deliberately set about a course of exercises in which small and purely arbitrary decisions were sharply carried out: "In ten minutes I will take another chair." "At five-thirty-eight I will walk around the block." "I will get out of bed at thirteen minutes to seven." The essence of this method is in its complete detachment. There is no temptation to be overcome, no difficulty to be met, nothing but a simple expression of will. Such exercises, carried on thoroughly, do develop the habit of executing one's decisions, and make it easy when there is something serious to be done.

With each trait to be acquired the Process was used; determination, self-suggestion, "making up the mind"—"I *will* think before I speak!" This was one of my most needed ones. The determination is forgotten, the thoughtless words go on, but after a while the memory revives—then welcome it, waste no moment in regret, say, "Ah, here you are!," and jam it in again, harder than before, "I *will* think before I speak!" You will remember it sooner next time, smile and jam it in again. At last the thought comes before the word, you catch yourself in the act and check the unkind or unwise speech—but only once that day. Twice the next day, then three times, and so slowly, not straining the new connection, until you have established the habit you desire.

One of my worst characteristics was bitterly bewailed by mother. "Shall I never teach you to think of other people! You *are* so thoughtless." She was right. I was not thoughtful of others, I could see that the characters I admired and strove to imitate were so, and I set to work to acquire this virtue. Evidently a large order, a year, perhaps two, required for its acquisition. First the firm determination, repeated as it recurred. When at last I thought of it in time, I'd gaze at some caller of mother's and consider what, if anything, I could do for that person: get a foot-stool, a glass of water, change a window-shade, any definitely conceived benefit. So with other people in other places, laboriously seeking to think of them. With this I undertook a course of minor self-denials, for the sole purpose of reversing the current, turning my mind from what I wanted to what other people wanted. This from no delusion of virtue; what I was after was the reversal of tendency, the turning of consciousness from self to others.

But this was too slow, too restricted, and I devised a larger scheme. There was a certain crippled girl, with a poor little mother, maker of lace caps for old ladies. Among the benevolent church members who cared for them were some of mother's cousins, and it was easy to be introduced to the poor invalid. Half-blind she was, wearing a shade over her eyes, lying curled up on her couch, a most unhappy object. Of this damsel I inquired, "Will you do me a service?"

She laughed with some bitterness at the idea that she could do anything for me, but I explained that I was quite in earnest, that she could help me most practically. "You see," I pursued seriously, "I don't think about other people, and I'm trying to learn. Now I don't care anything about you, yet, but I'd like to. Will you let me come and practise on you?"

This she thought to be merely a concealment of benevolent feelings, but it wasn't. I didn't care in the least about her, but I knew that I should if I did things for her; love grows by service. So I visited that unhappy creature, and studied what I could do to benefit her, beyond being amusing.

Her limitations were many and painful. I read to her, that was easy. Her eating was restricted, but she could smell, and I brought her flowers. Then, with a long, careful saving from my most narrow and uncertain resources, I bought her a small musicbox, for $3.00—a huge sum for me: it was a mere toy, but proved a great comfort to her. And sure enough, after a while I became quite fond of the girl.

In about two years I heard through a kind cousin that some old lady had said that she did like Charlotte Perkins—she was so thoughtful of other people. "Hurrah!" said I, "another game won!"

Each year I would lay out one, or perhaps two, desirable traits to acquire, and in a leisurely manner acquire them. We are told to hitch our wagons to a star, but why pick on Betelgeuse? I selected more modestly, more gradually, carefully choosing for imitation some admired character in history or fiction, not too far beyond me, and then catching up; followed by the selection of another more difficult. At the time when this long effort calamitously ended I had got as far as Socrates. . . .

One New Year's prayer heard during these years provoked me almost to interrupt. The minister was droning along in the "Thou knowest" style—(if it was plain "you know" how inelegant it would be!) "Thou knowest how a year ago we made good resolutions and have broken them. Thou knowest how we undertook to develop a better character and have failed." . . . I wanted to speak out and tell him that there was one person present who had undertaken to develop better character and succeeded, who had made good resolutions and kept them every one. But I was careful not to make too many at once. . . .

Among the many splendid movements of the late nineteenth century was one dear to my heart, that toward a higher physical culture. In Europe and then here the impulse was felt, building gymnasiums, practice of calisthenics even for girls, and the rapid development of college athletics. In this line of improvement I was highly ambitious. With right early training I could easily have been an acrobat, having good nervous coordination, strength, courage, and excellent balancing power.

High places never daunted me. As a child in Rehoboth I used to parade the ridge-pole of the barn and stand on the very end of it, to alarm people driving by—mischievous wretch! In the simple task of walking rails, railroad rails, I have kept on steadily over a hundred of them. Dancing would

have been a passion, but dancing was one of the many forbid-
dings of my youth.

What I did determine on and largely secure was the development of a fine physique. Blaikie's *How To Get Strong and
How To Stay So* was a great help. Early country life gave a
good start, and housework kept some muscles in use, the best
of it is scrubbing the floor. That is good back and arm work,
and not dusty or steamy like sweeping and washing.

Going to the art school gave me two miles' walk a day. In
the coldest weather I'd start off so briskly that before long
I'd have my mittens off and coat unbuttoned, smiling trium-
phantly at chillier people. All manner of "stunts" I delighted
to practise, that were within my range. There was one favorite,
which I will now try to describe—and a more difficult literary
task I never undertook!

Hold a yard-stick horizontally behind you, arms hanging
at your sides, palms front. Without changing this grip, raise
it behind and bring forward over your head until it is horizontal in front of you. Raise and somewhat advance the left-
hand end, lowering and drawing back the right to within a
foot of the floor directly before you. Raise the right foot and
put it outside the hand and inside the stick, while you balance
on the left foot. Then move your left hand forward and toward the right, never changing that grip, passing the stick
behind your head and downward, until you can lift your right
foot over it again and stand as you began. Repeat with the
other foot first. I used to do this with each foot three times
before going to bed. It is easy enough for slender, pliable
girls, but strong men, somewhat muscle-bound, cannot do it.

Needless to say that I never wore corsets, that my shoes
were "common sense" (and more people seemed to have common sense at the time), that all my clothing "hung from the
shoulder"—the custom being to drag all those heavy skirts
from the waist. I devised a sort of side-garter suspender, to
which skirts were buttoned, and, not a flat bandage to make
a woman look like a boy, but after many trials evolved a
species of brassiere which supported the breasts without con-

striction anywhere. It had elastic over the shoulder and under the arm, allowing perfect freedom for breathing and arm-motion, while snug and efficient as a support. . . .

My special efforts were not toward anything spectacular, but directed to the building up of a sound physique. Going twice a week, each day I ran a mile, not for speed but wind, and can still run better than many a younger woman. I could vault and jump, go up a knotted rope, walk on my hands under a ladder, kick as high as my head, and revel in the fly-ing rings. But best of all were the traveling rings, those wide-spaced single ones, stirrup-handled, that dangle in a line the length of the hall.

To mount a table with one of those in one hand, well drawn back, launch forth in a long swing and catch the next with the other, pull strongly on the first to get a long swing back, carefully letting go when it hung vertically so that it should be ready for the return, and go swinging on to the next, down the whole five and back again—that is as near flying as one gets, outside of a circus. I could do it four times in those days.

Life does not offer many opportunities for this exercise, but I had a chance at it when about thirty-six, again when somewhat over fifty, and last, lecturing in Oklahoma Uni-versity, I did it once, the whole row and back, at sixty-five. Whereby it is apparent that a careful early training in physi-cal culture lasts a lifetime. I never was vain of my looks, nor of any professional achievements, but am absurdly vain of my physical strength and agility. . . .

A lover more tender, a husband more devoted, woman could not ask. He helped in the housework more and more as my strength began to fail, for something was going wrong from the first. The steady cheerfulness, the strong, tireless spirit sank away. A sort of gray fog drifted across my mind, a cloud that grew and darkened.

"Feel sick and remain so all day." "Walter stays home and does everything for me." "Walter gets breakfast." October

10th: "I have coffee in bed mornings while Walter briskly makes fires and gets breakfast." "O dear! That I should come to this!" By October 13th the diary stops altogether, until January 1, 1885. "My journal has been long neglected by reason of ill-health. This day has not been a successful one as I was sicker than for some weeks. Walter also was not very well, and stayed at home, principally on my account. He has worked for me and for us both, waited on me in every tenderest way, played to me, read to me, done all for me as he always does. God be thanked for my husband."

February 16th: "A well-nigh sleepless night. Hot, cold, hot, restless, nervous, hysterical. Walter is love and patience personified, gets up over and over, gets me warm wintergreen, bromide, hot foot-bath, more bromide—all to no purpose."

Then, with impressive inscription: "March 23rd, 1885. This day, at about five minutes to nine in the morning, was born my child, Katharine."

Brief ecstasy. Long pain.
Then years of joy again.

Motherhood means giving. . . .

We had attributed all my increasing weakness and depression to pregnancy, and looked forward to prompt recovery now. All was normal and ordinary enough, but I was already plunged into an extreme of nervous exhaustion which no one observed or understood in the least. Of all angelic babies that darling was the best, a heavenly baby. My nurse, Maria Pease of Boston, was a joy while she lasted, and remained a lifelong friend. But after her month was up and I was left alone with the child I broke so fast that we sent for my mother, who had been visiting Thomas in Utah, and that baby-worshiping grandmother came to take care of the darling, I being incapable of doing that—or anything else, a mental wreck.

Presently we moved to a better house, on Humboldt Avenue near by, and a German servant girl of unparalleled virtues was installed. Here was a charming home; a loving and devoted husband; an exquisite baby, healthy, intelligent and good; a highly competent mother to run things; a wholly satisfactory servant—and I lay all day on the lounge and cried. . . .

In those days a new disease had dawned on the medical horizon. It was called "nervous prostration." No one knew much about it, and there were many who openly scoffed, saying it was only a new name for laziness. To be recognizably ill one must be confined to one's bed, and preferably in pain.

That a heretofore markedly vigorous young woman, with every comfort about her, should collapse in this lamentable manner was inexplicable. "You should use your will," said earnest friends. I had used it, hard and long, perhaps too hard and too long; at any rate it wouldn't work now.

"Force some happiness into your life," said one sympathizer. "Take an agreeable book to bed with you, occupy your mind with pleasant things." She did not realize that I was unable to read, and that my mind was exclusively occupied with unpleasant things. This disorder involved a growing melancholia, and that, as those know who have tasted it, consists of every painful mental sensation, shame, fear, remorse, a blind oppressive confusion, utter weakness, a steady brainache that fills the conscious mind with crowding images of distress.

The misery is doubtless as physical as a toothache, but a brain, of its own nature, gropes for reasons for its misery. Feeling the sensation fear, the mind suggests every possible calamity; the sensation shame—remorse—and one remembers every mistake and misdeeds of a lifetime, and grovels to the earth in abasement.

"If you would get up and do something you would feel better," said my mother. I rose drearily, and essayed to brush up the floor a little, with a dustpan and small whiskbroom, but soon dropped those implements exhausted, and wept again in helpless shame.

I, the ceaselessly industrious, could do no work of any kind. I was so weak that the knife and fork sank from my hands—too tired to eat. I could not read nor write nor paint nor sew nor talk nor listen to talking, nor anything. I lay on that lounge and wept all day. The tears ran down into my ears on either side. I went to bed crying, woke in the night crying, sat on the edge of the bed in the morning and cried —from sheer continuous pain. Not physical, the doctors examined me and found nothing the matter.

The only physical pain I ever knew, besides dentistry and one sore finger, was having the baby, and I would rather had had a baby every week than suffer as I suffered in my mind. A constant dragging weariness miles below zero. Absolute in capacity. Absolute misery. To the spirit it was as if one were an armless, legless, eyeless, voiceless cripple. Prominent among the tumbling suggestions of a suffering brain was the thought, "You did it yourself! You did it yourself! You had health and strength and hope and glorious work before you— and you threw it all away. You were called to serve humanity, and you cannot serve yourself. No good as a wife, no good as a mother, no good at anything. And you did it yourself!" . . .

The baby? I nursed her for five months. I would hold her close—that lovely child!—and instead of love and happiness, feel only pain. The tears ran down on my breast. . . . Nothing was more utterly bitter than this, that even motherhood brought no joy.

The doctor said I must wean her, and go away, for a change. So she was duly weaned and throve finely on Mellins' Food, drinking eagerly from the cup—no bottle needed. With mother there and the excellent maid I was free to go.

Those always kind friends, the Channings, had gone to Pasadena to live, and invited me to spend the winter with them. Feeble and hopeless I set forth, armed with tonics and sedatives, to cross the continent. From the moment the wheels began to turn, the train to move, I felt better. . . .

Leaving California in March, in the warm rush of its rich spring, I found snow in Denver, and from then on hardly saw the sun for a fortnight. I reached home with a heavy bronchial cold, which hung on long, the dark fog rose again in my mind, the miserable weakness—within a month I was as low as before leaving. . . .

This was a worse horror than before, for now I saw the stark fact—that I was well while away and sick while at home —a heartening prospect! Soon ensued the same utter prostration, the unbearable inner misery, the ceaseless tears. A new tonic had been invented, Essence of Oats, which was given me, and did some good for a time. I pulled up enough to do a little painting that fall, but soon slipped down again and stayed down. An old friend of my mother's, dear Mrs. Diman, was so grieved at this condition that she gave me a hundred dollars and urged me to go away somewhere and get cured.

At that time the greatest nerve specialist in the country was Dr. S. W. Mitchell of Philadelphia. Through the kindness of a friend of Mr. Stetson's living in that city, I went to him and took "the rest cure"; went with the utmost confidence, prefacing the visit with a long letter giving "the history of the case" in a way a modern psychologist would have appreciated. Dr. Mitchell only thought it proved self-conceit. He had a prejudice against the Beechers. "I've had two women of your blood here already," he told me scornfully. This eminent physician was well versed in two kinds of nervous prostration; that of the business man exhausted from too much work, and the society woman exhausted from too much play. The kind I had was evidently beyond him. But he did reassure me on one point—there was no dementia, he said, only hysteria.

I was put to bed and kept there. I was fed, bathed, rubbed, and responded with the vigorous body of twenty-six. As far as he could see there was nothing the matter with me, so after a month of this agreeable treatment he sent me home, with this prescription:

"Live as domestic a life as possible. Have your child with you all the time." (Be it remarked that if I did but dress the baby it left me shaking and crying—certainly far from a healthy companionship for her, to say nothing of the effect on me.) "Lie down an hour after each meal. Have but two hours' intellectual life a day. And never touch pen, brush or pencil as long as you live."

I went home, followed those directions rigidly for months, and came perilously near to losing my mind. The mental agony grew so unbearable that I would sit blankly moving my head from side to side—to get out from under the pain. Not physical pain, not the least "headache" even, just mental torment, and so heavy in its nightmare gloom that it seemed real enough to dodge.

I made a rag baby, hung it on a doorknob and played with it. I would crawl into remote closets and under beds—to hide from the grinding pressure of that profound distress. . . .

Finally, in the fall of '87, in a moment of clear vision, we agreed to separate, to get a divorce. There was no quarrel, no blame for either one, never an unkind word between us, unbroken mutual affection—but it seemed plain that if I went crazy it would do my husband no good, and be a deadly injury to my child.

What this meant to the young artist, the devoted husband, the loving father, was so bitter a grief and loss that nothing would have justified breaking the marriage save this worse loss which threatened. It was not a choice between going and staying, but between going, sane, and staying, insane. If I had been of the slightest use to him or to the child, I would have "stuck it," as the English say. But this progressive weakening of the mind made a horror unnecessary to face; better for that dear child to have separated parents than a lunatic mother.

We had been married four years and more. This miserable condition of mind, this darkness, feebleness and gloom, had begun in those difficult years of courtship, had grown rapidly worse after marriage, and was now threatening utter loss; whereas I had repeated proof that the moment I left home I began to recover. It seemed right to give up a mistaken marriage.

Our mistake was mutual. If I had been stronger and wiser I should never have been persuaded into it. Our suffering was mutual too, his unbroken devotion, his manifold cares and labors in tending a sick wife, his adoring pride in the best of babies, all coming to naught, ending in utter failure—we sympathized with each other but faced a bitter necessity. The separation must come as soon as possible, the divorce must wait for conditions.

If this decision could have been reached sooner it would have been much better for me, the lasting mental injury would have been less. Such recovery as I have made in forty years, and the work accomplished, seem to show that the fear of insanity was not fulfilled, but the effects of nerve bankruptcy remain to this day. So much of my many failures, of misplay and misunderstanding and "queerness" is due to this lasting weakness, and kind friends so unfailingly refuse to allow for it, to believe it, that I am now going to some length in stating the case.

That part of the ruin was due to the conditions of childhood I do not doubt, and part to the rigid stoicism and constant effort in character-building of my youth; I was "overtrained," had wasted my substance in riotous—virtues. But that the immediate and continuing cause was mismarriage is proved by the instant rebound when I left home and as instant relapse on returning.

After I was finally free, in 1890, wreck though I was, there was a surprising output of work, some of my best. I think that if I could have had a period of care and rest then, I might have made full recovery. But the ensuing fours years in California were the hardest of my life. The result has been a lasting loss of power, total in some directions, partial in others; the necessity for a laboriously acquired laziness foreign to both temperament and conviction, a crippled life.

But since my public activities do not show weakness, nor my writings, and since brain and nerve disorder is not visible, short of lunacy or literal "prostration," this lifetime of limitation and wretchedness, when I mention it, is flatly disbelieved. When I am forced to refuse invitations, to back out of work that seems easy, to own that I cannot read a heavy book, apologetically alleging this weakness of mind, friends gibber amiably, "I wish I had your mind!" I wish they had, for a while, as a punishment for doubting my word. What confuses them is the visible work I have been able to accomplish. They see activity, achievement, they do not see blank months of idleness; nor can they see what the work would have been if the powerful mind I had to begin with had not broken at twenty-four.

A brain may lose some faculties and keep others; it may be potent for a little while and impotent the rest of the time. Moreover, the work I have done has never been "work" in the sense of consciously applied effort. To write was always as easy to me as to talk. Even my verse, such as it is, flows as smoothly as a letter, is easier in fact. Perhaps the difficulty of answering letters will serve as an illustration of the weakness of mind so jocosely denied by would-be complimenters.

Here are a handful of letters—I dread to read them, especially if they are long—I pass them over to my husband—ask him to give me only those I must answer personally. These pile up and accumulate while I wait for a day when I feel able to attack them. A secretary does not help in the least, it is not the manual labor of writing which exhausts me, it is the effort to understand the letter, and make intelligent reply. I answer one, two, the next is harder, three—increasingly foggy, four—it's no use, I read it in vain, *I don't know what it says*. Literally, I can no longer understand what I read, and have to stop, with my mind like a piece of boiled spinach.

Reading is a simple art, common to most of us. As a child I read eagerly, greedily; as a girl I read steadily, with warm interest, in connected scientific study. No book seemed difficult. One of my Harvard boy friends told me no girl could read Clifford and understand him. Of course I got Clifford at once—and found him clear and easy enough.

After the debacle I could read nothing—instant exhaustion preventing. As years passed there was some gain in this line; if a story was short and interesting and I was feeling pretty well I could read a little while. Once when well over forty I made a test, taking a simple book on a subject I was interested in—Lucy Salmon on the servant question. I read for half an hour with ease; the next half-hour was harder, but I kept on. At the end of the third I could not understand a word of it.

That surely is a plain instance of what I mean when I say my mind is weak. It is precisely that, weak. It cannot hold attention, cannot study, cannot listen long to anything, is always backing out of things because it is tired. A library, which was once to me as a confectioner's shop to a child, became an appalling weariness just to look at.

This does not involve loss of clear perception, lack of logic, failure to think straight when able to think at all. The natural faculties are there, as my books and lectures show. But there remains this humiliating weakness, and if I try to drive, to compel effort, the resulting exhaustion is pitiful.

To step so suddenly from proud strength to contemptible feebleness, from cheerful stoicism to a whimpering avoidance of any strain or irritation for fear of the collapse ensuing, is not pleasant, at twenty-four. To spend forty years and more in the patient effort of learning how to carry such infirmity so as to accomplish something in spite of it is a wearing process, full of mortification and deprivation. To lose books out of one's life, certainly more than ninety per cent of one's normal reading capacity, is no light misfortune.

"But you write books!" Yes, I have written enough to make a set of twenty-five, including volumes of stories, plays, verse, and miscellany; besides no end of stuff not good enough to keep. But this was all the natural expression of thought, except in the stories, which called for composition and were more difficult—especially the novels, which are poor. The power of expression remained, fortunately for me, and the faculty of inner perception, of seeing the relation of facts and their consequences.

I am not skilled in mental disorders, and cannot say what it was which paralyzed previous capacities so extensively, while leaving some in working order. Perhaps another instance will be indicative. For nearly all these broken years I could not look down an index. To do this one must form the matrix of a thought or word and look down the list until it fits. I could not hold that matrix at all, could not remember what I

was looking for. To this day I'd rather turn the pages than
look at the index.

Worst of all was the rapid collapse of my so laboriously
built-up hand-made character. Eight years of honest conscientious nobly-purposed effort lost, with the will power that made
it. The bitterness of that shame will not bear reviving even
now. . . .

My Socialism was of the early humanitarian kind, based
on the first exponents, French and English, with the American enthusiasm of Bellamy. The narrow and rigid "economic
determinism" of Marx, with its "class consciousness" and
"class struggle" I never accepted, nor the political methods
pursued by Marxians. My main interest then was in the position of women, and the need for more scientific care for young
children. As to women, the basic need of economic independence seemed to me of far more importance than the ballot;
though that of course was a belated and legitimate claim, for
which I always worked as opportunity offered. . . .

Of the many people I met during these years I was particularly impressed by Elizabeth Cady Stanton. To have been
with her and "Aunt Susan," as we called the great Susan B.
Anthony, seemed to establish connection with a splendid period of real heroism. It amuses me when the short-memoried
young people of to-day introduce me as "one of the Pioneers."
The pioneers of the Woman's Movement began with Mary
Wollstonecraft, early in the last century, and ceased to be
such when their message was listened to politely. . . .

In great cities where people of ability abound, there is always a feverish urge to keep ahead, to set the pace, to adopt
each new fashion in thought and theory as well as in dress—
or undress. So in New York swept in with a rush the Freudian
psychology, with all the flock of "psycho-analysts."

Always it has amazed me to see how apparently intelligent
persons would permit these mind-meddlers, having no claim
to fitness except that of having read certain utterly unproven
books, to paddle among their thoughts and feelings, and ex-

tract confessions of the last intimacy. Men and women with no warrant in professional education, setting up offices and giving treatment—for handsome fees—became plentiful.

One of these men, becoming displeased with my views and their advancement, since I would not come to be "psyched," as they call it, had the impudence to write a long psycho-analysis of my case, and send it to me. My husband and I, going out in the morning, found this long, fat envelop with our mail. I looked at it, saw who it was from, and gave it to Houghton. "I don't want to read his stuff," I said. "You look it over and tell me what it is about." This he did, to my utter disgust. "Burn it up, do," I urged. "I haven't the least curiosity to know what this person thinks is the matter with me."

Fancy any decent physician presuming to send a diagnosis to some one never his patient, and who on no account would have consulted him! The joke is on him, in that his arrow never reached the mark, but the joke is on me because with a mind of that sort nothing could make him believe that a woman could have so little curiosity. . . .

Twenty-two years in New York. Twenty-two years in that unnatural city where every one is an exile, none more so than the American. I have seen it stated that there are but 7 per cent native-born, of native ancestors, in that city. Others give a larger proportion, perhaps 15 or 20 per cent. Imagine Paris with but a fifth of its citizens French! London with but a fifth English—Berlin with but a fifth German! One third of the inhabitants of New York now are Jews, and we know of the hundreds of thousands of Italians, Germans, and others.

One summer we went to the coast of Maine for a little. I could have hugged the gaunt New England farmers and fishermen—I had forgotten what my people looked like!

The petty minority of Americans in New York receive small respect from their supplanters. Why should they? What must any people think of another people who voluntarily give up their country—not conquered—not forced out—simply outnumbered and swallowed up without a struggle. After a speech of mine in Cooper Union a scornful German demanded from the floor—"What *is* an American?"

A good answer which I did not think of then would have been: "An American is the sort of person who builds a place like this for you to enjoy, free." But my real answer is this: "Americans are the kind of people who have made a country that every other kind of people wants to get into!" . . .

This new century, now past its first quarter, has seen the achievement of many of the things so ardently striven for in the last, but it is like climbing a mountain range, each surmounted peak only shows more and higher ones. For instance we have attained full suffrage for women. This was never to me the *summum bonum* it was to many of its advocates, but I did expect better things of women than they have shown.

They remain, for instance, as much the slaves of fashion as before, lifting their skirts, baring their backs, exhibiting their legs, powdering their noses, behaving just as foolishly as ever, if not more so. I have no objection to legs, as bare as faces when necessary. The one-piece bathing suit is precisely as right for women as for men. It is an exhilarating sight to see men and women, swimming together, walking or running on the beaches together, free, equal, not stressing sex in any way. But these gleaming "nudes," in the street-car for instance, have no *raison d'etre*, are merely an exhibition, neither timely, nor by any means always attractive. I have seen legs, yards of them one might say, with knee and thigh in full evidence, which so far from being desirable were fairly repellent.

The fine women who were making such advance in all manner of business and professional achievements are going on, in increasing numbers. More and more our girls expect to work, to earn, to be independent. But on the other hand, the "gold digger" is as rampant as ever, as greedy and shameless.

There is a splendid stir and push among our youth, what is called a "revolt," against pretty much everything that was before good, excellent, necessary—but what have they to propose instead? So far there has not been put forth by all this revolted youth any social improvement that I have heard of. Much is heard of the advantage of repudiating tradition, superstition, old legends, dogmas, conventions. Little is heard of any clear, newly established truth.

There is now nothing to prevent women from becoming as fully human in their social development as men; and although just now they seem more anxious to exhibit sex than ever, the real progress in humanness is there and will gradually overcome this backwash of primitive femininity.

It is amusing to find in this "advanced" period, some survivals of the mental attitudes of our decorous ancestors. For instance, I made myself, within a few years, a dress for the platform. Behold this aged amazon, stark and grim, covered from neck to wrist and ankle. Allow also for six layers of covering, the lace, the silk, the "slip" and so on inward.

Yet I was told confidentially, for my good, that people had criticized this costume as indelicate! They said it "showed the outline of the bust"! Two women and one man, it appears, had made this objection, with the added reproach, "At your age." When one considers the "outlines" now freely shown on our streets and in our parlors, to say nothing of the limitless exhibition elsewhere, and then looks at this grave and voluminous robe, such objection as this surely shows that there are still with us persons of a pure-mindedness difficult to fathom.

The Labor Movement, for which I worked as earnestly as for the advance of women, has now gone so far, achieved so much, with reduced hours, increased wages, and better conditions generally, that sympathy has given place to admiration. Further, there is a growing question on the part of the consumer as to where he comes in for advantages. The coal-miners fight for themselves, the coal operators fight for themselves, and the price of coal continues to go up.

Socialism, long misrepresented and misunderstood under the violent propaganda of Marxism, has been fairly obliterated in the public mind by the Jewish-Russian nightmare, Bolshevism. That "public mind" was never very clear on the subject, as was natural under the kind of talk they mostly heard; people used even to confuse Socialism with Anarchism—which are absolute opposites; and now there is such horror at the crimes and such contempt for the stupidities of the Russian Tyranny, that it is impossible to get a fair hearing for the most simple and advantageous steps in social progress if they seem to savor at all of Socialism. It may be years before that legitimate and gradual social advance can be presented with any hope of understanding.

One of the most important and most hopeful of all lines in advance is the rapid growth toward better education. From the post-graduate to the baby this gain is shown, and the baby end of it is most important. That intensely valuable period of life, the first four years, is at last recognized as deserving better care than can be given by solitary mothers and hired nurse-maids. We have now a name for this young person, "the pre-school child," and under this title earnest study is now being given to those first years and the best treatment for them. I sit and chuckle to see the most conscientious mamas proudly doing to their children what I was called "an unnatural mother" for doing to mine. Maternal instinct is at last giving ground a little before the resistless march of knowledge and experience. All this is good to see.

In our prehistoric status of "domestic industry" there is some progress, but not much. The increasing cost and decreasing efficiency of domestic servants teaches most women nothing. They merely revert to the more ancient custom of "doing their own work." But the double-pressure goes on; more and more professional women, who will marry and have families and will not be house-servants, for nothing; and less and less obtainable service, with the sacrifice of the wife and mother to that primal altar, the cook-stove. This pressure, which marks the passing of the period of domestic service and the beginning of professional service—cooked meals brought to the home, and labor by the hour—will gradually force that great economic change.

For some thirty-seven years, with voice and pen, I have

endeavored to explain and advocate this change, and the gain made in that time is probably all that could be expected in so deep-rooted a custom as that of to-every-man-his-own-cook. It would seem to one not accustomed to measure the glacial slowness of social progress, as if a change which would increase the income of a family and decrease its expenses by half, while at the same time greatly improving our health, would attract the most ordinary intelligence. But reason has no power against feeling, and feeling older than history is no light matter. . . .

Physically we seem to be improving. There is far more knowledge about health, more interest in hygiene and exercise, the death rate is being lowered, we are getting ahead of some diseases. In this line of progress there was no orthodoxy to be overcome.

Religion is in a very healthy commotion. The Romanists were perfectly right in foretelling that if we once began to divide we should keep on dividing. We have. That is the law of growth, the growth of living things. From the first step, the division of the fertilized cell, all the way onward, growth means division.

Also, the stony-minded orthodox were right in fearing the first movement of new knowledge and free thought. It has gone on, and will go on, irresistibly, until some day we shall have no respect for an alleged "truth" which cannot stand the full blaze of knowledge, the full force of active thought. We no longer—meaning educated people in general—believe as our forefathers did; and the uneducated, who probably know more than the educated of a few centuries ago, refuse to submit to dogmas and commands.

The religious need of the human mind remains alive, never more so, but it demands a teaching which can be *understood*. Slowly an apprehension of the intimate, usable power of God is growing among us, and a growing recognition of the only worth-while application of that power—in the improvement of the world.

As to ethics, unfortunately, we are still at sea. We never

did have any popular base for what little ethics we knew, except the religious theories, and now that our faith is shaken in those theories we cannot account for ethics at all. It is no wonder we behave badly, we are literally ignorant of the laws of ethics, which is the simplest of sciences, the most necessary, the most continuously needed. The childish misconduct of our "revolted youth" is quite equaled by that of older people, and neither young nor old seem to have any understanding of the reasons why conduct is "good" or "bad."

Perhaps the most salient change of the present period is the lowering of standards in sex relations, approaching some of the worst periods in ancient history. In my youth there was a fine, earnest movement toward an equal standard of chastity for men and women, an equalizing upward to the level of what women were then. But now the very word "chastity" seems to have become ridiculous. Even if complete promiscuity is avoided, there is a preliminary promiscuity of approach which leaves little to be desired.

The main influence accounting for this is the psychophilosophy, the sexuopathic philosophy, which solemnly advocates as "natural" a degree of indulgence utterly without parallel in nature. A larger knowledge of biology, of zoology, is what is wanted to offset this foolishness. In the widespread attacks upon marriage it is clearly shown that the attackers do not know that monogamy is a "natural" form of sex relationship, practised widely among both birds and beasts, who are neither "Puritan" nor "Mid-Victorian." These uneducated persons seem to think that all animals are either promiscuous or polygamous; and to add to their folly, forget that even such creatures have their definite season for mating.

These things I have seen happen. None of them give cause for as much anxiety, to an American, as the rapidly descending extinction of our nation, superseded by other nations who will soon completely outnumber us. This, with the majority rule of a democracy, means that our grandchildren will belong to a minority of dwindling Americans, ruled over by a majority of conglomerate races quite dissimilar.

But since it is no new thing in history to have a given nation fail, give way and disappear, while the progress of society continues in other hands, we should perhaps contentedly admit our failure and welcome our superseders. Perhaps they will do better than we.

Leaving New York with measureless relief, I came in 1922 to this old Connecticut settlement, Norwich Town. It is so beautiful as to have won the title, Rose of New England. This is my native state, and while the town is not my ancestral home it is my husband's, and in the larger sense of similarity in people and in tastes and habits, it has more of the home feeling than such a nomad as I had ever hoped for.

After New York it is like heaven. It is true that two-thirds of the population are aliens, but they are not so overwhelmingly in evidence as in the great city. The people I meet, and mostly those I see in the neighborhood, are of native stock. One may speak to them, to workmen of any grade, and get a cheerful man-to-man answer.

Here people can be friends, can see one another as often as desired without making a social function of it; here I can take my knitting or sewing and "run in"; or I can stop on my way down-town or up, for a little chat. Being a Connecticutter by birth, and my husband's family well known and loved here, I have been welcomed more than kindly.

Such nice people! Such well-educated, well-read, well-intentioned people! I had more accessible friends here in one year than in New York in twenty. Our Norwich Town is the early settlement; Norwich, now the city, is a later growth. The town lies to the north of it, a narrow strip between wooded hills and the Yantic River. The long streets are lined with trees, New England fashion, and the majestic old houses stand back under their great elms, a succession of noble pictures.

The most conspicuous religion of the place is ancestor worship—at least it looks like it. The town is labeled with the names of long-dead residents, not merely on gravestones, but on neat white signs hung on old houses, nailed on trees, set on the ground here and there. These were first put up in honor of the two hundred and fiftieth anniversary of the settlement, and have been piously maintained ever since. One somewhat irreverent friend suggested that I write a limerick on this local habit, with this result:

So proud of our grandsires are we,
Each old house wears a sign, as you see;
   If a house we have not,
   Then we label the lot,
And hang up the sign on a tree.

One of these signs commemorates "First child born in Norwich." Another prouder and more explicit, records "First male child." Our ancient mansion I found decorated with two, on either side the front door, one a list of ancestors, the other announcing, "Lydia Huntley Sigourney born here." The general effect of all these white records is of a sort of mural graveyard. . . .

Home-like and lovely as it is, no one with a sense of historical perspective can live in a New England town and not suffer to see its gradual extinction. Those noble houses, pillared porches, fanlights over rich doorways, wide sweeps of lawn under majestic elms, are no longer built. The old people who had sufficient wealth to live in those gracious mansions pass away, and the young people who have sufficient wealth prefer to spend it in other ways, in other places. Down go the gracious mansions and up spring the close-set "bungalows"; a different kind of people are taking over the place. But as yet there is dignity and beauty and peace, and I enjoy it with the delight of a returned exile.

ANCHOR BOOKS

AMERICAN HISTORY AND STUDIES